bake!

bake!

ESSENTIAL TECHNIQUES
FOR PERFECT BAKING *Nick Malgieri*

Photographs by
Quentin Bacon

Kyle Cathie Limited

DEDICATION
For Albert Kumin,
my teacher, and to
all my students

Published in Great Britain in 2011 by
Kyle Cathie Limited
23 Howland Street, London W1T 4AY
general.enquiries@kyle-cathie.com
www.kylecathie.com

ISBN: 978-1-85626-918-6

10 9 8 7 6 5 4 3 2 1

First published in 2010 by Kyle Books
an imprint of Kyle Cathie Limited
www.kylebooks.com

Text © 2010 by Nick Malgieri
Photographs © 2010 by Quentin Bacon
Book design © 2010 by Kyle Cathie Ltd

Project editor Anja Schmidt
Angliciser Lee Faber
Designer Dirk Kaufman
Photographer Quentin Bacon
Food Styling Liz Duffy
Prop Styling Roy Finamore
Copyeditor Janet McDonald
Production Lisa Pinnell and
Gemma John

A CIP catalogue record for this title is
available from the British Library.

Colour reproduction by Sang Choy
Printed and bound in China
by C & C Offset Printing Co.,Ltd.

contents

introduction

BAKE! is the book I've always wanted to write. More than 30 years of teaching people how to bake have clearly shown me that the easiest way to learn is to start with a basic recipe or technique and then prepare variations on it. And that's exactly what BAKE! is all about.

Each chapter starts with an Essential Technique—such as brioche dough, high-ratio cake batter or puff pastry—and the way to prepare that master recipe is shown in step-by-step photographs. Then you can use the master recipe in a variety of ways later in the chapter.

The 20 chapters cover all the main techniques of fine baking, starting with simple pastry dough and moving through puff pastry and Danish pastry, all sorts of breads, tea breads, cakes and biscuits.

Learning 'techniques' sounds a little dry and academic, like playing endless scales and other exercises in a music lesson. Nothing could be further from the truth: once you learn a baking technique (and most of them are really easy to do and easy to master), you'll also reap the benefit of having made something wonderful to enjoy.

Please don't buy into the fallacy that 'baking is a science': you'll only wind up intimidating yourself. Hundreds of everyday processes that people often use are also science; driving a car, using a telephone, even grilling a steak can be explained according to strict scientific principles. But we take all those processes for granted and we certainly aren't afraid of them.

I've been a fan of British baking for as long as I can remember and I'm proud and happy that my techniques and recipes are being presented to British readers and bakers for the first time.

And remember, I'm never really too far away if you have a question or want to see a video about one of the techniques. Visit my website, www.nickmalgieri.com, where you'll also find some new recipes based on the techniques in BAKE!

Enjoy, and above all, bake something!

Nick Malgieri
New York City, 2010

ingredients

FLOURS, OTHER GRAINS, STARCHES, AND GELATINE

Flour: Unbleached plain flour is fine for general use, but for the bread recipes, strong bread flour is preferred.

Polenta: I prefer stone-ground yellow polenta for its chewier texture.

Oats: Oats are regular porridge oats, not instant.

Cornflour: Plain cornflour is available in the supermarket.

Gelatine: I prefer the powdered gelatine that comes in a sachet since it's the form most widely available.

SUGARS AND SWEETENERS

Sugar: I use plain granulated sugar in all my recipes, never caster sugar.

Brown Sugar: I call for light and dark brown sugars in this book. The difference between them is the amount of molasses added back to the sugar after it's refined.

Icing Sugar: Icing sugar is finely pulverised granulated sugar. In the United States it has 3% cornflour added by weight, which is why I never use it in whipped cream.

Golden Syrup: Golden syrup is used to retain moisture and also impart smoothness in some preparations, such as ganache.

Honey: I buy dark, full-flavoured honey but not always one with a fancy pedigree.

Treacle: I use black treacle such as Lyles. For a milder flavour I use golden syrup.

RAISING AGENTS

Baking Powder: I use double-acting baking powder, which in the UK can be found online. The type sold in most supermarkets can be used but may not yield the same results. Always check the expiration date on the container.

Bicarbonate of Soda: Plain bicarbonate of soda – always crush lumps before using.

FLAVOURINGS

Salt: I usually use fine sea salt for both baking and seasoning food.

Extracts: Always buy 100% pure extracts.

Whole Vanilla Pods: Look for the best-quality vanilla pods you can find from a reliable source such as www.vanillapodsuk.com.

Ginger: Fresh, crystallised and ground gingers are all used in this book. Don't be tempted to substitute one for another. Each has a unique flavour and texture.

Spirits: A lesser-quality spirit or liqueur can instantly ruin a fine dessert. Here's my advice: if a large bottle of imported rum or other spirit or liqueur is expensive, buy a smaller bottle, rather than buying a lesser brand.

Chocolate: A range of chocolates is used here, including unsweetened (available online in the UK from www.melburyandappleton.co.uk), dark and milk chocolates. Remember that a chocolate dessert will only taste as good as the chocolate used to prepare it.

Cocoa Powder: I use alkalised (Dutch process) cocoa exclusively, which can be bought online in the UK. Alternatively, add $1/8$ teaspoon bicarbonate of soda to each 3 tablespoons of natural cocoa powder used.

Coffee: Brew triple-strength espresso (3 tablespoons coffee and 180ml boiling water) or use instant espresso.

Jam: Your favorite jam or conserve will work just fine.

NUTS AND NUT PRODUCTS

Nuts with the skin on are generally referred to as natural or unblanched. Those with the skins removed are referred to as blanched or skinless. Almonds, pistachios and hazelnuts are available both natural and blanched. Pecans and walnuts are not blanched but the skins are so thin that they don't need to be removed.

Store nuts in a plastic bag in the freezer. If you need to grind nuts in a food processor, bring them to room temperature before grinding. Cold nuts will clump up and never grind finely enough. Warm ones will turn almost immediately to nut butter.

EGGS

All the eggs called for here are medium eggs, 636–756 grams per dozen

DAIRY PRODUCTS

Butter: I use unsalted butter in the recipes here. All the recipes were tested with plain butter available at the supermarket. If you substitute butter with a higher fat content, you might get different results, especially in biscuit batters and pastry doughs. They will have a tendency to spread more and be highly fragile after baking. Butter is probably the most important ingredient in fine baking, so it needs to be fresh to be good. Unwrap a package of butter and scratch the surface with the point of a table knife. If the butter is lighter coloured on the inside than on the outside, it has oxidised and become stale. Such butter won't impart anything but a stale flavour to whatever you bake with it. If you stock up on butter during a sale, by all means store it in the freezer. If you intend to keep it for more than a month or so, wrap the packages in clingfilm and foil to keep them as airtight as possible.

Milk: When I call for milk, I mean full-fat milk, unless an alternative is indicated.

Buttermilk: Naturally low in fat yet rich in texture, buttermilk lends moisture and tenderness.

Cream: Whipping cream has a fat content of 35%, which is why it whips to a silky and luxurious consistency. Double cream (48%), whips the most easily and to the thickest consistency. Single cream, when called for, contains 18% butterfat.

Soured Cream: When I call for soured cream, I mean the full-fat version. Reduced fat or fat-free will not work in some baked goods.

Cheese: Freshly made ricotta and mozzarella taste better and have a better texture than their industrially made counterparts. True Parmigiano-Reggiano knows no substitute.

OILS

Vegetable Oils: When vegetable oil is called for, safflower, peanut, and rapeseed oils will all work fine. Look for 'cold-pressed' oil. In Europe, the term 'cold-pressed' is regulated, whereas US manufacturers may label oil as they wish. You will also see oils labelled 'expeller-pressed', which means they have been expressed without the use of chemical agents; but this does not necessarily mean the oil has not reached a high temperature during processing, which can destroy its flavour. (It can also make the oil resistant to high heat, desirable at times for cooking but rarely for baking.) Your best bet is to find a brand that you think smells and tastes good and stick with that.

equipment

BAKING TINS

Sandwich Tins: These are round cake tins. In this book they are 3.75–5cm deep and are always 23cm in diameter.

A 23cm tin that's 7.5cm deep may be used for the baked cheesecake recipe, but a springform tin is also good.

Rectangular Tins: For baking biscuits, Danish, or different kinds of large or individual pastries, you can use a baking sheet or a rectangular swiss roll tin. These come in a variety of sizes, including 33 x 25 x 3cm (domestic size) and 44 x 30 x 2.5cm commercial half-sheet tins. Thin, flexible baking sheets without sides are useful for moving dough and cake layers and for chilling pieces of dough in addition to baking biscuits. Insulated baking sheets are worth the expense if your oven has a tendency to burn things on the bottom. Only use them in the bottom of the oven, though. You can also get the same effect by stacking two tins together for baking in the bottom of the oven. A 23 x 33 x 5cm rectangular tin is called for in some recipes.

Tube Tins: This can be a 1- or 2-piece 24.5 x 10.5cm tube tin, or what's commonly referred to as a Bundt pan in the U.S. with the same capacity.

Loaf Tins: I use standard 1lb loaf tins.

Springform Tins: A springform tin has two parts: a flat base and a ring that closes with a clasp. All recipes that use springform tins in this book call for 23cm or 25cm tins.

Flan Tins: I use a loose-based flan tin with fluted sides, sometimes called a French tart tin. Recipes here call for 25cm and 30cm tins.

Muffin Tins and Mini Muffin Tins: I use the 12-hole muffin tins; each hole in the standard-size tins should hold about 120ml; the capacity of the holes in a mini muffin tin is variable. I always line full-size muffin tins with pleated paper liners.

Pizza Tin: The thin-crust pizzas in Chapter 8 are all about 25cm in diameter. Therefore, you may use anything from a 25–38cm diameter round tin or even a rectangular baking sheet or tin that's wider than 25cm for baking them.

Sauté Pan: The Tarte Tatin on page 59 is made in a 25cm non-stick sauté pan with sloping (not straight) sides.

HAND TOOLS

Knives: Three knives are essential in every kitchen: a good paring knife, a chopping (or chef's) knife and a serrated knife for slicing bread and through cake layers. A thin-bladed slicing knife is also useful for slicing cakes and other desserts at serving time.

Palette Knives and Spatulas: Palette knives are essential for evenly spreading out batters before baking, spreading fillings onto dough and finishing cakes. I also like to use a wide spatula for moving finished cakes and desserts and a rubber spatula for mixing doughs and batters.

Graters: A box grater with diagonally set holes, large and small, is better than one that has only holes that look like they were formed by a nail piercing the sheet metal. Microplane and Cuisipro are two brands of graters that come in all sizes and degrees of fineness for grating zests, nutmeg or cheese or shaving chocolate.

Pizza Wheel: A plain sharp one and a serrated one (sometimes both come

mounted on the same handle) are useful for cutting dough and of course, pizza.

Thermometers: A small instant-read thermometer looks like a dial set at the top of a very long nail. It's useful for determining the internal temperature of dough and for testing doneness, as well as in heated mixtures such as meringue.

Rolling Pin: I prefer the wooden type without handles that is a straight cylinder, about 40 x 5cm.

Pastry Brush: A natural bristle pastry brush works better than one with synthetic bristles. Silicone brushes with thin bristles work well for brushing egg wash or sprinkling syrup on cake layers.

Spray Bottle: A spray bottle is used to spritz the oven when baking certain types of bread. Be careful not to hit the pilot light and knock out your oven heat.

X-Acto Knife or Single-Edged Razor: Either of these blades make nice deep cuts when slashing the tops of breads.

Baking Stone: A baking stone gives your breads a crisp bottom crust, but you can also use an upside-down swiss roll tin that doesn't warp under intense heat.

Pastry Bag and Tips: Nylon or cloth bags can be cleaned in the top rack of a dishwasher or in a washing machine. I use a 1.25cm plain piping tube (Ateco size 6) and a 1.25cm open star tube (Ateco size 4).

PAPERS AND FOIL

Baking Paper: Try to find baking paper that comes in large individual sheets, rather than on a roll.

Silicone Tin Liners: These reusable liners are great for anything that spreads. Don't use them as tin liners for general baking. That way they don't get worn out.

Cake Boards: These are available in a variety of sizes and shapes. Round ones the same diameter as your cake will make cake finishing a breeze. Rectangular ones make unmoulding easy.

MEASURING TOOLS

Liquid Measures: These are usually made from glass or clear plastic. Newer measuring cups make it possible to read the quantity from the top, rather than the side of the cup – a definite improvement. One litre jugs are widely available in the UK and are useful to measure fluid ounces and millilitres.

Dry-Measure Cups: Americans measure dry ingredients such as flour, icing sugar or cornflour in measuring cups. We have used metric weights throughout for this edition.

Measuring Spoons: Graduated metal measuring spoons are essential. I like to have several sets so that if one gets wet measuring liquid ingredients, there is another set of dry ones waiting.

Kitchen Scales: There are any number of fairly inexpensive kitchen scales available. These make quick work of weighing out ingredients.

ELECTRICALS

Mixer: A heavy-duty mixer such as a KitchenAid is an essential baker's tool. You could use a heavy-duty handheld mixer, but they are much less convenient. If you are investing in a mixer, buy an extra bowl and whisk. They will save you time when you need to whisk several mixtures for a single dessert.

Food Processor: A food processor (fitted with its metal blade) is useful for grinding nuts and mixing doughs.

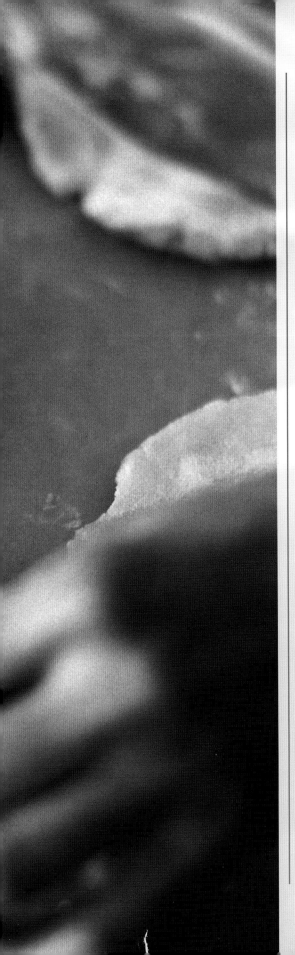

01

sweet pastry & tarts

Sweet-crusted tarts are a welcome dessert, teatime sweet, or snack any time of the year. All the tarts in this chapter are made with a sweet, crumbly crust that is as delicious as it is easy to prepare. And aside from being easy both to mix and to work with, the dough bakes to golden perfection every time. Fillings vary from the humble sweet potato to flavourful combinations of chocolate, nuts, citrus and other fruit. Serve any of these and you'll quickly gain a reputation as an accomplished baker.

A

B

sweet pastry dough

If you've long shied away from preparing pastry, this is a perfect dough to begin with as you conquer your fear. It's easy both to make and to use, and it always bakes through dry and golden on the bottom, ensuring a successful tart with no filling leaks or inconsistent patches.

Makes about 500g dough, enough for two 25cm tarts, or the bottom and top crust for a 25cm pie

260g plain flour

75g sugar

½ teaspoon baking powder

¼ teaspoon salt

110g unsalted butter, cold, cut into 10 pieces

2 medium eggs

1. To mix the dough by hand, combine the flour, sugar, baking powder and salt in a medium bowl and stir well to combine.

2. Cut each piece of butter into 4 or 5 smaller pieces and add all of them to the bowl.

3. Use both hands, palms upward, to reach under the dry ingredients to the bottom of the bowl and lift them up through the contents of the bowl several times to distribute the pieces of butter evenly among the dry ingredients (A).

4. Use your fingertips to pinch the pieces of butter into smaller pieces, alternating with rubbing the mixture between the palms of your hands and occasionally repeating step 3. Continue rubbing in the butter until no visible pieces remain and the whole mixture is cool and powdery.

5. Add the eggs and use a fork to break them up. Use one hand to move the bowl back and forth across the work surface in a straight line while you stir up from the bottom with the fork until the dough is almost completely mixed (B).

6. Turn the dough onto a floured work surface (C) and gently knead it into a consistent mass (D and E). Continue with step 10.

7. To mix the dough in a food processor, combine the flour, sugar, baking powder and salt in the work bowl fitted with the metal blade. Pulse several times to mix.

8. Add the butter and pulse repeatedly at 1-second intervals until the butter is finely mixed into the dry ingredients.

9. Add the eggs and pulse again until the dough forms a ball. Turn the dough onto a floured work surface and carefully remove the blade.

10. Divide the dough in half, then flatten each half into a disc. Use immediately or wrap in clingfilm and refrigerate for up to 3 days.

variations

Nut dough: Add 50g ground nuts such as almonds or hazelnuts to the dough. No adjustments are necessary, since the ground nuts won't absorb the eggs.

Cocoa dough: Use 215g plain flour and 3 tablespoons alkalised (Dutch process) cocoa powder, sifted after measuring, in place of the 260g flour.

C

D

E

essential tips for sweet pastry dough

- Sweet dough is easy to work with because of its relatively low butter content. Most pastry doughs contain much more butter (both for tenderness and flavour), and therefore they may soften to an unmanageable consistency if your kitchen is warm or you take too long rolling out the dough. Usually less butter means less tenderness, but in this case, sugar provides the extra tenderness needed to achieve a baked crust that isn't tough or hard.

- Baking powder is another ingredient that contributes to this dough's ability to bake through dry and golden even under a liquid filling. Normally when we add baking powder to a dough, it causes it to puff up. In this case, however, the filling exerts enough weight to prevent the dough from rising upward, causing it to press firmly against the bottom of the tin when it expands, so that it maintains constant contact with the hot tin base and bakes through efficiently. The most common cause of a tart's bottom crust not baking through is the dough shrinking slightly and losing contact with the hot tin base.

- Because of this dough's ability to bake through so efficiently, it never needs to be partially pre-baked, saving time and fuss whenever you bake a tart.

forming a tart crust from sweet pastry dough

Makes one 25 cm tart crust

½ batch Sweet Pastry Dough (page 14)

Flour for the work surface and dough

One 25cm loose-based fluted flan tin

Because of its relatively high sugar content, Sweet Pastry Dough can become soft and sticky if excessively handled. Follow the instructions for using the chilled dough until you feel confident enough to try rolling freshly prepared dough. Whether working with chilled or fresh dough, try the alternative method for rolling the dough directly on the tart tin base (step 6) to simplify transferring the dough to the tin.

1. Remove one of the pieces of dough from the refrigerator, unwrap it and place it on a floured work surface. Gently knead the dough until it is slightly softened and malleable. Shape it into a disc again and use the palm of your hand to press it about 5mm thick.

2. Flour the work surface and the dough and gently roll the dough to a 33cm diameter disc, adding pinches of flour under and on top of the dough as needed. Picture the dough as the face of a clock: Roll back and forth from 6 to 12 and back again, without rolling over the edges in either direction. Slide the dough around to make sure it doesn't stick to the work surface, then add a few more pinches of flour to both the work surface and the surface of the dough. Turn the dough a little so that the spot that was at 12 o'clock is now at 2 and repeat. After you have rolled over the dough 3 or 4 times, turning it a little in between, it should be large enough for the tin and still an even thickness.

3. Fold the dough in half and slide both hands under it, palms upward, and transfer it to the tin, lining up the fold with the diameter of the tin. Unfold the dough into the tin. Don't be concerned if the dough cracks or tears – you can always press it back together. Evenly fit the dough into the tin, making sure it's flat against both the base and sides of the tin.

4. Trim away any excess dough at the rim of the tin by rolling over the rim with the rolling pin or scraping away excess dough with the back of a paring knife.

5. Finish off the top edges of the crust by using your thumb to press the dough from inside the tin against the side of the tin and at the same time using your index finger to press down on the top of the crust.

6. Alternatively, remove the base from the flan tin and place it on the work surface. Flour the metal disc, place the disc of dough in the centre of it, and roll the dough as in step 2 (A). When the dough reaches the edge of the tin base, flour the work surface around the dough and roll it to 5cm more in diameter or 2.5cm beyond the edge of the metal disc. Run a thin palette knife under the overhanging perimeter of dough to make sure it isn't stuck to the work surface (if it is, gently slide a long palette knife or a thin flan tin base underneath). Fold the extra dough inward all around onto the rolled dough on the metal disc and gently transfer the tin base to the flan tin (B). Lift the folded-over dough and press it against the side of the tin, then perform steps 4 and 5 above (C).

7. Use the crust immediately or wrap it in clingfilm and chill for up to 24 hours.

A

B

C

essential tips for rolling tart crusts

- Always knead and gently soften the dough before attempting to roll it. A chilled, hard dough will break apart when rolled.

- Flouring the work surface and dough is essential to prevent sticking. Use small pinches of flour and repeat, adding them often, and you won't add more than a couple of teaspoons of extra flour to the dough.

- You can also roll the dough on a thin, flexible chopping board. After the dough is rolled, slide a long palette knife or other thin knife under it to make sure it isn't stuck, then slide the dough to the edge of the board. Line up the edge of the chopping board with the far end of the flan tin and gently slide the disc of dough off the chopping board and into the tin.

- Make sure you have pressed the dough against the side of the tin (step 3) before cutting off any excess or the tin sides might not be completely covered with dough.

- Practice finishing off the top edges of the crust by pressing inward on the side with your thumb and downward on the top with your forefinger at the same time (see photo C at left), making a straight, even, finished edge that won't crack when baking.

chocolate hazelnut tart

Makes one 25cm tart, 8–10 servings

225g whole hazelnuts

350g golden syrup

110g sugar

110g dark chocolate, (55-65% cocoa solids) cut into 5mm pieces

55g unsalted butter, cut into 8 pieces

3 medium eggs

Pinch of salt

2 tablespoons dark rum or bourbon, optional

One 25cm tart crust made from Sweet Pastry Dough (page 14)

The filling of this tart recalls *gianduja*, the delicious chocolate hazelnut confection of Italy's Piemonte region. I like to use a plain crust with this filling so that all the chocolate emphasis is within, plus the pale crust and dark filling provide fun colour contrast. Purchasing hazelnuts with their skins already removed makes preparing the filling much easier.

1 Set an oven rack in the lowest level of the oven and preheat to 180°C/gas mark 4.

2 If the hazelnuts are not already skinned, place them in a small roasting tin or swiss roll tin and toast them in the oven until the skins darken and loosen, 10–15 minutes. Pour the hazelnuts onto a clean tea towel and rub them vigorously in the towel to loosen their skins, then go over them one by one and peel off any remaining skins (if you purchased skinned hazelnuts, toast them lightly). Place the skinned nuts on a swiss roll tin and set a small saucepan on top of them. Rock the saucepan back and forth over the nuts, applying firm pressure, to crush them into halves and quarters.

3 Combine the golden syrup and sugar in a medium saucepan and stir well to mix. Place on a medium heat and bring to the boil, stirring occasionally. Off heat, add the chocolate and butter and gently shake the pan once or twice to submerge them. Wait 2 minutes, then whisk smooth.

4 Whisk the eggs into the chocolate mixture, one at a time, followed by the salt and rum, if using. Stir in the hazelnuts.

5 Pour the filling into the prepared crust and bake the tart until the dough is baked through and deep golden on the top edges and the filling is set, 35–40 minutes.

6 Cool the tart on a rack. Unmould the cooled tart and slide it from the tin base to a serving plate.

Serving: Serve the tart in wedges. A spoonful of whipped cream is a nice touch.

Storage: Keep the tart loosely covered at room temperature until serving. Wrap and store leftovers at room temperature.

variations

Walnuts, pecans, toasted almonds, and macadamia nuts all make excellent substitutes for the hazelnuts. One of the best fillings for this tart I've ever made used an assortment of odds and ends of nuts I had in the freezer.

old-fashioned sweet potato tart

Makes one 25cm tart, 8–10 servings

3 medium sweet potatoes, 675–800g

110g sugar

½ teaspoon ground cinnamon

Generous pinch of freshly grated nutmeg

Pinch of salt

3 medium eggs

240ml single cream

1 teaspoon vanilla extract

One 25cm tart crust made from Sweet Pastry Dough (page 14)

A delicious change from the traditional pumpkin pie, sweet potato tart is as American Southern as you can get. This version is loosely based on one by Leah Chase, proprietor of the Dooky Chase restaurant in New Orleans, Louisiana. There seems to be a lot of confusion about sweet potatoes versus yams and some people even use the terms interchangeably. You can easily find a sweet potato in a supermarket or farmers' market and the colour of its flesh or skin varies. Yams are another species of tuber altogether, which have a completely different flavour. They grow mostly in South America, though I'm sure some Caribbean markets carry them.

1 Set an oven rack in the lowest level of the oven and preheat to 190°C/gas mark 5.

2 Bake the sweet potatoes in the oven until they feel soft when pressed with a fingertip at the thickest part, about 1 hour. Cool and peel them, trimming away any dry spots on the pointed ends after peeling.

3 Place the sweet potatoes in a shallow bowl and use a potato masher to reduce them to a thick purée. Stir in the sugar, spices and salt.

4 Whisk in the eggs, one at a time, followed by the cream and vanilla.

5 Pour the filling into the prepared crust. Place the tart on the lowest rack of the oven and immediately reduce the temperature to 180°C/gas mark 4. Bake until the edge of the crust is deep golden and the filling is set, about 40–45 minutes.

6 Cool the tart on a rack. Unmould and slide the tart from the tin base to a serving plate. Serve at room temperature.

Serving: In New Orleans they often decorate each portion of the tart with a pecan half, then serve it with whipped cream or vanilla ice cream.

Storage: Keep the tart at a cool room temperature until serving, or wrap and refrigerate. Bring to room temperature before serving.

variations

Add 30g finely ground pecans to the dough when preparing it. Scatter 55g chopped pecans over the filling before baking.

pear & walnut tart

Makes one 25cm tart, 8 servings

POACHED PEARS

2 litres iced water

2 tablespoons lemon juice

5 ripe Williams pears, about 900g

110g sugar

1 vanilla pod

1 cinnamon stick

1 tablespoon clear pear brandy, optional

WALNUT FILLING

110g walnut pieces

100g light brown sugar

¼ teaspoon ground cinnamon

Pinch of salt

85g unsalted butter, softened

1 medium egg

1 medium egg yolk

4 tablespoons plain flour

½ teaspoon baking powder

55g walnut pieces, finely chopped

APRICOT GLAZE

225g apricot jam

2 tablespoons water

Icing sugar for finishing

One 25cm tart crust made from
Sweet Pastry Dough (page 14)

variations

For the filling, use pecans or blanched almonds, granulated sugar for brown, and 1 teaspoon vanilla for cinnamon.

Cover the crust with 300g blueberries, spreading the filling over them before sprinkling with the nuts. Omit the glaze.

Substitute peeled peach or nectarine quarters or unpeeled apricot, plum or prune halves, for the pears.

This was always one of the most popular items sold by my Total Heaven Baking Company in the early 1980s. Poaching the pears first is a little extra work, but you can do it for up to five days in advance of assembling the tart; just chill them in their poaching liquid. The variations to this tart are almost infinite – just change the fruit or the nuts in the filling.

1 To poach the pears, half-fill a 4-litre pan with iced water and add the lemon juice. Pare, halve, and use a melon-ball scoop to core and stem the pears, adding each half to the iced water. Skim out the ice and pour away all the water except what's needed to cover the pears by 2.5cm. Add the sugar, vanilla pod and cinnamon stick and stir gently. Cut a piece of baking paper the same diameter as the pan and cut six to eight 2.5cm holes in it. Press the paper down on top of the pears so that it is fully submerged. (This will keep the pears from floating up while they are cooking.) Place the pan over a medium heat and bring to the boil. Cover, remove from the heat and allow the pears to sit in the hot liquid until completely cooled. If the pears are perfectly ripe, they won't need any more cooking; if they are less ripe, boil them for another 2 minutes. Once the pears are cool, use a slotted spoon to lift them gently to a plastic container and pour the pear brandy, if using, over. Pour in enough of the poaching syrup to cover the pears and transfer the vanilla pod to the container. Cover and refrigerate until needed.

2 Set a rack in the lowest level of the oven and preheat to 180°C/gas mark 4.

3 For the filling, combine the walnut pieces, sugar, cinnamon and salt in the bowl of a food processor fitted with the metal blade. Pulse until finely ground. Use a thin palette knife to scrape away any mixture stuck to the bottom and sides of the bowl. Add the butter, egg and egg yolk and pulse until smooth. Mix the flour and baking powder together, then add to the bowl and pulse again until absorbed. Scrape the sides of the bowl again and pulse 2 or 3 more times. Remove the blade and scrape any filling stuck to it into the prepared tart crust. Scrape the remaining filling into the crust and smooth the top. Evenly scatter the chopped walnuts on top.

4 Drain the pear halves on kitchen paper and arrange them on the filling, wider sides close to the edge of the crust, ends pointing toward the centre. (Do a dry run on a plate and trim the sides of the pear halves if necessary.) Bake until the edge of the crust is deep golden and the filling is set, about 30 minutes.

5 Cool on a rack. Meanwhile, prepare the glaze. Stir together the jam and water in a small saucepan and bring to the boil, stirring occasionally, over a low heat. Strain into a bowl, then rinse the pan and return the strained glaze to it.

6 Dust the tart well with icing sugar and wait until it melts on the pears. Blot the pears with kitchen paper. Reheat the glaze and reduce it slightly, then pour a small spoonful of glaze onto each pear. Unmould and slide the tart to a serving plate.

Serving: Cut the tart into wedges with one pear half in the centre of each serving.
Storage: Keep the tart loosely covered with foil (clingfilm will stick to the glaze) until serving. Wrap and store leftovers at room temperature.

citrus-scented chocolate tart

Makes one 25cm tart, 8–10 servings

300ml single cream

70g sugar

85g unsalted butter,
cut into 10 pieces

225g dark chocolate (55–65% cocoa
solids), cut into 5mm pieces

3 medium eggs

Pinch of salt

1 teaspoon finely grated lemon zest

2 teaspoons finely grated orange zest

1 tablespoon lemon juice, strained
before measuring

2 tablespoons orange juice, strained
before measuring

1 tablespoon orange liqueur, such as
Cointreau or Triple Sec, optional

1 teaspoon vanilla extract

One 25cm tart crust, made from Sweet
Pastry Dough, Cocoa Dough variation
(page 14)

The flavour of this creamy chocolate filling is beautifully enhanced by lemon and orange zests and a little of each fruit's juice, both of which tie into the chocolate's natural acidity. I like to bake it in a cocoa-flavoured crust to emphasise the tart's chocolate richness, but you may also use a plain or nut-enriched sweet dough. This tart also makes a delicious base for berries or orange or tangerine segments, or try hiding a thin layer of sliced bananas under the chocolate filling.

1   Set an oven rack in the lowest level of the oven and preheat to 180°C/gas mark 4.

2   Whisk the cream and sugar together in a small saucepan, place over a medium heat and bring to the boil. Off heat, add the butter and chocolate to the saucepan and shake the pan to submerge them. Let stand for 1 minute, then whisk smooth.

3   Add the eggs and salt; whisk them in, followed by the citrus zests, juices, liqueur, and vanilla.

4   Pour the filling into the prepared crust and bake until the crust is baked through and the filling is set, about 25 minutes.

5   Cool the tart on a rack. Unmould it and slide it from the tin base to a serving plate.

Serving: Serve the tart at room temperature with some slices of peeled orange or decorate the edge of the tart with halved orange slices.

Storage: Keep the tart at room temperature until serving. Wrap and store leftovers at a cool room temperature.

variations

For a pure chocolate flavour, omit the citrus zests and juices. Or scatter 120g fresh raspberries on the crust before pouring over the plain or citrus-scented filling; don't be tempted to add more berries, as they'll exude a lot of juice during baking. Or thinly slice a couple of poached pear halves (see Pear and Walnut Tart, page 20) and arrange them on the crust before adding the plain filling.

shredded apple custard tart

Makes one 25cm tart, 8–10 servings

3 large tart apples such as Granny Smith, about 675g

70g sugar

3 tablespoons plain flour

3 medium eggs

1 teaspoon vanilla extract

150ml single cream

Ground cinnamon for sprinkling on the filling

55g walnut pieces, coarsely chopped

One 25cm tart crust made from Sweet Pastry Dough (page 14)

I remember the pastry chef at the hotel where I worked in Zurich in the early 1970s improvising a tart like this one afternoon when we didn't have a lot of work to do. It's also a model for tarts made with other fruits.

1 Set a rack in the lowest level of the oven and preheat to 180°C/gas mark 4.

2 Pare, halve, and core the apples. Set a box grater in a shallow bowl and grate the apple halves over the grater's largest holes, or use the largest grating blade of your food processor. Scrape the grated apples into a large sieve and set it back over the bowl for the apples to drain while preparing the other ingredients. Don't be concerned if the apples darken slightly, but don't take too long with the rest of the filling either.

3 Evenly whisk the sugar and flour together in a mixing bowl. Add the eggs and vanilla and whisk smooth. Whisk in the cream.

4 Stir the drained apples into the custard mixture and scrape it into the prepared tart crust. If the apples mound in the centre of the tart, use a fork to distribute them more evenly.

5 Sparingly sprinkle the top of the tart with cinnamon and evenly scatter on the chopped nuts. Bake the tart until the edge of the crust is deep golden and the filling is set, 40–45 minutes.

6 Cool the tart on a rack, then unmould and slide it from the tin base to a serving plate.

Serving: Cut the tart into wedges. It needs no accompaniment.

Storage: Keep the tart at a cool room temperature until serving. Wrap and refrigerate leftovers and bring them to room temperature before serving again.

variations

Scatter 425g rinsed, dried and picked over blueberries onto the tart crust and pour the custard cream over them. Omit the cinnamon and walnuts. Substitute 425g blackberries or raspberries for the blueberries, but just pick through them for any stems or blemished berries – washing either will turn them to purée.

Substitute 4 or 5 ripe peaches (about 900g), peeled and halved, with each half cut into 3 wedges. Arrange the peach wedges cut side up on the tart crust, making one row of wedges perpendicular to the edge of the tart and filling in the centre with the remaining wedges. Pour the custard cream over the peaches, omitting the cinnamon and walnuts. The top may be glazed with the apricot glaze from the recipe for Pear and Walnut Tart, page 20. Substitute unpeeled quarters of apricots or plums for the peaches.

You may finish the top of the tart with an unbaked crumb topping for any of the variations above, including the apple tart. Use the crumb topping in the recipe for Strawberry Cream Cheese Crumble Tart, page 45, omitting the almonds.

bakewell tart

One 25cm unbaked tart crust made from Sweet Pastry Dough (see pages 14 and 16)

4 tablespoons strawberry or seedless raspberry jam

225g marzipan, cut into 1cm cubes (see Note)

55g sugar

3 medium eggs

110g unsalted butter, softened

1 tablespoon lemon juice

5 tablespoons plain flour

variation

Bordeaux Fruit Tart: This is my take on the old-fashioned French tart Infante de Bordeaux that calls for an icing to be spread over baked almond filling. I like to use it as a base for really juicy fruit, such as pineapple, oranges or perfectly ripe strawberries, which would drain too much liquid into a typical tart crust spread with crème pâtissière.

Prepare the tart filling using the ground almonds and sugar (see Note) instead of the marzipan, and using melted butter in place of the softened butter. Omit the jam and spread the filling in the crust and bake. Cool the tart and arrange 340g sliced fruit on the surface. Just before serving, blot excess moisture from the surface of the fruit and brush on apricot glaze (see page 20) for light-coloured fruit, or raspberry glaze (see page 46) for red fruit. Use a very sharp knife to cut the tart since there is nothing to adhere the fruit to the filling beneath.

I love British recipes like this one for Bakewell Tart – the only definitive statement you can make about it is that absolutely no one can agree on what it is. According to some, it was originally a custard tart with some ground almonds added for flavour and a layer of jam spread on the crust. Some time late in the 19th century, the almonds became more prominent in the filling. Purists like to refer to it as Bakewell pudding, probably from the British tradition of referring to all sweets served at the table as 'puddings'. My thoroughly delicious, but non-authentic, version calls for a type of frangipane filling made with marzipan (or you can easily substitute ground almonds). By the way, Bakewell is a town in Derbyshire, not a reference to the quality of the outcome. Thanks to my dear friend Kyra Effren for guiding me through the intricacies of Bakewell.

1   Set a rack in the lowest level of the oven and preheat to 180°C/gas mark 4.

2   Use the tines of a fork to pierce the bottom of the crust all over at 2.5cm intervals. Evenly spread the jam on the tart crust and set aside.

3   Combine the marzipan and sugar in the bowl of an electric mixer fitted with the paddle attachment. Beat on a medium speed until reduced to small crumbs. Add one of the eggs and continue beating until the mixture is smooth and free of lumps.

4   Use a rubber spatula to scrape the side of the bowl and the beater, beat again for a minute, then add the butter. Continue beating until the mixture lightens somewhat, 2–3 minutes.

5   Beat in the lemon juice and the second egg, continuing to beat until smooth. Scrape the bowl and beater again and add the last egg. Beat until smooth and decrease to the lowest speed. Add the flour and beat until it is just absorbed.

6   Use a large rubber spatula to give a final mixing to the batter and scrape it into the prepared crust. Use a small palette knife to spread the filling evenly.

7   Bake the tart until the crust is deep golden and the filling is set and a light golden colour, 30–40 minutes.

8   Cool on a rack; unmould and slide the tart from the tin base to a serving plate.

Serving: Serve wedges of the tart with spoonfuls of whipped cream.

Storage: Keep the tart at room temperature before and after serving. Cover leftovers with clingfilm.

Note: If you don't have any marzipan, combine 110g blanched almonds, 110g sugar and ½ teaspoon almond essence in the bowl of a food processor fitted with the metal blade. Pulse until finely ground, then let the machine run continuously for 1 minute at a time until the mixture starts to become pasty. Stop the machine and use the end of a narrow palette knife to scrape the bottom and sides of the bowl, pulse again a few times for even consistency, and use instead of the marzipan.

flaky pastry & tarts

When I first tried baking, back when I was a teenager, I hated making flaky pastry dough. All the caveats about keeping everything cool, over-handling, and worst of all, the variable amount of water needed to pull the ingredients together to form a dough so filled me with dread that the dough and subsequent tart were ruined before I even got started. This dough takes all the fear out of preparing a rich, flaky crust. No variables, ease of mixing and handling and best of all, a perfectly baked result every time will make you look forward to working with this type of dough. The tarts are both sweet and savoury, including a free-standing version of everyone's favourite, apple pie. Two types of tangy lemon tart, a chocolate cream tart, and my favorite savoury combinations – spinach and bacon, cheese and onion and smoked salmon and avocado – round out the assortment.

flaky pastry dough

Flaky dough makes a wonderful container for many sweet and savoury fillings. Its fragile texture after baking is more than equalled by its subtle buttery flavour, which always enhances but never competes with delicate fillings.

Makes about 500g dough, enough for two 25cm tart crusts or one double-crust pie

260g plain flour

½ teaspoon salt

1 teaspoon baking powder

170g unsalted butter, chilled, cut into 12 pieces

2 medium eggs (see Note)

Note: In the UK, medium eggs vary between 53–63g each. If you happen to use the two smallest eggs in the dozen, the dough might not start to form a ball after 4 or 5 pulses. If this happens, add ½ teaspoon water or a little more, if required.

A

1 To mix the dough by hand, combine the flour, salt and baking powder in a medium bowl and stir to combine.

2 Cut each piece of butter into 4 or 5 smaller pieces and add the pieces to the bowl. Using both hands, palms upward, reach under the dry ingredients to the bottom of the bowl and lift them up through the contents of the bowl several times to distribute the pieces of butter evenly.

3 Use your fingertips to pinch the pieces of butter into smaller pieces, alternating that with rubbing the mixture between the palms of your hands, as well as occasionally repeating step 2.

4 Continue rubbing in the butter until the largest pieces are no more than 5mm across, but the whole mixture is still cool and powdery.

5 Add the eggs and use a fork to break them up. Move the bowl back and forth on the work surface while you stir from the bottom up with the fork until the dough is almost completely mixed.

6 Turn the dough out onto a floured work surface and gently press it into a cohesive mass. Continue with step 11.

7 To mix the dough in a food processor, combine the flour, salt and baking powder in the bowl fitted with the metal blade. Pulse several times to mix.

8 Add the butter and pulse repeatedly at 1 second intervals until the butter is in small pieces as in step 4 (A).

B

9   Add the eggs and pulse just until the dough almost forms a ball; pulsing too much at this point will incorporate the butter smoothly and cut down on flakiness.

10   Turn the dough out onto a floured work surface and carefully remove the blade. Gently press the dough into a cohesive mass (B).

11   Divide the dough in half, then flatten each half into a disc. Wrap in clingfilm and refrigerate until firm or as long as 3 days.

essential tips for flaky pastry dough

- The small pieces of butter turn into irregular layers when the dough is rolled out. When the dough begins baking, the butter melts and leaves tiny spaces throughout the dough. When the liquid in the dough evaporates, it forms steam, which slightly inflates all those little spaces. Once the starches in the dough coagulate, those spaces provide the open-textured flakiness characteristic of this dough.

- Starting with cold butter is important. If the butter melts during mixing or later during rolling, it forms a paste with the flour rather than remaining in separate pieces. No pieces of butter equals no flakiness.

- Unlike a dough that contains sugar, a flaky dough develops a slightly stronger elasticity during both mixing and rolling. Proteins in the flour change shape due to the addition of moisture and the presence of friction and they form elastic strands of gluten. Overmixing can form too strong a gluten, causing a dough to shrink excessively (all pastry doughs shrink a little) during baking and become tough. Mix quickly and efficiently, allow the dough to chill and rest after mixing and again after rolling and shrinkage will be minimised and tenderness maximised.

forming a tart crust from flaky pastry dough

Makes one 25cm tart crust

½ batch Flaky Pastry Dough (page 26)

Flour for the work surface and dough

One loose-based 25cm flan tin

essential tips for rolling tart crusts from flaky dough

- A thin baking sheet with no sides or a thin flexible chopping board are helpful when rolling a flaky dough. If the kitchen is warm and the dough starts to soften, slide the baking sheet or chopping board under the dough and refrigerate it until it is firm, about 10–15 minutes.

- Continue rolling directly on the baking sheet or chopping board and transfer it to the tin as in step 3.

- A flaky dough tart crust needs to chill and rest after being rolled too. Rolling activates the strands of gluten again and may cause excessive shrinkage if the crust is baked immediately. Give the crust at least a couple of hours of chilling before baking for best results.

Because of its relatively high butter content, Flaky Pastry Dough can become soft and sticky if excessively handled. Follow the instructions for using the chilled dough until you feel confident enough to try rolling the freshly prepared dough. In either case, you may also try the alternative method for rolling the dough directly on the flan tin base (step 6) to simplify transferring the dough to the tin.

1 Remove one of the pieces of dough from the refrigerator, unwrap it and place it on a floured work surface. Use the rolling pin to press the dough, gently at first, in a series of strokes that are both parallel and close together. Turn the disc of dough clockwise about 30 degrees and repeat. While you're rolling the dough, be sure to add pinches of flour under and on the dough to prevent sticking. Moving the dough 30 degrees every time you roll it will help to keep it round. Continue rolling the dough until it is pliable and about 5mm thick.

2 Flour the work surface and the dough and gently roll the dough to a 33cm diameter disc, adding pinches of flour under and on the dough as needed. If you picture the dough as the face of a clock, roll back and forth from 6–12 and back again, without rolling over the edges in either direction. Slide the dough around to make sure it isn't stuck to the work surface (if it is, gently slide a long palette knife or a thin flan tin base underneath), then add a few more pinches of flour to both the work surface and the dough. Turn the dough so that the spot that was at 12 o'clock is now at 2 and repeat. After you have rolled over the dough 3 or 4 times, turning it a little in between, it should be large enough for the tin.

3 Fold the dough in half and slide both hands under it, palms upward, and transfer it to the tin, lining up the fold with the diameter of the tin. Unfold the dough into the tin. The dough will be slightly elastic after rolling, so it won't break apart unless it has softened excessively. Evenly fit the dough into the tin, making sure it's flat against both the base and sides of the tin.

4 Use the back of a knife or scissors to trim away all but 1cm of excess dough at the rim of the tin. Fold the extra dough inward against the inside of the tin to reinforce the side of the crust. (This isn't necessary if the tart is going to be made into a pie and have a top crust – in that case, just leave the extra dough in place until you add the top crust.)

5 Finish off the top edges of the crust by using your thumb to press the dough from inside the tin against the side of the tin and at the same time using your index finger to press down on the top of the crust.

6 Alternatively, remove the base from the flan tin and place it on the work surface. Flour the metal disc, place the disc of dough in the centre of it and roll the dough as in step 2. When the dough reaches the edge of the tin base, flour the work surface around the dough and roll it to 5cm more in diameter or 4cm beyond the edge of the metal disc. Run a thin palette knife under the overhanging perimeter of dough to make sure it isn't stuck to the work surface. Fold the extra dough inward all around onto the rolled dough on the metal disc and gently transfer the tin base to the flan

tin. Lift the folded-over dough and press it against the side of the tin (see photos on page 17), then perform steps 4 and 5 above. Wrap the flan tin in clingfilm and chill for at least 3 hours or up to 24 hours.

7   For a *full top crust*, roll the dough to a 28cm disc, slide it to a baking sheet or the back of a swiss roll tin, cover with clingfilm and chill it until ready to fill and finish the pie. For a *lattice top crust*, roll the dough to an 28cm square by starting with a square of dough and turning it 90 degrees every time you roll over it. Wrap and chill as in step 6.

> ESSENTIAL TECHNIQUE

baking an empty tart crust

Often a tart crust needs to be fully baked before adding a filling that doesn't require baking. This technique is known as baking it 'blind'. It's simple to do, but you'll need some dried beans to weigh down the crust during the initial baking time when it might puff up and distort.

One tart crust made from Flaky Pastry Dough, see opposite page, chilled

1   When you are ready to bake the tart crust, set a rack in the centre of the oven and preheat to 180°C/gas mark 4.

2   Pierce the chilled crust at 2.5cm intervals with a fork. Line the bottom and sides of the crust with a 35.5cm disc of parchment paper (A) and fill with dried beans.

3   Bake the tart crust until it is dry-looking and set, about 10 minutes. Remove the paper and beans and continue baking until the crust is evenly light golden, 15–20 minutes more.

4   Cool the crust on a rack and use it the same day you bake it.

A

lattice-topped apple pie

Makes one 25cm tart, about 10 servings

APPLE FILLING

1.35kg tart apples, pared, halved, cored, and cut into 1cm dice (see Note)

110g granulated sugar

55g light brown sugar

3 tablespoons plain flour

1 teaspoon ground cinnamon

30g cold unsalted butter

FINISHING

2 tablespoons granulated sugar

One 25cm unbaked tart crust, edges untrimmed and a square of dough for the top crust, both made from Flaky Pastry Dough (pages 26 and 28–29)

Note: The most traditional apples for the filling are Bramleys. A combination of equal parts Golden Delicious and Granny Smith also works well, but cut the Granny Smith apples into smaller dice since they're so firm – otherwise they'll take too long to soften.

variations

Add the (unbaked) crumb topping on page 31 (omit the almonds or substitute walnut pieces) instead of the lattice.

Try adding 170g raisins or dried currants to the filling by reserving 2/3 of the seasoned filling and folding the raisins into the rest of the filling. Scrape the raisin-studded filling into the bottom crust, then top with the reserved filling to avoid burnt raisins at the top of the tart. Dried cranberries work well, too.

This is so much more practical to prepare and serve than a standard apple pie baked in a sloping pie tin. It's free-standing on a serving plate and only needs to be cut into wedges, with none of the sometimes destructive digging underneath the bottom crust to extract wedges from the other type of tin. It's also much more elegant looking than a plain apple pie. I like to use a little flour to thicken the juices of an apple filling such as this one – it's easy to do (just mix the flour with the sugar) and unless you use too much, it provides just the slight thickening needed so the juices in the baked pie aren't watery. Dicing the apples makes them bake through more quickly than cutting them into wedges, plus it makes the filling less bulky when placed in the bottom crust, creating only a small gap between the filling and top crust after the tart is baked.

1 Set a rack in the lowest level of the oven and preheat to 190°C/gas mark 5. Slide a sheet of aluminium foil onto the bottom of the oven to catch drips when the filling comes to the simmer close to the end of the baking time.

2 Put the apples in a large bowl and mix the sugars, flour and cinnamon in a small bowl. Scatter 2 tablespoons of the sugar mixture onto the bottom of the tart crust. Scatter the rest over the apples and use a large rubber spatula, repeatedly digging upward from the bottom of the bowl to mix.

3 Scrape the filling into the prepared crust and redistribute the apple pieces so that the top of the filling is level rather than domed. Dot the filling with shreds of the butter.

4 Use some water and a brush to moisten the extra dough at the edge of the tin. Use a pizza wheel or serrated pastry wheel to cut the square of dough into ten 2.5cm strips. Place 5 of the strips parallel and equidistant from each other on the filling, letting the ends of the strips touch the moistened area of the bottom crust. Place the next 5 strips at either a 45- or 90-degree angle to the first strips.

5 Use moistened fingers to press the ends of the strips gently against the overhanging edge of the bottom crust. Use the back of a knife to trim the overhanging dough even with the rim of the tin.

6 To finish, gently brush a little water on the strips of dough and scatter on the sugar. Bake the tart until the crust is well coloured and baked through and the filling is gently bubbling, about 45–55 minutes.

7 Cool the tart on a rack. Slide it from the flan tin base to a serving plate to serve.

Serving: Cut wedges of the tart and serve with a scoop of vanilla ice cream if you wish.

Storage: Keep the tart at room temperature on the day it's baked. For longer storage, continue to keep it at room temperature, but cover loosely with clingfilm.

shaker lemon tart

Makes one 25cm tart, about 10 servings

450g lemons, about 3 medium
or 4 small

450g sugar

5 large eggs

¼ teaspoon salt

Sugar, for finishing

One 25cm unbaked tart crust, made from
Flaky Pastry Dough (page 26)

This is my version of what's often known as Shaker lemon pie. The Shakers were a Christian religious sect that practised communal living and have left behind a legacy of delicious plain cooking and beautifully designed hand-crafted furniture and household accessories. This four-ingredient lemon filling is a perfect example of Shaker cooking at its best. This is usually made with thin lemon slices. I find it easier to quarter the lemons and remove the pips and then chop them in the food processor.

1 Place the lemons in a large saucepan or casserp;e and cover them by 5cm with cold water. Place on a medium heat and bring to the boil. Pour off the water and replace with fresh cold water, then bring to the boil and continue cooking at a steady boil for 10 minutes. Use a slotted spoon to remove the lemons to a bowl and cover them with cold water. Let the lemons stand until completely cooled, then drain them.

2 Set a rack in the lowest level of the oven and preheat to 190°C/gas mark 5.

3 Quarter the lemons and catch any pips in a sieve set over a bowl, so that any juice is collected in the bowl.

4 Place the solid lemon pieces into a food processor and pulse them until they are chopped into pieces no larger than 5mm. Pour the contents of the work bowl into the bowl with the lemon juice and stir in the sugar, eggs and salt. Pour into the tart crust.

5 Bake the tart until the crust is deep golden and the filling is set, about 30–35 minutes.

6 Cool the tart on a rack. Unmould it and slide the tart to a serving plate to serve.

Serving: Serve wedges of the tart with lightly sweetened whipped cream.

Storage: Keep the tart at room temperature if serving the same day. Wrap and refrigerate leftovers and bring them to room temperature again before serving.

chocolate meringue tart

Makes one 25cm tart, 8–10 servings

CHOCOLATE CREAM FILLING

480ml full fat milk

110g sugar

1 7.5cm cinnamon stick

3 7.5cm strips orange zest, removed with a vegetable peeler

240ml single cream

40g cornflour

4 medium eggs

225g dark chocolate (65 to 70% cocoa solids), cut into 5mm pieces

2 teaspoons vanilla extract

MERINGUE TOPPING

4 medium egg whites

170g sugar

Pinch of salt

One 25cm tart crust made from Flaky Pastry Dough (pages 26 and 28–29), baked and cooled

variation

Lemon cream meringue tart: Decrease the milk to 240ml; combine the milk and cream with the sugar in step 1. Omit the cinnamon stick, orange zest, and chocolate. Whisk the cornflour and eggs into 120ml lemon juice, strained before measuring, instead of the cream in step 2.

Though a chocolate cream tart is often covered with whipped cream, it's more traditional to use a light meringue. For best results, don't have the chocolate cream too cold or a layer of watery condensation will develop between the filling and the meringue.

1 For the chocolate cream, combine the milk and sugar in a medium saucepan and whisk to dissolve the sugar. Add the cinnamon stick and orange zest. Set the pan over a low heat and bring to the boil.

2 Meanwhile, pour the cream into a large heat-proof bowl and whisk in the cornflour. Whisk the eggs into the cream mixture, one at a time.

3 When the milk mixture boils, remove the pan from the heat and use a slotted spoon to remove and discard the cinnamon stick and strips of zest. Whisk about 180ml of the hot milk into the cream and egg mixture.

4 Return the remaining milk to the boil and, beginning to whisk before pouring, whisk the cream and egg mixture into the boiling milk, continuing to whisk constantly until the cream comes to the boil. Cook, whisking, for 30 seconds.

5 Remove the pan from the heat and whisk in the chocolate until it is melted and the cream is smooth. Whisk in the vanilla.

6 Scrape the chocolate cream into the cooled tart shell and spread it evenly. Press clingfilm against the surface of the cream and refrigerate the filled tart until the cream has cooled to about 21°C.

7 Once the filling has cooled, remove the tart from the refrigerator. Set a rack in the centre of the oven and preheat to 200°C/gas mark 6.

8 For the meringue, fill a saucepan halfway with water and bring it to the boil. Decrease the heat so that the water boils gently. Combine the egg whites, sugar and salt in the bowl of an electric mixer and place the bowl over the pan of simmering water. Whisk gently until the egg whites are hot (about 60°C) and the sugar is dissolved, about 2 minutes.

9 Place the bowl on the mixer with the whisk attachment and whisk the meringue on a medium-high speed until it has risen in volume and is very fluffy, 2–3 minutes. Decrease the speed to medium and continue whisking until the meringue cools to room temperature. Press the palm of your hand against the outside of the bowl; if you can't feel any heat, the meringue is ready.

10 Use a rubber spatula to scrape the meringue onto the chocolate filling. Spread the meringue evenly over the filling, making sure that it touches the edge of the crust all around. Bake the tart until the meringue is golden, 3–4 minutes, watching it constantly.

11 Cool the tart on a rack, then chill until serving. Unmould the tart and slide it from the flan tin base to a serving plate.

Serving: Use a thin, sharp knife to cut the tart, wiping the knife after each cut.

Storage: Wrap leftovers and store in the refrigerator.

spinach & bacon tart

Makes one 25cm tart, about 10 servings

450g baby spinach or 280g frozen spinach, thawed

110g thin-sliced streaky bacon, cut into 5mm dice

85g finely diced white or yellow onion

Salt

Freshly ground black pepper

Freshly grated nutmeg

360ml single cream

110g coarsely grated mature cheddar, Gouda, or Swiss Gruyère cheese

3 medium eggs

One 25cm unbaked tart crust made from Flaky Pastry Dough (page 26)

Tart fillings made from greens such as spinach are always difficult to salt properly: too much and the tart's inedible, too little and you risk expiring from boredom after a forkful or two. Adding bacon to this spinach filling helps, because the spinach itself may then be very lightly salted since you'll have little bursts of salty bacon flavour in every bite.

1 For the filling, rinse the spinach and place it in a colander to drain. Place the spinach in a large saucepan and place over a high heat. Cover the pan and let the spinach steam, uncovering and stirring it occasionally, until it is completely wilted and cooked through, about 5 minutes. Drain in the same colander and allow to cool. Once cooled, squeeze the moisture from handfuls of the spinach, then coarsely chop by hand. If using frozen spinach, just wring out the excess moisture.

2 Cook the bacon over a medium heat in a shallow sauté pan, stirring occasionally to keep the pieces separate. Once the bacon has coloured nicely, take off the heat and use a slotted spoon to transfer the cooked bacon to a plate lined with kitchen paper. Pour off all but 1 tablespoon of the bacon fat from the pan.

3 Set a rack in the lowest level of the oven and preheat to 190°C/gas mark 5.

4 Place the pan on a medium heat and add the onion. Once it starts to sizzle, decrease the heat to low and continue cooking, stirring occasionally, until the onion is wilted and just beginning to colour, about 10 minutes. Add the spinach and bacon to the pan and season with a little salt, several grindings of pepper, and a tiny pinch of nutmeg. Stir everything together until evenly combined.

5 Scrape the mixture into a bowl and stir in the cream and grated cheese. Taste for seasoning. At this point, it should taste like well-seasoned creamed spinach. Add a little more salt and pepper if necessary. Whisk in the eggs one at a time. Scrape the filling into the prepared crust and spread it evenly.

6 Bake the tart until the crust is well coloured and baked through and the filling is set, about 35–40 minutes.

7 Cool the tart on a rack and unmould it. Slide it from the flan tin base to a serving plate to serve.

Storage: Keep the tart at room temperature on the day it's baked. Loosely cover with clingfilm and store leftovers at room temperature for up to one day.

smoked salmon & avocado tart

Makes one 25cm tart, 8–10 servings

2–3 perfectly ripe Hass avocados, about 450–560g

2 tablespoons lime juice

1 tablespoon finely chopped seeded jalapeño or serrano chilli, or a few drops chilli sauce, optional

Salt

Freshly ground black pepper

4 tablespoons finely chopped white onion

2 medium ripe plum tomatoes, about 225g, stemmed, halved, seeded and cut into 5mm dice

110g best smoked salmon, thinly sliced and cut into 1cm squares

3–4 large leaves of cos or iceburg lettuce, rinsed, thoroughly dried, any thick ribs removed, and shredded

1 bunch chives, finely sliced, about 55g or chopped coriander leaves

One 25cm tart crust made from Flaky Pastry Dough (page 26), baked and cooled

No, I shouldn't admit it, but, yes, I could eat a whole one of these. Smoked salmon and avocados are two of my favourite foods, and I like them even better together. I first tasted the combination at Bouley restaurant in New York. It came in a tiny portion served as an 'amuse bouche' right after my friends and I had ordered our lunch. I resolved to try it as a tart and this is the result. Make sure the lettuce in the bottom of the tart shell is completely dry or it will defeat its purpose of keeping the crust from softening from contact with the moist avocado and salmon. Normally I would prefer not to cut smoked salmon into small pieces, but it's essential here or it would be impossible to cut through the tart without having the soft avocado mixture squish out in all directions.

1 For the filling, halve one of the avocados and remove the stone. Scoop the flesh from the skin into a mixing bowl. Quickly repeat with the remaining avocado(s). Sprinkle on the lime juice, chilli sauce, if using, a large pinch of salt and a couple of grindings of pepper. Use a small rubber spatula to fold in the seasonings, being careful not to overmix and mash the avocado. Press clingfilm against the surface and refrigerate until right before serving.

2 Half an hour before serving the tart, use a large fork to mash the avocados so that there are no pieces larger than about 5mm. Taste for seasoning and adjust, remembering that the salmon is salty. Add the finely chopped chilli (if using), onion, tomatoes and salmon to the avocado; use a small rubber spatula to fold everything together.

3 Evenly scatter the lettuce in the bottom of the tart crust. Scrape the avocado mixture onto the lettuce in 6 or 8 places to make it easier to spread. Use a small palette knife to spread the filling smoothly in the crust.

4 Sprinkle the chives on top of the filling. Unmould the tart and slide it from the flan tin base to a serving plate. Serve immediately or within 20 minutes at the latest.

Serving: Use a thin, sharp knife to cut the tart into wedges. Garnish with lime wedges if you wish.

Storage: Try to avoid having leftovers; this isn't a good keeper.

gommer cholera

(Swiss potato & cheese pie from Goms in the Valais)

Makes one 23cm pie, about 10 servings

55g unsalted butter

2 large white onions (about 450g), peeled and finely chopped

2 large tart apples (about 450g) such as Granny Smith, pared, halved, cored and thinly sliced

Salt

Freshly ground black pepper

Freshly grated nutmeg

1 batch Flaky Pastry Dough (page 26), divided into two pieces, one slightly larger than the other

450g waxy potatoes, boiled until tender, cooled, peeled, and sliced 5mm thick

450g Goms or other Swiss raclette cheese, rind removed and thinly sliced

Egg wash: 1 egg well beaten with a pinch of salt

One 23 x 5cm round cake tin, buttered

No one seems to really know how this delicious pie came to be named after a disease. One flimsy explanation states that people stayed indoors and cooked what they had, rather than venturing out to do food shopping during the 1830 cholera epidemic. The village of Goms in the Upper Valais is also well known for the quality of the cheese produced there, but any real Swiss raclette cheese will do nicely. This makes an excellent brunch or lunch dish served with a salad and then some sorbet and crisp biscuits for dessert.

1   For the filling, melt the butter on a medium heat in a sauté pan or casserole with a lid. Add the chopped onion and cook until it starts to sizzle. Reduce the heat, cover the pan and let the onion sweat until very soft, about 20 minutes. Add the sliced apples and continue to cook uncovered until the apples are tender and their moisture has evaporated. Cool slightly and season with salt, pepper and nutmeg.

2   When you're ready to bake the pie, set a rack in the lowest level of the oven and preheat to 190°C/gas mark 5.

3   Roll the larger piece of dough on a floured surface and fit it into the tin, letting any excess dough hang over the edge of the tin. Place a layer of half the sliced potatoes into the tin and season sparingly with salt and pepper. Spread half the onion and apple mixture over them, then top with half the cheese slices. Repeat with the remaining potatoes, onion and apple mixture and cheese.

4   Trim the excess dough at the rim of the pan to 1cm and fold it in over the filling.

5   Roll the remaining dough to a disc the size of the top of the pie and trim evenly. Arrange on the filling so that the top crust comes right to the edge of the tin and gently press it to the downturned edge of the bottom crust. Brush with the egg wash and trace a lattice pattern on the top crust with the back of a fork.

6   Bake the pie until the crust is deep golden and the filling is well heated through, about 45 minutes. Cool briefly on a rack and serve warm or at room temperature.

Storage: Keep at room temperature on the day it is baked. Wrap leftovers tightly in clingfilm and store at room temperature for up to two days. Reheat at 180°C/gas mark 4 for 15 minutes and cool slightly before serving.

03

shortcrust pastry & tarts

The French name for shortcrust pastry, *pâte sablée* (sandy pastry), says it all: When baked, this dough has a crumbly, sandy texture that pairs well with rich, creamy fillings. Preparing the dough in the food processor is especially efficient when you use ground nuts as an ingredient, as the nuts are processed and then simply left in the work bowl. Fillings range from a rich and elegant layered combination of chocolate and chestnut creams, to the smooth and satisfying cream cheese and soured cream filling for a New York cheesecake – which actually isn't a tart at all, but does use a baked shortcrust pastry crust as a base.

baked shortcrust pastry tart crust

I like to include some ground almonds in this dough for extra flavour and texture, but you may omit them. Since the almonds don't absorb any liquid, the dough will work exactly the same way with or without them; no need to make adjustments. This recipe makes enough for two crusts as do all the other pastry dough recipes, but the instructions in steps 4 to 12 are for rolling and baking a single crust from half the dough.

Makes about 675g of dough, enough for two 25cm tart crusts

30g slivered or whole blanched almonds, optional

85g icing sugar, sifted

325g plain flour

¼ teaspoon salt

225g unsalted butter, cold, cut into 16 pieces

2 medium egg yolks

1 teaspoon vanilla extract

One 25cm loose-based flan tin

A

D

1   Combine the almonds and icing sugar in the bowl of a food processor and pulse repeatedly until finely ground, about 1 minute. No visible pieces of almond should remain. Use a thin palette knife to scrape away any of the mixture caked up in the corner where the base meets the side of the bowl.

2   Add the flour and salt and pulse a couple of times to mix. (If not using the nuts, start here and add the sugar.) Add the butter and pulse repeatedly until no visible pieces remain. Add the egg yolks and vanilla and pulse until the dough forms a ball.

3   Turn the dough out onto a floured surface and carefully remove the blade. Divide the dough into 2 equal pieces. Shape each piece of dough into a thick disc and wrap individually in clingfilm. Refrigerate until firm, at least 1 hour. You may prepare the dough several days in advance and keep it refrigerated, or double wrap and freeze the second piece, defrosting it in the refrigerator overnight before use.

4   To form a tart crust, remove one of the pieces of dough from the refrigerator and allow it to soften at a cool room temperature for about 20 minutes, just until it is soft enough to roll without cracking, but still firm. Unwrap it and place it on a floured surface. Use the palm of your hand to press it to a thickness of 5mm.

5   Flour the dough and gently roll it out into a 33cm disc, adding pinches of flour under and on top of the dough as needed (A and B).

6   Fold the dough in half and slide both hands under it, palms upward, and transfer it to the tin, lining up the fold with the diameter of the tin. Unfold the dough into the tin. If the dough cracks or tears you can press it back together (C and D).

7   Evenly fit the dough into the tin, making sure it's flat against both the base and side of the tin (E). Trim away any excess dough at the rim of the tin by rolling over it with a rolling pin (F) or scraping it away with the back of a paring knife.

8   Finish off the top edges by pressing outward against the side of the tin with your thumb and down at the same time at the top of the crust with your index finger.

9   Slide the flan tin onto a baking sheet, cover it with clingfilm and refrigerate it for several hours or overnight before baking.

10 Set a rack in the centre of the oven and preheat to 180°C/gas mark 4. Pierce the chilled tart crust all over at 2.5cm intervals with a fork. Line the crust, bottom and sides, with a 35.5cm disc of parchment paper and fill with dried beans or other small weights (G).

11 Bake the tart crust until it is dry looking and set, about 10 minutes. Remove the paper and beans and bake until the crust is evenly light golden, 15–20 minutes.

12 Cool the crust on a rack and use it the same day you bake it.

new york cheesecake

This isn't a tart, but it does utilise a shortcrust pastry base – my favourite way of preparing a cheesecake. A baked pastry base makes the cheesecake so easy to unmould, even if you use a springform tin and it tastes much better than those biscuit crumb crusts that are so loaded with butter that they never really become firm.

Makes one 23cm cheesecake, about 12 servings

½ batch Shortcrust Pastry Dough (page 40), made with or without ground almonds

CHEESECAKE BATTER

450g cream cheese, softened at room temperature for at least 3 hours

225g sugar

4 medium eggs

360ml soured cream

2 teaspoons vanilla extract

1 tablespoon lemon juice, strained before measuring

One 23 x 7.5cm round cake tin or a 23cm springform tin, the base buttered and lined with a disc of baking paper; one small roasting tin to hold the cake in water

Serving: A rich cheesecake needs no accompaniment, but some crushed, sugared strawberries wouldn't hurt either. Bring the cake to room temperature at least 2 hours before serving.

Storage: Store the cake wrapped in clingfilm in the refrigerator for several days before serving.

1 Roll the shortcrust pastry dough to a 24cm disc according to the directions on page 40. Slide the piece of rolled dough onto a flexible baking sheet or chopping board. Place the tin on the dough and cut around the base of the tin using a paring knife or small pizza wheel. Remove the scraps and slide the disc of dough into the prepared tin. Press it into place and about 3mm up the side of the tin to allow for shrinkage during baking. Chill the dough-lined tin for up to 1 day or at least 1 hour before proceeding.

2 When you are ready to bake the cheesecake, set a rack in the lower third of the oven and preheat to 160°C/gas mark 3.

3 Combine the cream cheese and sugar in the bowl of an electric mixer fitted with the paddle attachment and beat on a low speed until smooth, about 30 seconds. Use a rubber spatula to scrape down the bowl and beater.

4 Add 1 egg, beat just until smooth, still on a low speed, and scrape. Repeat for each of the 3 remaining eggs.

5 In a bowl, whisk the soured cream with the vanilla and lemon juice and add to the mixer bowl. Mix on a low speed until just combined. Set the filling aside. If you notice any lumps, use a small rubber spatula to pass the batter through a fine-mesh sieve into a clean bowl.

6 If using a springform tin, wrap the base and sides of the tin in a double layer of aluminium foil. Pierce the chilled dough at 2.5cm intervals with the tines of a fork and bake it until it is dry and golden, about 15 minutes.

7 While the crust is baking, set the roasting tin on the hob. Have ready a 1 litre measuring jug filled with hot water.

8 As soon as the crust is baked, place it in the roasting tin and butter the side of the tin. Pour the cheesecake batter over the baked crust. Quickly add 1cm hot water to the roasting tin and place it in the oven. This quick succession of steps is necessary to ensure that the crust doesn't cool after baking and possibly shrink.

9 Bake the cheesecake until the top is lightly coloured and it is set in all but the very centre, 45–55 minutes. Remove the tin from the bain marie and place the cheesecake on a rack. Immediately run the point of a small paring knife around the inside of the tin at the top to loosen the top 1cm of the cake from the side of the tin. This will prevent cracking.

10 Cool completely, wrap loosely in clingfilm and chill for several hours or overnight before serving.

11 To unmould the chilled cheesecake, have a couple of round cake boards, clingfilm and a serving plate ready. Use a small paring knife to loosen the cake from the side of the tin. Place the tin over a high heat for a couple of seconds to melt the butter under the paper and loosen the cake from the tin. If you used a springform, remove the side of the tin.

12 Cover the top of the cake with clingfilm and a cake board and invert. Lift off the tin and paper. Replace with another cake board and invert again. Remove the top cake board and clingfilm. Slide the cheesecake from the cake board onto the serving plate or wrap the cake, still on the cake board and refrigerate until needed.

chocolate chestnut tart

Makes one 25cm tart, about 10 servings

CHESTNUT FILLING

675g fresh chestnuts, or one 400g tin or jar of peeled chestnuts

1 teaspoon salt

480ml milk

70g sugar

1 vanilla pod, split lengthways

1 tablespoon dark rum

55g unsalted butter, softened

CHOCOLATE FILLING

150ml whipping cream

2 tablespoons sugar

200g dark chocolate (65–70% cocoa solids), melted and cooled

30g unsalted butter, very soft

10 crystallised violets or large chocolate shavings for finishing

One 25cm Shortcrust Pastry Tart Crust (page 40), with or without ground almonds, baked and cooled, but left in the tin

This is a showstopper dessert for an autumn or winter party. The crumbly shortcrust pastry crust contrasts perfectly with the rich chestnut and chocolate fillings, which form elegant layers when the tart is cut. Fresh chestnuts are readily available from October through to January, the best time to enjoy this type of dessert. You may substitute peeled chestnuts that come in a jar or tin, but they tend to be really expensive.

1 For the chestnut filling, pierce the rounded end of each chestnut with the point of a small knife and place the nuts in a large saucepan. Cover with water and bring to the boil. Add the salt and continue cooking at a low boil until the chestnuts are tender and one peels easily, 30–45 minutes. If using chestnuts from a jar, rinse, drain, and taste a small piece of one for tenderness. If they seem hard, boil them as above for 30 minutes.

2 Drain the chestnuts in a colander and cover with a tea towel to keep them warm so that they peel easily. Peel the chestnuts, removing the outer shell and as much of the interior brown skin as possible.

3 Rinse the pan and return the peeled chestnuts to it along with the milk, sugar and vanilla pod. Use a potato masher to crush the chestnuts into small pieces, but not a purée. Bring to the boil over a medium heat and decrease the heat so that the milk just simmers. Cook, stirring often, until the chestnuts are very soft, about 20 minutes. If the liquid becomes too thick before the chestnuts are tender, add water a couple of tablespoons at a time to prevent scorching. Remove the vanilla pod.

4 Cool the cooked chestnuts to room temperature and then purée them in a food processor for 30 seconds, scrape down the sides, and continue to alternate puréeing and scraping until when you taste a small spoonful of the cream there is no graininess at all in it. Once they are reduced to a perfectly smooth cream, add the rum and the butter and pulse to mix in.

5 Scrape the filling into the crust and use a small palette knife to spread it evenly.

6 For the chocolate filling, combine the cream and sugar in a small saucepan and whisk to dissolve the sugar. Place over a medium heat and cook until the sugar is dissolved and the mixture is hot, about 25°C. Pour the cream into a bowl to cool to room temperature.

7 Pour the cooled cream into the cooled chocolate and whisk smooth. Whisk in the butter (if it's not very soft, the butter will form lumps).

8 Scrape the chocolate filling over the chestnut filling and use a small palette knife to spread it evenly. Arrange 10 crystallised violets equidistant from each other on the chocolate filling next to the crust, or sprinkle with chocolate shavings. Unmould the tart and slide it from the flan tin base to a serving plate.

Serving: Use a thin, sharp knife wiped with a damp cloth after each cut to divide the tart into wedges.

Storage: Cover leftovers with clingfilm and keep at a cool room temperature or in the refrigerator. If refrigerated, bring to room temperature again before serving.

strawberry cream cheese crumble tart

Makes one 25cm tart, about 8 servings

ALMOND CRUMB TOPPING

160g plain flour

70g sugar

¼ teaspoon baking powder

¼ teaspoon ground cinnamon

⅛ teaspoon salt

4 tablespoons flaked or whole blanched almonds, coarsely chopped into 5mm pieces

110g unsalted butter, melted

STRAWBERRY CREAM CHEESE FILLING

450g cream cheese, softened

110g icing sugar, sifted

1 teaspoon finely grated lemon zest

1½ teaspoons vanilla extract

450g strawberries, rinsed, hulled and halved or quartered if large, or left whole if very small (reserve 1 perfect whole berry)

Icing sugar in a shaker, for finishing

1 unbaked Shortcrust Pastry Tart Crust (page 40), prepared up to the end of step 9

Swiss roll tin lined with parchment paper or foil for baking the crumb topping

I've often confessed in the past to being addicted to crumb topping. Recently I even found a new way to enjoy it – atop a tart that has a pre-baked crust and a creamy filling. This does necessitate the extra step of baking the crumb topping separately, but you can do that while baking the tart crust. The crisp crumb topping with a hint of chopped almonds is a perfect contrast to this tart's light cream cheese filling and juicy strawberries.

1　Set racks in the upper and lower thirds of the oven and preheat to 180°C/gas mark 4.

2　For the topping, in a medium bowl stir together the flour, sugar, baking powder, cinnamon and salt. Stir in the almonds. Use a rubber spatula to stir in the butter. Let the mixture stand for a few minutes, then use your fingertips to break the mixture into 5mm–1cm crumbs. Scatter the crumbs on the prepared tin.

3　Bake the tart crust in the lower third of the oven and the crumb topping in the upper third. After 10 minutes, remove the paper and beans from the tart crust and place it on the upper rack and the crumbs on the lower one.

4　Continue baking the tart crust until it is dry and light golden, another 15–20 minutes. Bake the crumb topping until it is deep golden and firm, another 10–15 minutes.

5　Cool the crust and the topping on racks. If the crumbs have clumped together during baking, let them cool completely and then use a dough scraper or table knife to chop them coarsely.

6　For the cream cheese filling, place the cream cheese in the bowl of an electric mixer fitted with the paddle attachment and beat on medium speed just until it is smooth. Beat in the icing sugar, lemon zest and vanilla and continue beating until lightened, about 1 minute.

7　To assemble the tart, spread half the cream cheese filling on the base of the tart crust and arrange the berries on it, cut side down. Spread the remaining filling over the berries. Evenly scatter the crumb topping over the filling. Right before serving, lightly dust the topping with icing sugar and place the reserved berry in the centre of the tart.

Serving: Unmould the tart and slide it off the flan tin base to a serving plate. Serve wedges of the tart; it needs no accompaniment.

Storage: You may have all the components ready, but don't assemble the tart until a few hours before you intend to serve it. Keep it at a cool room temperature until you do. Wrap and refrigerate leftovers and bring to room temperature before serving again. The crust will soften after it has been refrigerated.

variations

Substitute raspberries or blueberries or use a combination of all three berries. Skinned and diced perfectly ripe peaches or mangoes are also good choices.

french raspberry tart

Makes one 25cm tart, 8–10 servings

CRÈME PÂTISSIÈRE

180ml full fat milk

60ml whipping cream

55g sugar

3 medium egg yolks

2 tablespoons plain flour

1 teaspoon vanilla extract

RASPBERRIES AND GLAZE

225g seedless raspberry jam

2 tablespoons water

450g fresh raspberries, picked over but not washed

25cm Shortcrust Pastry Tart Crust (page 40), with or without ground almonds, baked and cooled, but left in the tin

This is a classic: a shortcrust pastry crust topped with a thin layer of crème pâtissière, lots of flavourful fresh raspberries and a bit of raspberry glaze to bind them together. Strawberries are an obvious substitute, but I only like to make this with small, perfectly sweet, height-of-season strawberries. Larger, out-of-season berries have less flavour and produce a lot of water when they are cut. Mulberries, blackberries and blueberries in season sidestep the water issue. See the variations for making an accompanying glaze for these berries.

1 For the crème pâtissière, whisk the milk, cream and half the sugar in a small saucepan. Place over a low heat and bring to the boil.

2 Meanwhile, in a bowl, whisk the egg yolks and then whisk in the remaining sugar. Sift over and whisk in the flour.

3 When the milk mixture boils, whisk it into the yolk mixture. Strain the mixture back into the pan and place over a medium heat. Use a small, pointed-end whisk to whisk constantly, being sure to reach into the corners of the pan, until the cream comes to the boil and thickens. Continue to cook, whisking constantly, for 30 seconds. Off heat, whisk in the vanilla.

4 Scrape the cream into a glass or stainless-steel bowl and press clingfilm against the surface. Chill until cold.

5 A few hours before you intend to serve the tart, make the glaze. Combine the jam and water in a small saucepan. Bring to the boil over a medium heat, stirring often. Strain the glaze into a bowl, rinse the saucepan, return the glaze to the saucepan, and cook over a low heat until reduced to about 120ml, about 10 minutes.

6 Use a small palette knife to spread the cooled crème pâtissière in the tart crust.

7 Put the berries in a bowl and drizzle on the slightly cooled glaze. Use a small rubber spatula to fold the berries and glaze together gently. Scrape the berries into the tart crust on top of the crème pâtissière and arrange them in an even mound.

8 Unmould the tart and slide it from the flan tin base to a serving plate.

Serving: Use a sharp, thin knife to cut the tart into wedges.

Storage: Keep at a cool room temperature until serving. Wrap and chill leftovers.

variations

Omit the glaze, arrange the berries in the crust and dust with icing sugar immediately before serving.

Substitute strawberry jam for the glaze. Arrange strawberries on the crème pâtissière and use a pastry brush to apply a thin coat of the glaze.

To substitute any of the other berries mentioned above, use a neutral-flavoured jelly such as currant or apple instead of the jam. Omit the water. Crush 110g of the berries, add them to the jelly, and bring to the boil over a medium heat, stirring occasionally. Strain and reduce the glaze as above. Continue with the recipe at step 6, above.

quick puff pastry

Some purists may still make the laborious type of puff pastry that involves preparing a dough and wrapping it around a square of softened butter before beginning the rolling and folding process. I abandoned it a long time ago, especially since I know that no one, including me, has the time for long versions of recipes when equally good and faster versions exist. Making quick puff pastry, sometimes also referred to as rough puff pastry, is a one-step mixing process immediately followed by rolling and folding that's completed without chilling the dough either after mixing or after any of the folds. It does take a bit of time to prepare, but still only about a third of the time (or less) that the traditional version takes. If you're really pressed for time, there is an even faster version made in the food processor that will take about twenty minutes.

A

> ESSENTIAL TECHNIQUE
quick puff pastry

There is only one inviolable rule for preparing quick or any other kind of puff pastry: Make sure it's cool in your kitchen or the dough will turn into a gooey mess. That said, mixing the dough is no more complicated than making any other pastry dough – in fact, you can do part or all of the mixing in the food processor. Keep a ruler handy as you roll or you might end up with an odd-shaped piece of dough that's difficult to manoeuvre.

Makes about 675g dough

280g unsalted butter, cold

260g plain flour

3/4 teaspoon salt

150ml cold water

Storage: The dough keeps well in the refrigerator for up to 5 days. Some people like to add a couple of teaspoons of distilled white vinegar to that first amount of water added to the dough in step 4 as a preservative. Double wrap and freeze for up to 1 month. Defrost the dough in the refrigerator overnight before using.

1 Cut 225g of the butter into 5mm cubes. Scrape them onto a plate in one layer and refrigerate them.

2 Put the flour and salt in a bowl and stir a couple of times to combine. Cut the remaining 55g of butter into thin slivers and add to the bowl. Rub in the butter, squeezing it with your fingertips, rubbing the butter and flour mixture between the palms of your hands and reaching down to the bottom of the bowl. Repeat until the flour and butter are evenly mixed. This only takes a couple of minutes; the mixture should remain cool and powdery. Alternatively, pulse the flour, salt, and butter slivers in a food processor fitted with the metal blade until no visible pieces of butter remain, then pour the mixture into a bowl.

3 Add the chilled butter cubes (A) and use a rubber spatula to fold them in.

4 Set aside 2 tablespoons of the measured water and pour the remaining water on the flour and butter mixture (B). Use the rubber spatula to fold everything together, scraping from the bottom of the bowl upward (C). If there are a lot of dry bits of unmoistened flour, sprinkle on the remaining water, 1 tablespoon at a time, folding it in as before.

5 Scrape the dough from the bowl to a floured work surface and lightly flour the dough. Use your hands to squeeze and shape the dough into a cylinder, and then press down to flatten it into a rectangle (D).

6 Flour the surface and the dough and starting at the narrow end of the rectangle farthest from you, use a rolling pin to press the dough firmly in parallel strokes close to each other (E). If there are sticky pieces of butter on the surface of the dough, seal them with a large pinch of flour, making sure to clean off anything stuck to the rolling pin before continuing. Repeat the pressing motion again from the nearest to furthest narrow end of the dough.

7 Press the dough once along the width; it should now be a rectangle about 1/2–1cm thick. Once again, flour under and on top of the dough and roll the dough away and back toward you in the length and once in the width, without rolling over the ends in the same direction, to make a rectangle about 46cm long and 20cm wide.

B

C

D

E

F

G

H

8 Fold the two 20cm ends of the dough in toward the middle of the rectangle,
   leaving a 2.5cm space in the middle. Fold the bottom up to the top to form
   4 layers of dough (F, G, and H). Reposition the dough so that the folded edge
   that resembles the spine of a book is on your left. Rolling and folding the
   dough is known as 'giving the dough a turn'.

9 Repeat steps 6, 7 and 8.

10 Repeat steps 6, 7 and 8 again.

11 Wrap the dough and refrigerate it for at least 3 hours to firm up and rest its
   elasticity before attempting to use it. ❯

variation

Food Processor Mixing Prepare the first part of the dough in the food processor as described in step 2, but leave it in the work bowl. Add the chilled butter cubes and give three 1-second pulses. Add half the water and pulse once; add the remaining water and pulse twice. The dough will not form a ball. Remove the blade by its handle and do step 5, page 50. Press the dough in both directions as in step 6, then roll it to a rectangle that's about 25 x 50cm. Fold the 25cm side furthest from you down over the middle and the 25cm side closest to you over that to make a 3-layered rectangle that's about 15 x 25cm. Position one of the 15cm sides closest to you and roll upward, swiss roll-style, to make a fat cylinder. Flour the work surface, position the cylinder of dough with the seam on the bottom, flour the top of the dough, and press with the palm of your hand to make the dough into a rectangle. Resume at step 11.

> ESSENTIAL TECHNIQUE

rolling puff pastry

Follow these simple instructions for all the recipes in this chapter. Some recipes might call for the dough to be rolled in sugar instead of flour, but the technique remains the same.

1 Flour the work surface and place the chilled puff pastry on it. Flour the dough. Press the dough in parallel and successive firm strokes with a rolling pin in both directions, until it is somewhat more pliable. Repeat dusting the surface and the dough with pinches of flour.

2 Roll back and forth away and back toward you without rolling over the ends (which would make them thinner and possibly make them stick to the surface).

3 To roll in the other direction, move the piece of dough 90 degrees and repeat step 2.

4 Keep a ruler nearby and measure the dough to see whether it is the size specified in the recipe. Repeat rolling in both directions until the dough is about 1cm larger all around than the size you need.

5 Slide the dough to a baking sheet (if it's a large piece, you might have to fold it and then unfold it on the sheet) and cover loosely with clingfilm.

6 Chill the dough until firm for easier cutting and shaping.

essential tips for quick puff pastry

- Quick puff pastry works like the flaky pastry dough on page 26, except here the butter is in larger pieces, consequently making larger layers throughout the dough. There is even more butter than flour by weight, so the dough not only bakes up flaky, but the many spaces that fill with steam actually rise up (puff) away from each other.

- When mixing the liquid into the dough, be careful not to overmix, which might render the dough elastic and consequently difficult to roll and form the layers.

- Cold, cold, cold: make sure everything is cold before you start mixing the dough. If you're the least bit apprehensive, or if the butter seems to be softening before you start rolling the dough, refrigerate the dough, wrapped in clingfilm, for 1 hour after step 5.

- Pay attention to the corners of the dough every time you roll over it. You want real 90-degree corners, so that the dough folds up into a symmetrically layered package that's easy to roll out again. A dough scraper is a handy tool for straightening the corners: Hold it perpendicular to the work surface and push in on the dough with the flat side of the blade to straighten it.

- As with all pastry doughs, resting is as important as careful mixing and rolling. Let the dough rest after turning it, then again once you've formed a pastry from the dough.

- Save any scraps generated by cutting out rounds of dough. Wrap and chill them and when they are firm, press them together, then roll them into a rectangle twice as long as it is wide. Fold the dough over to make a square, wrap and refrigerate. This dough is best used for the base of the thin apple tart, the cheese straws or the sugared puff pastries that follow.

- If you intend to keep the puff pastry in the refrigerator and use it over the course of several days, when preparing the dough, stir a tablespoon of strained lemon juice or distilled white vinegar into the water. The acidity will help prevent the dough from becoming grey as it sits.

'thin' apple tart

tarte fine aux pommes

This name refers to what I call a bistro apple tart – a dinner-plate-size or two-portion puff pastry tart topped with thin apple slices and a bit of glaze. It's a lovely tart, but it's pretty impractical if you are serving more than a couple of guests. The recipe below incorporates all the same elements, but with a slightly more generous yield. It's more practical, too, since it can be baked in advance and reheated if you want to serve it warm.

Makes one large 25 x 38cm tart, about 12 servings

½ batch (340g) Quick Puff Pastry (page 50)

APPLE TOPPING

4 large Golden Delicious apples, about 1kg

55g unsalted butter, melted

70g demerara sugar

APRICOT GLAZE

225g best-quality apricot jam

2 tablespoons water

Crème fraîche or sweetened whipped cream for serving

One 25 x 38cm swiss roll tin lined, base and sides, with buttered foil

1 Roll the dough to a 30 x 40cm rectangle, according to the instructions on page 50.

2 Fold the dough in quarters and arrange it in the tin, unfolding it to fit the tin. Press the dough into the base and sides of the tin and leave the excess dough at the rim of the tin untrimmed for the moment. Cover loosely with clingfilm and chill until a few hours before you intend to serve the tart.

3 When you are ready to serve the tart, set a rack in the lowest level of the oven and preheat to 200°C/gas mark 6.

4 Pare, halve, and core the apples. Use a small sharp paring knife to slice through each apple half across the core, to make 3mm slices. Keep the apple halves together as you slice through them to make arranging the apples easier.

5 Remove the tart crust from the refrigerator and pierce it all over with a fork at 2.5cm intervals.

6 Eliminate the first couple of smaller slices from the ends of each apple half and press on it gently with the palm of your hand to fan it out away from you so that it's about 15cm long. Slide a palette knife under the apple slices and arrange them in the top left corner of the tin in the length of the tin. Repeat with another apple half, then use an apple quarter to fill in the first row. Make 2 more rows right next to each other in the same way.

7 Paint the apple slices with the butter and evenly sprinkle with the sugar. Bake the tart until the pastry is baked through and the apples have taken on some colour, about 30 minutes.

8 Place the tart on a rack and use a sharp paring knife to trim away the overhanging pastry. Cool the tart completely and keep it at room temperature until you intend to serve it.

9 For the glaze, stir the apricot jam and water together in a small saucepan and bring to the boil over a low heat, stirring occasionally. Strain into a bowl, rinse the pan, return the glaze to the pan, and bring the glaze to the boil again. Let it reduce until slightly thickened, about 5 minutes.

10 If you wish to serve the tart warm, reheat for 10 minutes at 180°C/gas mark 4 and cool slightly. Pull on the foil lining to slide the tart to a chopping board. Flatten the foil that was on the side of the tart and slide a long palette knife between the tart and the foil. Pull away the foil, holding the tart in place with your other hand. Paint the apples with the glaze.

Serving: Use a sharp knife to slice the tart into three 38cm strips. Cut each strip into quarters to make 12 servings. Arrange each serving on a dessert plate and spoon some crème fraîche or whipped cream beside it.

Storage: Wrap leftovers and keep at room temperature for a day or two. Leftover apple tart benefits from reheating.

A   B   C

minced beef empanadas
empanadas de picadillo

Makes eight 15cm empanadas

²⁄₃ **batch (450g) Quick Puff Pastry (page 50)**

PICADILLO

2 small (about 225g total) waxy potatoes

½ large white or yellow onion (about 110–140g), peeled and coarsely chopped

1 small red or green pepper (about 110–140g), coarsely chopped

3 large cloves garlic, crushed, peeled, and coarsely chopped

3 tablespoons olive or mild vegetable oil

1 teaspoon ground cumin

450g lean beef mince

180ml tomato passata

180ml water

½ teaspoon salt

1 teaspoon distilled white vinegar

2 tablespoons capers in brine, rinsed and drained

3 tablespoons sliced pimento-stuffed green olives

¼ teaspoon hot chilli powder, or to taste (optional)

One baking sheet or swiss roll tin lined with parchment paper or foil

Typical empanadas are made from complicated, ancient forms of puff pastry and are usually fried. I recently had leftover puff pastry and leftover picadillo and decided to try some baked empanadas; these are the result. Picadillo (*picado* means 'chopped' in Spanish) is a fairly dry ragout made from beef mince and seasonings. This quantity is about twice as much as you need for eight empanadas. Serve the rest with rice.

1 Roll the dough according to the instructions on page 52 to a 30cm square. Slide the dough to a baking sheet and refrigerate until firm, about 15 minutes. Cut the square of dough into two 15 x 30cm rectangles and roll each to a 30cm square. Stack them on a baking sheet with clingfilm between and on top and refrigerate until you are ready to form the empanadas.

2 For the picadillo, put the potatoes in a small saucepan and cover them with water. Bring to the boil over a medium heat and boil for a minute. Slide the pan off the heat and leave the potatoes in the water until you need to add them to the picadillo; they'll be about three-quarters cooked when you do.

3 Put the onion, pepper and garlic in a food processor fitted with the metal blade and pulse to chop finely, but do not purée.

4 Put the oil in a wide saucepan or casserole with a lid and add the vegetables. Cook over a medium heat until they start to sizzle, then decrease to medium-low and cook, stirring occasionally, until they are soft and beginning to turn golden, about 20 minutes. Stir in the cumin and cook, stirring, for 30 seconds.

5 Add the beef mince and use a wooden spoon to mash it into the vegetables, continuously jabbing the spoon downward into the meat so that it cooks in separate grains and not clumps. Continue jabbing and stirring until the meat is reduced to fine granules and is starting to sizzle in the pan, about 5 minutes.

6 Add the tomato passata, water, salt and vinegar and stir them in. Bring to the boil, then regulate the heat so that the mixture simmers actively for about 10 minutes. If the liquid seems to be evaporating too quickly, decrease the heat.

D   E   F

7. Peel and cut the potatoes into 1cm dice. Add the potatoes, capers, olives, and chilli powder, if using, to the pan and stir. Simmer until the potatoes are tender and most of the liquid has boiled off, 15–20 minutes more.

8. Cool the picadillo completely before filling the empanadas. When you are ready to bake, set a rack in the centre of the oven and preheat to 200°C/gas mark 6.

9. Cut each piece of chilled dough into four 15cm discs (A and B), refrigerating them again as you cut them. Wrap and refrigerate the scraps for another use.

10. Place one of the discs on a floured surface and sprinkle lightly with flour. Roll over once away and back toward you to make a 20cm oval (C). Brush some water on the edge of the oval closest to you and place 3 tablespoons of the filling on it (D). Fold the bottom half of the oval over to join the top edge (E) and transfer to the pan. Use your finger to press the two layers of dough firmly together, about 3mm from the edge (F). Repeat with the rest of the dough and filling.

11. Use the point of a paring knife to cut a 2.5cm vent hole in each empanada over the thickest part of the filling. Bake until the empanadas are deep golden and the filling is bubbling slightly, about 20 minutes.

12. Slide to a rack and cool the empanadas for 5 minutes before serving on a platter.

Serving: Empanadas make a great lunch with a salad. They're also good at room temperature or for a picnic. Cool them on a rack to keep them crisp if you want to serve them that way.

Storage: You can assemble the empanadas and bake them later the same day, but they have to be eaten on the day they're baked. Wrap and refrigerate leftovers, reheat them at 180°C/gas mark 4 for 10 minutes, and cool them slightly before serving.

variation

Chicken Empanadas Substitute 450g skinless boneless chicken thighs cut into 2.5cm dice for the beef mince. Cook the same way, stirring occasionally (no need to jab) after adding the meat to the vegetables. Before adding the potatoes, use 2 forks to shred the meat.

just add sugar

There are any number of wonderful puff pastries that only require rolling the dough in sugar before shaping it. Though these are simple, absolutely nothing can equal the flavour of fresh-from-the-oven, all-butter puff pastry that has had sugar caramelised on it. When you begin rolling the dough, the amount of sugar it has to absorb might seem excessive. Every time you roll over the dough, redistribute half the sugar underneath it and half on top of it and roll with a firm but gentle pressure to avoid making the dough too thin too quickly. Remember that any leftover sugar can either be sprinkled on the pastries before they're baked or, as in the case of the Butterfly Wings, the pastries can be dipped into the sugar after they are cut and before they are placed on the tin.

½ batch (340g) Quick Puff Pastry (page 50)

225g sugar

2 baking sheets or swiss roll tins, lined with baking paper

ox tongues

This is the easiest and most simple variation.

Makes 24 individual pastries

1 Roll the dough according to the instructions on page 52 to a 20 x 30cm rectangle. If the dough gets soft, slide it onto a baking sheet and refrigerate it for 15 minutes.

2 Use a 5 cm plain round cutter to cut the dough into 24 discs. Wrap and refrigerate the scraps and use them for another pastry.

3 One at a time, place the discs on a heavily sugared work surface and sprinkle with additional sugar. Roll over the disk to make it into a 9cm oval.

4 Arrange the ovals on the prepared tins and refrigerate them for 30 minutes.

5 When you are ready to bake them, set a rack in the centre of the oven and preheat to 190°C/gas mark 5.

6 Pierce the chilled ox tongues all over with a fork and sprinkle more sugar on them. Bake one tin at a time until the sugar is caramelised to a deep golden colour, 10–15 minutes.

7 Watch the ox tongues carefully after half the baking time has elapsed. Hotter areas in the oven and other variables such as the thickness of the dough will cause them to be done at different times. If necessary, use a wide palette knife to remove individual pastries from the tin to a cooling rack as they are done.

8 Cool on a rack and serve them on the day they are baked for best flavour.

Storage: Keep leftovers between baking paper in an airtight container.

banderillas

Named for the darts that are used during a bullfight, these are a popular Mexican puff pastry.

Makes 16 individual pastries

1 Cover the work surface with half the sugar and the top of the dough with the other half, then roll the dough, according to the instructions on page 52, to an 20 x 30cm rectangle. If the dough gets soft, slide it onto a baking sheet and refrigerate it for 15 minutes.

2 Use a sharp pizza wheel to trim the edges of the dough and then to cut it into two 20 x 15cm rectangles. Pierce the dough all over with the tines of a fork.

3 Cut one of the pieces of dough into eight 2.5 x 15cm strips. Place the strips on one of the prepared tins as they are cut. Repeat with the second piece of dough.

4 Arrange the pastries on the prepared tins and refrigerate them for 30 minutes.

5 Bake and cool as for ox tongues, above.

butterfly wings

A variation of the ever-popular palmier, or elephant ear, these are more tailored and elegant in appearance.

Makes about 24 individual pastries

1. Cover the work surface with half the sugar, then top the dough with the remainder, and, according to the instructions on page 52, roll to an 20 x 30cm rectangle. If the dough gets soft, slide it onto a baking sheet and refrigerate it for 15 minutes.

2. Use a sharp pizza wheel to trim the edges of the dough. Fold each of the 30cm sides of the dough in almost to the centre, leaving a 2cm gap where they meet. Fold the left (10cm) side of the dough over to meet the right side. Finally, fold the top (now 15cm) side down to meet the bottom edge. Give the layered strip of dough a good press with the palm of your hand and wrap and refrigerate for 1 hour. Reserve the extra sugar on the work surface.

3. Cut the chilled package of dough into 5mm slices. Working with one at a time, dip the bottom cut side into the reserved sugar and place the pastry on one of the tins, leaving 5cm all around to allow for expansion.

4. Bake and cool as for ox tongues, opposite.

sacristains

The name of these pastries means sacristan or church/sacristy caretaker in French. All my efforts to find out why they have this name have been unsuccessful, but I can attest to the fact that they're delicious.

Makes about 48 small individual pastries

½ batch (340g) Quick Puff Pastry (page 52)

Egg wash: 1 egg well beaten with a pinch of salt

70g ground almonds

140g sugar

½ teaspoon ground cinnamon

2 swiss roll tins lined with parchment paper

1. Roll the dough according to the instructions on page 52 to a 30cm square. Paint with the egg wash. Mix the almonds, sugar and cinnamon together and evenly sprinkle on a 15 x 30 rectangle of the dough. Fold the other half of the dough over the sugar and almonds and press to adhere. Refrigerate until firm, about 15 minutes.

2. Set racks in the upper and lower thirds of the oven and preheat to 190°C/gas mark 5.

3. Roll the dough back to a 30cm square and use a pastry wheel to cut into two 11cm wide strips. Twist one of the strips into a corkscrew shape by pressing in opposite directions at the same time with the palms of each hand.

4. Arrange 12 sacristains on each of the prepared tins, pressing the ends against the side of the tin to prevent them from unravelling while baking.

5. Bake until deep golden, about 15 minutes, switching the tins from top to bottom and vice versa and rotating them from front to back at the same time halfway through the baking time.

6. Immediately remove the sacristains to a chopping board, trim off the ends, and cut them in half lengthways. Work quickly because the pastry is still flexible when it's hot, but it becomes crisp as it cools and would shatter when cut.

variation

Cheese Straws Substitute 85g finely grated Parmigiano-Reggiano cheese for the almonds and sugar. Spread the cheese on the egg-washed dough and sprinkle with ½ teaspoon salt (it brings out the flavour in the cheese) and 2 teaspoons sweet Hungarian paprika. Proceed as for Sacristains, above.

NOTE: To substitute the grated cheese and paprika in the recipes for the Ox Tongues, Banderillas or Butterfly Wings, roll the dough to the size and shape specified in the recipe. For the Ox Tongues, cut the dough, brush the tops with egg wash, and sprinkle with half of the cheese, salt and paprika. Turn them over, repeat the egg wash, cheese, salt and paprika, then roll them into ovals. For the Banderillas, paint the two rectangles of dough with egg wash and sprinkle with half the cheese, salt and paprika. Invert, paint, and sprinkle and then cut and place on tins. For the Butterfly Wings, paint the surface of the dough with the egg wash and sprinkle with the cheese, salt and paprika before folding.

caramelised apple tart

tarte tatin

Makes one 23–25cm tart,
about 8–10 servings

½ batch (340g) Quick Puff Pastry,
page 50, or ½ batch (about 250g)
Flaky Pastry Dough, page 26

1.1kg Golden Delicious apples

170g sugar

1 tablespoon lemon juice, measured
after straining

1 tablespoon water

45g unsalted butter,
cut into 8 pieces

One 23–25cm non-stick slope-sided
sauté pan

Serving: Serve the tart at room
temperature with some whipped cream.

Storage: Keep the tart loosely covered
at room temperature before and after
serving. Reheat leftovers for best flavour.

I first encountered Tarte Tatin in early 1974, when I lived briefly with the Pinelli family at their small hotel in Monte Carlo. Raymonde Pinelli loved apples in all forms and had beautiful 19th-century earthenware Calvados jugs in the shape of apples, which I have to confess I coveted. Raymonde's method of preparing Tarte Tatin involved repeatedly turning wedges of her favourite apples, *les Golden*, in a buttery caramel in a flimsy aluminium tart tin set atop a flame tamer on her big commercial range. She used a tender sweet dough to cover the apples before baking, which is pleasant enough, but buttery puff pastry, especially in combination with caramel, is much better. I retained one thing from her recipe, though: the apples need plenty of caramel and butter to achieve the best flavour.

1   Roll the dough according to the directions on page 52 to a 27.5cm disc. Slide onto a baking sheet, loosely cover with clingfilm and refrigerate while making the filling.

2   Pare, halve and core the apples. Cut each half into 3 wedges. Cover and set aside while preparing the caramel.

3   Set a rack in the centre of the oven and preheat to 180°C/gas mark 4.

4   Combine the sugar, lemon juice, water and butter in the sauté pan and use a wooden spoon to mix. Place over a medium heat and bring to the boil, stirring often so that the butter is absorbed by the syrup and does not separate from it.

5   At the boil, decrease the heat to medium-low and continue cooking until the syrup begins to colour. Check the colour of the syrup by picking up a spoonful and letting it drip back into the pan; the caramel always looks darker when concentrated in the pan. Pull the pan from the heat as the caramel continues to darken but is not quite finished; it will continue to cook and colour more deeply from the heat retained by the pan. If it stays too light, return the pan to the heat and cook until only slightly darker, removing the pan again and checking the colour after a minute. At this point the caramel is safe from over-darkening.

6   Arrange the apple wedges in the caramel rounded side down, crowding them close together in a row perpendicular to the side of the pan. Fill in the centre with more wedges, then scatter over any remaining apple pieces.

7   Place the pan over a low heat to melt the caramel again. Remove from the heat and slide the disc of chilled dough onto the apples. Push the dough inward towards the centre of the pan so that it fits inside the pan even though it's larger. This will compensate for any shrinkage while the dough is baking.

8   Bake the tart until the dough is baked through and the apples have absorbed the caramel and are no longer watery, about 50–60 minutes.

9   Cool the tart in the pan on a rack until it is lukewarm. To unmould the tart, invert a plate onto the pan and invert again, firmly grasping the plate with one hand and the handle of the pan with the other. Protect both hands with oven mitts in case some hot syrup drips out of the pan. Lift off the pan.

fig & raspberry croustades

Makes nine 12cm croustades

CROUSTADES

½ batch (340g) Quick Puff Pastry (page 50)

Egg wash: 1 egg well beaten with
a pinch of salt

CRÈME ANGLAISE

240ml full-fat milk

240ml whipping cream

70g sugar

½ vanilla pod, split lengthways

3 7.5cm strips lemon zest removed
with a vegetable peeler

5cm cinnamon stick

6 medium egg yolks

FIG AND RASPBERRY FILLING

340g fresh black or green figs

225g fresh raspberries

225g seedless raspberry jam

1 baking sheet or swiss roll tin lined
with parchment paper or foil

Serving: Place each croustade on
a dessert plate and pass the crème
anglaise at the table in a bowl or
sauce boat.

Storage: Keep the croustades at room
temperature and use them on the day
they are baked.

A

D

Although I love this fig and raspberry combination, these
tailored croustades can be filled with any sweet or savoury
mixture you like. Here fresh figs are mixed with whole
raspberries, bound with some raspberry glaze, and finished
with an unglazed fig half and berries and crème anglaise.
Another presentation might use the crème pâtissière on page 46
on the bottom, topped with any single fruit or assortment of
fruit you have on hand. Or try savoury mixtures like creamed
mushrooms, cultivated or wild; shredded roast duck (I buy a half
roast duck in Chinatown), quickly stir-fried with spring onions
and a dash of hoisin sauce; or diced Japanese aubergine sautéed
in olive oil and garlic with seeded, diced fresh tomatoes and a
handful of shredded basil. The recipe calls for a half batch of puff
pastry, which makes 9 croustades. Place any extra unbaked ones
on a baking sheet in the freezer until they're frozen solid, wrap
them individually in clingfilm, and store in a sealed plastic bag in
the freezer; they'll defrost in a few minutes.

B

C

E

F

1 Roll the dough according to the directions on page 52 to a 38cm square. Slide onto a baking sheet or flexible chopping board and chill until firm, about 15 minutes.

2 Use a sharp pizza wheel to trim the edges and cut the dough into nine 12cm squares. Fold over each square of dough to form a triangle. Make a cut over the fold on either side, 1cm from the cut edge to within 1cm of the point of the triangle (A). Unfold the triangles back into squares.

3 Pierce the inner squares at 1cm intervals with a fork (B) and paint them lightly with the egg wash. Fold the outer corners of each square over to the opposite inside corners, one at a time (C and D). With a floured fingertip press the borders down and indent the sides of each croustade at 5mm intervals with the dull side of a paring knife (E and F). Arrange on the prepared tin and refrigerate until firm or cover and refrigerate overnight.

4 When you are ready to bake the croustades, set a rack in the centre of the oven and preheat to 190°C/gas mark 5.

Arrange the chilled croustades on the prepared tin. Bake the croustades until they are well risen and deep golden, 25–30 minutes. Remove the tin from the oven and cool the croustades on a rack and use them the day they are baked.

5 For the crème anglaise, whisk together the milk, cream, sugar, vanilla pod, lemon zest and cinnamon stick in a saucepan. Bring to the boil over a low heat. Meanwhile, set a fine sieve over a bowl and set the bowl in a larger bowl of ice water. Whisk the yolks in a third bowl. When the milk mixture boils, use a slotted spoon to remove and discard the vanilla pod, lemon zest and cinnamon stick. Whisk about a third of the hot milk mixture into the yolks. Return the remaining milk mixture to the boil and, beginning to whisk before you pour, whisk in the yolk mixture. Continue whisking until the cream thickens slightly, about 15 seconds (the cream thickens only a little now, but thickens further as it cools). Immediately strain the cream into the prepared bowl and remove the sieve. Whisk the hot cream until it cools slightly, about 30 seconds. Let it continue to **>**

cool in the ice water bath. Once the cream is cold, pour it into a plastic container, cover and chill until needed.

6 For the filling, reserve 5 whole figs and 18 whole raspberries to finish the croustades. Stem, peel, and dice the remaining figs and place them in a mixing bowl with the remaining raspberries. Cover and reserve at room temperature.

7 All the previous steps may be done up to one day in advance. Only proceed to the steps below when you are ready to serve the croustades; if the fruit sits after it's combined with the jam, before or after filling the croustades, it will turn watery.

8 Cook the jam in a small saucepan over a low heat until it comes to the boil, stirring occasionally. Let the jam reduce slightly, about 5 minutes, then pour it into a bowl to cool for at least 15 minutes.

9 To assemble the croustades, fold the cooled raspberry jam into the fruit mixture, then spoon some of the mixture into the centre of each croustade. Finish the top with a stemmed fig half, cut side up, and a couple of raspberries. Spoon some of the crème anglaise next to it on the plate.

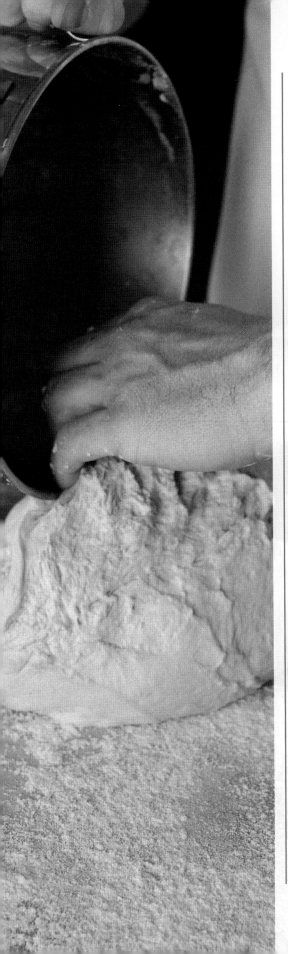

05

one-step breads & rolls

These are one-step breads in the sense that to make the dough, you will simply combine all the ingredients at once rather than creating a sponge separately that's mixed into the rest of the dough ingredients after it has fermented. I would like to correct a misconception about bread baking right up front: you do not need to beat up your dough. Rather, the gentle mixing method used here assures maximum flavour, because flavour-bearing pigments in the flour don't dissipate as they do with prolonged mixing. Another misconception about bread baking is that it requires a big time commitment. This is only half right: you do need to be around in order to take care of the various steps, but none of the individual steps is actually time-consuming. Because I've designed these recipes using the one-step process, these are breads to bake and eat in one day, unlike their artisan cousins, which can take four or five days to create.

A

B

one-step bread dough

Using this new mixing technique means this bread is ready in hardly any time at all. I like to add a little olive oil to this dough for flavour as well as tenderness – a little secret touch that many bread bakers use.

Makes 800g dough, enough for any of the loaves or rolls in this chapter

475g bread flour or unbleached plain flour

1½ teaspoons non-iodized salt or fine sea salt

7g sachet active dried yeast

315ml warm tap water, about 38°C

1 tablespoon olive oil, plus ½ teaspoon for oiling the bowl

1 Mix the flour and salt together in a small bowl and set aside.

2 In a large bowl, whisk the yeast into the water. Wait 30 seconds, then whisk again to make sure all the yeast is dissolved. Whisk in the oil.

3 Use a large rubber spatula to mix in half the flour to make a paste. Add about half the remaining flour, mixing it in by repeatedly digging down to the bottom of the bowl with the spatula until the spatula is parallel to the bottom of the bowl and folding upward (A). Add the last of the flour and repeat the folding motion until all the flour is absorbed and there are no dry bits stuck to the side of the bowl (B).

4 Cover the bowl with a clean tea towel or clingfilm and let the dough rest for 10–15 minutes (C).

5 Repeat the digging and folding motion in the dough using a clean rubber spatula (D). Cover and let the dough rest for 10–15 minutes again.

6 Lightly oil a bowl large enough to hold twice the quantity of dough you now have. Scrape the dough onto a lightly floured work surface. Flour your hands, not the top of the dough and pat the dough into a rough rectangle. Fold one of the narrow ends of the dough over the middle, then fold the other end over to make 3 layers. Turn the dough 90 degrees so that the folded side is facing you and repeat the folding. Invert the dough into the oiled bowl and cover it with a tea towel or clingfilm. Let the dough rest for 15 minutes, then repeat the folding.

7 Lightly oil the bowl again if necessary and put the dough back into the bowl. Turn the dough over so that the top is oiled. Cover with clingfilm and let the dough rise until it has doubled in size, 45 minutes to 1 hour.

8 Use the dough immediately to shape any of the loaves or rolls in this chapter.

C

D

variations

Part Wholemeal Dough: Substitute
130g wholemeal flour for an equal
amount of the white flour in the recipe.

Mixed Grain Dough: Substitute 65g
wholemeal flour and 65g wholegrain
rye flour for 130g of the white flour in
the recipe.

essential tips for one-step bread dough

- Using bread flour makes this dough and the resulting bread even easier to
prepare. Once difficult to obtain, strong white bread flour has become a
common supermarket item.

- Make sure the water is no hotter than 43°C or the yeast might die as soon as it
hits the water. This is the single greatest cause of failure in home bread baking.

- Mixing, resting, mixing and turning the dough makes it smooth and elastic
without any of the effort of kneading. There really isn't any need to use a mixer,
as none of the mixing is strenuous.

- Controlled mixing helps preserve the natural sweet wheat flavour in flour.
That flavour dissipates when dough is mixed too long or too fast.

- The short rests followed by the rising contribute to developing flavour in the
dough. Never try to rush the dough by putting it in an excessively warm place.

- The initial mixing and turning will take about 1 hour at a 21°C room temperature.
The rising until doubled in the bowl should take another 45 minutes to 1 hour –
longer if it's cooler in the room and shorter if it's a little warmer.

- Time the preparation of the dough so that you can proceed immediately to the
shaping, rising and baking of your dough.

- If you know you'll have, or need, 3 or 4 hours between mixing and baking the
bread, cover and refrigerate the dough at the beginning of step 1. Deflate the
dough and bring it back to room temperature before forming.

crusty ring bread

Makes one 25cm ring-shaped loaf

1 batch One-Step Bread Dough (page 64)

Flour for shaping

Polenta or baking paper for the tin

Baking sheet, swiss roll tin, or round pizza tin (only for the ring loaf) at least 30cm in diameter

Spray bottle filled with warm water

Serving: Use a sharp serrated knife to cut the loaf into thick slices.

Storage: Keep the loaf uncovered on the day it is baked. If it's humid and the crust softens, crisp it in a 180°C/gas mark 4 oven for a few minutes and cool it again before serving.

This loaf, like a giant bagel, increases the surface area for crust and makes for a chewy, crusty loaf that's great for serving with a meal, especially if a hearty soup or tasty sauce is on the menu. See the end of the recipe for other easy shapes. This and any of the variations that follow may be made with any of the dough variations on page 65.

1 Turn the risen dough out onto a floured surface, scraping it from the bowl without folding it over on itself. Turn the dough over so that what was the smooth top surface when it was rising is now uppermost.

2 Gently round the piece of dough without deflating it too much by pushing inward at the bottom with your flat upturned palms all around the piece of dough; you'll see the outside skin of the dough tighten and it will become more spherical. Cover the dough with a clean flat-weave tea towel and let it rest for 10 minutes.

3 Gently press the ball of dough to flatten it. Lightly flour the top of the dough and the fingertips of one hand. Point these fingertips and use them to make an opening in the center of the flattened dough. Once your fingertips are touching the work surface, rotate your hand to widen the opening (A and B).

4 Dust the tin with polenta and transfer the loaf to it (C and D). Widen the opening in the centre of the loaf by pushing outward with one hand from the inside, until it is about 12cm in diameter. Cover with the tea towel and let rise until almost doubled, about 1 hour at a 21°C–24°C room temperature.

5 About 20 minutes before the loaf is risen, set a rack in the lower third of the oven and preheat to 200°C/gas mark 6.

6 Remove the towel and use a single-edged razor or X-Acto knife to make 4 diagonal slashes through just the outside skin at the very top of the loaf. Place the tin in the oven and spray water all over the sides of the oven to create steam; quickly close the oven door.

7 Five minutes later, repeat the spraying. Continue baking until the loaf is deep golden and has an internal temperature of over 93°C–99°C, a total of 30–40 minutes.

8 Slide the loaf to a rack to cool.

variations

Boule Loaves: A boule (ball) is a French name for a spherical loaf. After step 2 above, use a dough scraper or knife to divide the dough into 2 equal pieces (they'll bake better and more quickly than a large loaf). Round both loaves as in step 2 and place them on the semolina-dusted tin and resume at covering in step 4. At step 6, slash the top of the loaf in a diagonal lattice pattern – 4 or 5 cuts parallel and equidistant from each other in one direction, then another 4 or 5 at a 45 degree angle to the first ones. Bake as above, but they should be done in a little less than 30 minutes.

Bâtard Loaves: No, I'm not going to provide a translation... A bâtard is a fatter form of a baguette and is easy to shape. Divide the risen dough in half and round each piece separately. Cover and let rest 10 minutes. Working with one ball of dough at a time,

A

B

C

D

invert it and pull it into a rough rectangle with the long ends facing you. Roll the far end of the dough over about 1 inch and gently press it into place. Continue rolling and sealing until you get to the end. Pinch the last edge into place. Invert and cover. Repeat with the second piece of dough and let rest 5–10 minutes. Keeping the seam on the bottom, roll the dough back and forth under your palms into a fat sausage shape that is a little shorter than the length of your tin. Roll over and taper the ends. Place the loaves on the semolina-dusted tin. Cover and let rise until almost doubled. Before baking, slash each loaf in 7cm cuts in the centre of the loaf that are almost parallel to the sides. Bake as for the boules, above.

Seeded Twist:

145g white sesame seeds, or equal parts black and white seeds

Form the dough as for bâtards, but roll each piece to about 50cm. You may need to stop and cover the dough and let it rest for 10 minutes to avoid tearing when making it so long. Don't point the ends. Position one of the lengths of dough parallel to the edge of the work surface and bring one end to meet the other in a hairpin shape. Twist the opposite ends 2 or 3 times in opposite directions at the same time. Repeat with the other piece of dough. Paint one loaf with water and slide it onto a piece of parchment paper. Generously sprinkle the entire outside of the loaf with half the seeds, letting the excess fall onto the paper. Use the palm of one hand to press the seeds gently to make them adhere. Transfer the loaf to the tin and repeat with the other loaf. Bake as for bâtards, above.

tiger rolls

Also called Dutch crunch rolls, these have a crisp topping made from rice flour, and are popular in both the Netherlands and the UK. In the US, they're found largely in San Francisco. The tasty topping derives a lot of its flavour from the yeast in it and its crunch from the rice flour, which, being mostly starch, contributes no elasticity and therefore bakes to a hard, crunchy texture. Rice flour is available in most health food shops. Dutch crunch topping is equally appropriate on a larger loaf, such as a bâtard, page 66, or twist, page 67. However, in the case of the bâtard, no slashing is necessary before baking the loaf.

Makes 12 rolls

1 batch One-Step Bread Dough (page 64) or the part wholemeal variation (page 65)

7g sachet active dried yeast

75ml warm water, about 38°C

2½ teaspoons sugar

¼ teaspoon salt

2 teaspoons olive or vegetable oil

65g rice flour

Baking sheet or swiss roll tin lined with parchment paper or foil

1 Turn the risen dough out onto a floured work surface without folding it over on itself. Turn the dough over and without deflating it too much, pull it into a rough rectangle. Cut the dough into 12 equal pieces.

2 Round each piece of dough under the cupped palm of your hand on a clean, flour-free work surface. Arrange the rolls on the prepared tin, cover with a clean tea towel and set aside.

3 For the topping, whisk the yeast into the warm water, then whisk in the remaining ingredients, one at a time. Cover the bowl and set aside for 15 minutes.

4 Once the topping has rested for about 15 minutes, stir it down and evenly spread it on the rolls with the back of a spoon or a small palette knife. Don't overload the rolls with topping or it will puddle underneath.

5 Let the rolls continue to rise, uncovered, until they have doubled in size, about 45 minutes to an hour. About 20 minutes before the loaf is risen, set a rack in the centre of the oven and preheat to 190°C/gas mark 5.

6 Bake the rolls until the topping is set, crackled and lightly coloured, 25–30 minutes. Cool the rolls on a rack and serve them on the day they are baked.

Serving: These rolls make good little sandwiches or even dinner rolls.

Storage: Keep the rolls uncovered at room temperature the day they are baked. Wrap and freeze for longer storage. Defrost; reheat at 180°C/gas mark 4 for about 5 minutes, then cool before serving.

variations

Round or Long Sandwich Rolls: Use any of the variations of One-Step Bread Dough on pages 64–65 for these. After rounding off the rolls in step 2 above, cover and let them rest again. For round rolls, leave them as they are. For long rolls, one at a time, roll over them with the palm of one hand to elongate and make them about 2cm in diameter and about 11 cm long. Arrange the rolls on the prepared tin as they're formed. For the round rolls, use the palm of your hand to flatten them once they are on the tin to retain a round shape. Omit the crunch topping and dust the rolls with flour before covering. Bake as above.

Poppy Seed Knots: You can use sesame seeds, white or black or a combination; nigella seeds; or even caraway seeds if using any rye flour (see Variations on page 65). Apply just a pinch of caraway seeds, though – don't encrust the entire roll with them.

140g poppy seeds in a small bowl

Form the rolls as above. One at a time, pick up a cylinder of dough and stretch it to about 15cm in length. Tie it into a loose single knot so that one of the ends is on the bottom of the roll and the other protrudes slightly at the top. Arrange the rolls on the work surface. Brush a roll with water and invert it into the poppy seeds, pressing gently to make the seeds adhere. Arrange on the prepared tin. Allow to rise and bake as for Tiger Rolls.

salt sticks

These, like good bagels and bialys, used to be a New York standby but seem to have all but disappeared from the typical bagel shop assortment. These are more tender than the classics, but not a bad substitute, all things considered. If you can get some chunky opaque pretzel salt, by all means use it; the rolls will taste pretty much the same, but they'll look terrific.

Makes 16 15cm rolls

1 batch One-Step Bread Dough (page 64)

Egg wash: 1 medium egg white, well beaten in a small bowl

Coarse sea salt or other coarse salt

2 baking sheets or swiss roll tins lined with parchment paper or foil

1 Turn the risen dough out onto a floured work surface without folding it over on itself. Turn the dough over and, without deflating it too much, pull it into a rough rectangle. Cut the dough into 16 equal pieces, each about 125g.

2 Round each piece of dough under the cupped palm of your hand on a clean flour-free work surface. Cover with a clean tea towel and let them rest for 5 minutes.

3 One by one, roll over the pieces of dough with the palm of one hand to elongate to about 15cm, without pointing the ends.

4 Arrange the rolls on the prepared tins 5cm apart all around to allow for expansion. Cover the rolls with a tea towel and let them rise until they just start to puff, about 20 minutes.

5 Set racks in the upper and lower thirds of the oven and preheat to 190°C/gas mark 5.

6 Once the rolls have begun to rise, brush them with the egg white and sprinkle with a couple of pinches of salt. Let the rolls continue to rise, uncovered, until they have doubled in size.

7 Bake the rolls until they're deep golden and firm, 20–25 minutes, switching the bottom pan to the top rack and vice versa and also turning the pans from back to front halfway through the baking time.

8 Cool the rolls on a rack and serve them on the day they are baked.

Serving: These rolls are great with butter for breakfast, warmed or not, or even split and toasted.

Storage: Keep the rolls uncovered at room temperature the day they are baked. Wrap and freeze for longer storage. Defrost; reheat at 180°C/gas mark 4 for about 5 minutes, then cool before serving.

variation

Soft Sesame Breadsticks: These are a slightly longer and thinner version of the salt sticks above.

145g white sesame seeds

2 baking sheets or swiss roll tins lined with baking paper or foil

1 Prepare salt sticks up to the end of step 2. Elongate them as in step 3, but make them about 20cm long.

2 Have ready a bowl of water and the sesame seeds arranged in a wide 20cm area on a piece of baking paper.

3 One by one, use one hand to dip a formed breadstick into the water, then lift it out, letting it drain and arrange it on the sesame seeds. Use the dry hand to coat it all over with the seeds and then transfer it to the work surface. Repeat with the remaining sticks.

4 Dry the water dipping hand and use both hands to transfer the breadsticks to the prepared tins, allowing 5cm all around for expansion. Resume with step 4, above.

Serving: These are more of a snack, or a good accompaniment to hors d'oeuvre or first courses, but not really a bread roll.

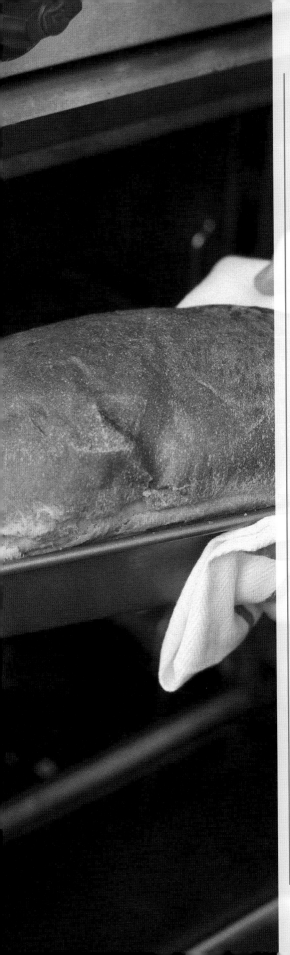

06

tin loaves

Tin loaves are versatile and easy to shape. As their name indicates, they're risen and baked in a tin – usually a loaf tin – which makes them perfect for slicing. They're great for sandwiches, toast, croutons and all manner of bread-based dishes, both sweet and savoury. Because the dough for these breads is quickly made by machine, this type of loaf can become a flavourful substitute for commercially-made white bread. The same dough also makes excellent dinner rolls and perfect beefburger baps and hot dog rolls. The flavouring variations in the recipes that follow the chapter's master recipe all expand upon the almost endless possibilities of this simple bread. Use them as guidelines for developing your own combinations; just remember not to overdo the quantity of anything you decide to add to the dough to flavour it.

A

B

perfect white loaf

Makes two standard loaves

850g bread flour

1 tablespoon sugar

1 tablespoon salt

55g unsalted butter, cut into 8 pieces

360ml full fat milk, scalded

240ml warm tap water, about 43°C

7g sachet active dried yeast

Two standard 1lb loaf tins, buttered or oiled

E

Despite its wonderful texture and flavour, a loaf such as this is more than easy to prepare. In addition, it's the basis for all the recipe variations in this chapter; some use a full recipe, some use half. After you try this once, you'll never settle for supermarket sandwich bread again. Many thanks to my friend Kyra Effren for sharing all her wisdom about this bread, which she has been making two to seven times a week for 50 years.

1 Stir the flour, sugar and salt together and set aside.

2 Stir the butter into the hot milk, pour it into a shallow bowl and let it cool to room temperature.

3 Once the milk has cooled, pour the water into the bowl of an electric mixer and whisk in the yeast. Wait 1 minute, then whisk again to make sure the yeast is completely dissolved. Whisk in the cooled milk and butter mixture.

4 Use a large rubber spatula to stir in about half of the flour mixture. Stir in the rest in 3 or 4 additions to form a rough dough in which there is no longer any unmoistened flour.

5 Place the bowl on the mixer fitted with the dough hook and beat on medium speed until the dough is somewhat smoother but not perfectly smooth, about 2 minutes. Stop the mixer and allow the dough to rest for 10 minutes.

6 Beat the rested dough on medium speed until it is smoother and more elastic, about 2 minutes more.

7 Scrape the dough into a lightly oiled bowl large enough to hold twice the amount of dough and turn the dough over so that the top is now oiled. Gently press oiled clingfilm against the surface of the dough. Let the dough rise until it has doubled in size. At a room temperature of 24°C, it should take about 1 hour.

8 Turn the dough out onto a lightly floured work surface and turn it over. Press to deflate the dough (A) and repeat step 7.

9 After the dough has risen for the second time, use a small flexible scraper to turn the dough out onto a lightly floured work surface. Divide the dough in half. Without deflating the dough too much, pull and stretch each piece into a rough 20–23cm

C

D

square. Starting at the far end of the dough, tightly roll it toward you swiss roll style, pinching the edge in place when you get to the end (B and C).

10 Place the formed loaves in the tins, seam side down, evenly pressing into place so that the top of each loaf is level (D). Cover with oiled clingfilm and let rise until doubled, about 1 hour. When risen, the dough should be at least 2.5cm above the rims of the tins (E).

11 When the loaves are almost completely risen, set a rack in the centre of the oven and preheat to 200°C/gas mark 6.

12 Once the loaves are completely risen, uncover and place them on the rack in the oven, short side inward and equidistant from each other and the sides of the oven. Bake until the bread is well risen, deep golden, and firm, with an internal temperature of over 93°C, about 45 minutes.

13 Unmould each loaf to a rack and cool on its side to prevent falling. If you want the crust to be very soft, have a tablespoon of melted butter ready when you unmould the breads and use a pastry brush to paint all surfaces of each loaf with the butter.

Serving: Wait until the bread cools before attempting to slice it with a sharp serrated knife. Slice the bread about 1cm thick and use for sandwiches or toast.

Storage: Keep the loaves at room temperature on the day they are baked. Slide leftovers into a plastic bag and keep at room temperature. Freeze for longer storage.

variations

To mix the dough by hand, use the method described on page 64 for One-Step Bread Dough. Resume the recipe above with step 7.

Beefburger or Sandwich Baps: You can make 6 large rolls or 8 smaller ones from a half batch of the dough. After dividing the dough in half and forming a loaf, divide the remaining dough into 6 or 8 equal pieces. Round each and place on a parchment paper-lined baking sheet or swiss roll tin. Cover and let rest for 15 minutes. Press each with the palm of your hand to flatten it. Cover again and let rise until doubled in size, 20–30 minutes. Bake until firm and golden, about 20 minutes. For hot dog or sausage rolls, round the dough, then cover and let rest 10 minutes. Roll each round by hand to form an even 15cm long cylinder. Place on the tin and continue as for beefburger baps.

essentials for tin breads

- Review Essentials for One-Step Bread Doughs, page 65.

- As in all other yeast-risen baked goods, the most important part of this recipe is having the water between 38°C and 43°C when you add the yeast. If the water is too hot, the yeast will die immediately and you'll wait in vain for the dough to rise.

- Avoid deflating the dough too much by pressing on it while forming the loaf. The shaping process will deflate the dough enough.

- Don't skimp on the rising time either in the bowl or before baking or the loaf will be tough and dry after baking.

- Refrigerating baked bread will hasten staling. If you want to bake a few in advance for a special occasion, double-wrap completely cooled loaves in clingfilm and freeze them. Defrost at room temperature and warm slightly at 180°C/gas mark 4 for 5 minutes, then cool before serving.

gruyère & walnut bread

Makes two standard loaves

1 batch dough for Perfect White Tin Bread (page 72), completed up to the end of step 5

225g coarsely grated Swiss Gruyère cheese, chopped into 5mm pieces

225g chopped walnuts, lightly toasted

2 teaspoons coarsely ground black pepper or crushed red pepper, optional

Two standard 1lb loaf tins, buttered or oiled

Serving and Storage: As in the master recipe.

Gruyère and other aged cheeses are a perfect pairing with the slight bitterness of walnuts in this easy and delicious bread.

1 Add the cheese and nuts to the mixer bowl before beginning with step 6, and then continue with the master recipe. In a mixer fitted with the dough hook, beat the rested dough on a medium speed until it is smoother and more elastic, about 2 minutes more. Remove the dough to a lightly oiled bowl and turn it over so that the top is oiled. Press clingfilm against the surface and let the dough rise until it has doubled in size.

2 Continue with the rising, shaping, proofing and baking in the master recipe.

variations

Substitute any aged cheese such as sharp Cheddar, Cantal or Parmigiano-Reggiano for the Gruyère. Grate the Parmigiano fine as you would for serving with pasta. You can also substitute chopped toasted pecans for the walnuts.

oat & honey bread

Makes two standard loaves

PORRIDGE

120g porridge oats

4 tablespoons dark flavourful honey

30g unsalted butter, cut into 5 or 6 pieces

360ml boiling water

DOUGH

500g white bread flour

250g wholemeal bread flour

1 tablespoon salt

360ml warm tap water, about 43°C

10.5g (1½ sachets) active dried yeast

120g uncooked porridge oats for finishing

Two standard 1lb loaf tins, buttered or oiled

This makes an excellent breakfast or brunch bread when toasted; the best way to enjoy this moist-textured bread. The addition of wholemeal flour to the dough emphasises the nutty flavour of the oats.

1 For the porridge, place the oats in a stainless-steel bowl and drizzle the honey over them. Scatter the pieces of butter over all. Pour over the boiling water and stir once to mix. Let the mixture cool to room temperature.

2 Follow the instructions on page 72 for Perfect White Tin Bread; substitute the combination of white and wholemeal bread flours for the white bread flour. At the middle of step 4, add the cooked porridge along with the second half of the flour.

3 Continue with the master recipe to the end of step 9.

4 Place the uncooked porridge oats on a piece of baking paper and form them into a rectangle roughly equal to size of the top of one loaf.

5 Paint the top of one of the loaves with water and invert it onto the oats. Let the dough remain there for 1 minute, then lift and invert it into one of the prepared tins so that the oat-encrusted part is uppermost. Repeat with the other loaf.

6 Let rise, bake, and cool as in the master recipe.

Serving: Wait until completely cool before attempting to slice with a sharp serrated knife. Slice the bread a little under 1cm thick and use it for sandwiches or toast.

Storage: Keep the loaves at room temperature on the day they are baked. Slide leftovers into a plastic bag and keep at room temperature. Freeze for longer storage.

chocolate
spiral bread

Makes two standard loaves

**1 batch dough for Perfect White Loaf
(page 72), up to the end of step 5**

60ml milk

¼ teaspoon ground cinnamon

**85g dark chocolate (55–65% cocoa
solids), melted and slightly cooled**

4 tablespoons white bread flour

1 tablespoon melted butter, for finishing

Two standard 1lb loaf tins, buttered
or oiled

**Once you've mixed the Perfect White Loaf up to the end of
step 5, you can use it to make a couple of striking loaves that
have a spiral of chocolate dough running through them. In
this recipe, the chocolate colours the dough really well and
imparts a faint chocolate flavour, but don't think that biting
into a slice of this is going to be anything like chewing on
a brownie.**

1   Divide the dough into two pieces, one of which is twice as large as the other. Put
    the larger piece of dough into an oiled bowl and turn it so that the top is oiled;
    cover with clingfilm and allow to rise until doubled. Return the smaller piece
    of dough to the mixer, still fitted with the dough hook

2   Whisk the milk and cinnamon into the chocolate and scrape the mixture into
    the mixer bowl. Mix on the lowest speed until the dough evenly absorbs the
    chocolate liquid. Let the dough rest 10 minutes, then mix again on low for 2 more
    minutes. Put the chocolate dough into an oiled bowl and turn it so that the top is
    oiled; cover with clingfilm and allow to rise until doubled in size.

3   Deflate the white and chocolate doughs and return them to the bowls to rise again
    until doubled in size.

4   Scrape the white dough from the bowl to a floured work surface and roll or press
    the dough into a 40cm square (the square of dough is not as wide as the two
    tins, but will stretch an extra centimeter or two when it's being rolled). Press or
    roll the chocolate dough into an 20 x 40cm rectangle. Brush the surface of the
    white dough with water. Position the rectangle of chocolate dough on it, leaving a
    2.5cm margin of white dough on the edge closest to you.

5   Fold over the inch of white dough onto the chocolate dough and then roll up the
    whole package swiss roll-style to make one long cylinder of dough. (The extra
    white dough at the end attractively frames the chocolate spiral within.)

6   Cut the roll in half lengthways and press each roll into one of the prepared tins,
    seam side down. Cover the tins with oiled clingfilm and set aside to rise until
    doubled in size, about 1 hour. When risen, the dough should be at least 2.5cm above
    the rim of the tin.

7   When the loaves are almost completely risen, set a rack in the centre of the oven
    and preheat to 200°C/gas mark 6.

8   Once the loaves are completely risen, uncover them and place them on the rack
    in the oven, short side inward. Bake until the bread is well risen, deep golden, and
    firm, with an internal temperature of 93°C–99°C, about 45 minutes.

9   Unmould to a rack and cool the loaves on their sides. If you want the crust to be
    very soft, have a tablespoon of melted butter ready when you unmould the bread
    and use a pastry brush to paint all surfaces of the loaves with the butter.

dark caraway rye bread

Makes one standard loaf

500g strong white bread flour

180g wholegrain or medium rye flour

2 teaspoons salt

2 teaspoons ground caraway seeds

2 teaspoons whole caraway seeds, optional

480ml warm tap water, about 43°C

7g sachet active dried yeast

2 tablespoons treacle

One standard 1lb loaf tin, buttered or oiled

Many rye breads are made using a sourdough starter since rye flour can only develop gluten in the presence of acidity. Without using a sourdough, the best solution is to use a combination of rye flour and strong bread flour to impart the necessary elasticity to the dough, but even then part-rye doughs like this one tend to remain quite sticky. Try not to use too much flour in shaping the dough or it might not grow together well while it's rising and baking. I was amazed when I learned years ago that the flavour I had always associated with rye bread didn't come from rye flour, but from the addition of ground caraway seeds to the dough. If you can't find ready-ground caraway, just grind up some seeds in a spice grinder. Treacle adds a note of dark richness to this bread and it ties in perfectly with the earthy rye flavour. Please note that the dough only rises once before being formed unlike the other doughs in this chapter.

1　In a bowl, mix the flours, salt, ground caraway seeds and whole caraway seeds, if using. Set aside.

2　Pour the water into the bowl of an electric mixer and whisk in the yeast. Let stand 2 minutes, then whisk again. Add the flour mixture, then the treacle.

3　Use a large rubber spatula to mix the ingredients to a rough dough.

4　Place on the mixer fitted with the dough hook and continue with the master recipe from steps 5 through 7, on page 72.

5　Continue with the master recipe at step 9 (pages 72–73) but remember to form only a single loaf from the dough.

6　Let the loaf rise and bake it as in the master recipe, page 73.

Serving: Though delicious as toast, I love this untoasted as sandwich bread. Thinly sliced baked ham and Gruyère with dark mustard and a garlicky gherkin elevate this bread to the realm of haute cuisine.

Storage: Keep the loaves at room temperature on the day they are baked. Slide leftovers into a plastic bag and keep at room temperature. Freeze for longer storage.

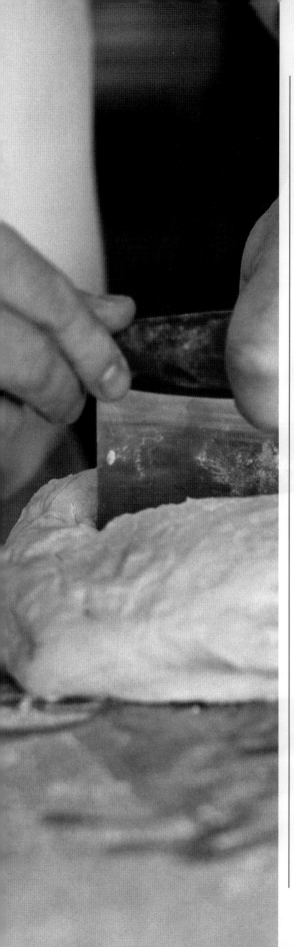

two-step & wholegrain breads

Using a sponge to make bread is nothing more than preparing a small amount of dough in advance and allowing it to rise in the refrigerator, usually overnight or over the course of the day. Sponges are easy to prepare, and the yeast multiplies in the sponge, so that when you add the sponge to the final dough it has much more impact than the same amount of yeast would have in a one-step dough. Consequently, since you are using less yeast in the final dough, the wheat flavour of the flour you are using stands out more. A bread made with a sponge has excellent flavour, a crisp crust, and an open crumb dotted with holes (though I would argue that it's not necessarily superior to a one-step bread – just different).

yeast-based sponge

Makes about 250g

½ teaspoon active dried yeast

180ml

room temperature tap water, about 23°C–27°C

130g bread flour

Though this sponge (also known as a starter or pre-ferment) needs more than 8 hours to rise completely before it can be used, it takes about 5 minutes to prepare, so it really doesn't add extra work to baking a loaf of bread. Using a sponge as part of a baked dough naturally increases the amount of yeast cells in the dough without using a large amount of yeast at the outset. This imparts a better flavour to the baked bread.

1 In a 1- to 2-litre bowl, whisk the yeast into the water. Wait a minute, then whisk again to make sure the yeast is completely dissolved.

2 Stir in the flour smoothly; the sponge will be like a thin batter. Cover the bowl with clingfilm and let it rise for at least 1 hour at room temperature. The sponge will rise slowly.

3 Stir down the sponge and refrigerate it for 8–12 hours before using it in a recipe.

Storage: You may keep the sponge refrigerated for up to 16 hours, but after that the sponge will start to acquire an overly sour flavour.

essential tips for sponges & sponge-based bread dough

- Make sure the water is just room temperature when you add the yeast, or the sponge will rise too quickly.

- Never try to rush the sponge or the resulting dough, or you'll defeat the entire purpose of using it. Each needs to rise slowly to develop the best possible flavour and texture.

- Note: This is emphatically not a sourdough sponge; that's made from flour and water only and ferments due to the natural yeasts in the wheat, not in the air as some erroneously believe. Sometimes a yeast-rich ingredient such as the water used to rinse raisins is added to boost the sourdough fermentation along.

- Although this sponge-based dough is mixed by machine, you still need to let it rest between gentle mixings. Mixing too fast or for too long overheats the dough and also destroys the natural flavour components in the flour.

- You can make this sponge and bread dough work around your schedule; it can be left alone for a few hours after mixing, but only if the room is cool. Letting either the sponge or dough ferment too much, however, will give an excessively yeasty taste to the dough and make the dough overly sticky and difficult to shape.

sponge-based bread dough

Use this recipe as a model for the variations in this chapter. Once the sponge is made, the dough comes together relatively quickly. This dough may also be formed and baked in the same way as any of the one-step breads in Chapter 5. Here, I'm giving you a machine mixing method, but you can also mix this by hand as for the One-Step Bread Dough, page 64.

Makes about 1.1kg dough

390g white bread flour

2 teaspoons salt

½ teaspoon active dried yeast

240ml warm tap water, about 38°C–43°C

1 batch Yeast-Based Sponge, opposite

1 Mix the flour and salt together and set aside.

2 In the bowl of an electric mixer fitted with the dough hook, whisk the yeast into the water. Wait 2 minutes, then whisk again to make sure all the yeast is dissolved. Use a large rubber spatula to stir in the sponge.

3 Use the same rubber spatula to stir the flour and salt into the liquid all at once.

4 Mix on a medium speed for 2 minutes. Stop the mixer and let the dough rest for 10 minutes.

5 Mix again on a medium speed for 2 minutes.

6 Lightly oil a bowl large enough to hold twice the quantity of dough you now have. Cover the bowl with clingfilm and let the dough rest until it starts to puff visibly, about 30 minutes.

7 Scrape the dough from the bowl to a lightly floured work surface. Flour your hands, not the top of the dough, and pat it into a rough rectangle. Fold one of the narrow ends of the dough over the middle, then fold the other end over that to make 3 layers. Turn the dough 90 degrees so that the folded side is facing you and repeat the folding. Lightly oil the bowl again if necessary and invert the dough into the oiled bowl and cover it.

8 Let the dough rest for 15 minutes, then repeat step 7.

9 Lightly oil the bowl again if necessary and put in the dough. Turn the dough over so that the top is oiled. Cover with clingfilm and let the dough rise until it has doubled in size.

variation

Part Wholemeal Dough: Substitute 130g wholemeal bread flour for 130g of the white bread flour.

Wholemeal Hazelnut Bread The nutty flavor of wholemeal flour pairs naturally with any nuts, but I like the flavour of hazelnuts with it best. Purchase the hazelnuts already skinned if you can; sometimes the skins are difficult to remove. Adding a handful of raisins or dried currants to this dough further complements the wholemeal flavour.

Use this part wholemeal variation of the dough; add 225g toasted, skinned and coarsely crushed hazelnuts (or lightly toasted and coarsely chopped walnut or pecan pieces) about halfway through step 5 in the master dough recipe above. Follow the Apulian Olive Bread recipe on page 84 starting at step 2.

ciabatta
'slipper' bread

Makes two 25cm long loaves

260g bread flour

1½ teaspoons salt

½ teaspoon active dried yeast

180ml cool tap water, about 24°C

1 batch Yeast-Based Sponge
page 80 (see Note)

Olive oil for the rising bowl

Baking stone or inverted heavy duty
swiss roll tin

Polenta for the peel

Spray bottle filled with hot water
for baking

Peel or rectangle of stiff cardboard

variation

Ciabatta Rolls: Unless you are a master
at handling a peel, bake these on a tin
dusted with polenta or lined with baking
paper. In step 10, right, gently pull the
dough into a 25cm square. Use the dough
scraper to cut it into 9 equal squares.
Gently round each one by inverting and
pulling the corners together. Invert again
onto the prepared tin. Cover the rolls
with a tea towel or oiled clingfilm and
let them rise until well puffed, but not
completely double, about 30 minutes.
Place the tin in the preheated oven (the
stone isn't necessary) and mist with
water. Repeat the misting again after
5 minutes. Bake the rolls as above until
they are deep golden and light for their
size, about 15 minutes. Cool on a rack
and use or freeze.

A

Ciabatta's justly deserved popularity is due to its crusty exterior and airy interior, making it the ultimate crust-lovers' bread. Small versions make excellent sandwich rolls. Here we're using the sponge on page 80 and making a very soft dough. Don't be afraid to handle such a soft dough; just use plenty of flour on your hands and under the dough. You can brush away excess flour from the tops of the loaves before placing them in the oven, but many bakers leave a floury coating on the bread. It's best to use a baking stone for ciabatta, but if you don't have one and don't want to buy one, an overturned swiss roll tin that won't warp when heated will do the trick. Use a wooden peel for sliding the loaves into the oven or improvise one with a piece of stiff cardboard. If you don't want to fuss with the peel or cardboard, just place the two loaves on a polenta-dusted or baking paper-lined swiss roll tin. After placing it in the oven, spray, and then continue with the recipe at step 12.

1 Mix the flour and salt together and set aside.

2 In the bowl of an electric mixer fitted with the paddle attachment, whisk the yeast into the water. Use a large rubber spatula to scrape in and stir the sponge into the yeast and water.

3 Stir in the flour and salt; the dough will be very soft.

4 Beat on medium-low for 3 minutes. Stop and let the dough rest for 10 minutes.

B

5 Repeat step 4.

6 Continue with steps 6, 7 and 8 on page 81.

7 Turn the dough over so that the fold is underneath and form it into a 20cm square. Cover with clingfilm and a clean tea towel and let rise until puffed, about 30 minutes.

8 About 20 minutes before the dough is fully risen, set a rack in the centre of the oven and place your baking stone or inverted swiss roll tin on it (long side parallel to the oven door); preheat to 250°C/gas mark 9 or the highest temperature on your oven.

9 Once the dough has risen, generously flour the work surface. Have the peel nearby and generously dust it with polenta. Place the spray bottle close to the oven.

10 Use an oiled dough scraper to cut the dough (cut straight down repeatedly, don't drag the blade through the dough) into two 10 x 20cm rectangles (A).

11 Slide your flat upturned palms under one of the pieces of dough from the short ends until your fingertips meet in the middle. Lift the dough to the outermost edge of the peel, pulling it slightly until it is about 25cm long (B). Open the oven and quickly slide the loaf from the peel to the far side of the baking stone or tin. Quickly close the oven and scatter more polenta on the peel and repeat with the second loaf, positioning it on the half of the stone closer to the oven door. Generously spray the inside of the oven with water to create steam.

12 Wait 5 minutes, then spray again.

13 Bake the ciabatte (the plural) until they are deep golden and their internal temperature is over 93°C, about 20–25 minutes. Transfer to a rack to cool.

Serving: Ciabatta is good with everything. For some no-nonsense hors d'oeuvre to serve with drinks before dinner, split a ciabatta or two horizontally and fill with thinly sliced prosciutto and mozzarella cheese, a drizzle of olive oil and some torn fresh basil. Replace the top of the loaf and cut lengthways and then crossways into 4cm pieces. Ciabatta is equally good with smoked salmon, a thin smear of cream cheese, plenty of ground pepper and some finely cut chives or spring onions.

Storage: Keep the ciabatta at room temperature on the day it is baked. This type of bread grows stale quickly, so wrap and freeze the second loaf if you don't need it immediately. Defrost and reheat at 180°C/gas mark 4 for 10 minutes, then cool and serve.

Note: Many bakers use a firmer Italian-style sponge called *biga* for making ciabatta, but this one works well too. Make sure the sponge is well risen for best flavour and texture.

apulian olive bread

Real Cerignola green olives from Puglia make the best version of this bread. They're flavourful and somewhat firm and don't turn to purée when you're beating them into the dough. I often bake this as two smaller loaves – just divide the dough in half and round both pieces. For ease, you can also bake the loaf or loaves on a polenta-dusted or baking paper-lined swiss roll tin.

Makes one round 23 or 25cm loaf

1 batch Sponge-Based Bread Dough (page 81)

170g Cerignola or other large green olives, pitted and coarsely chopped

Polenta for the peel

Baking stone or inverted heavy duty swiss roll tin

Spray bottle filled with hot water for baking

Peel

1 Add the chopped olives about halfway through step 5 in the master dough recipe on page 81. Follow the master recipe to the end of step 9.

2 Turn the dough out onto a floured work surface without folding it over on itself. Turn the dough over so that what was the smooth top surface when it was rising is now uppermost. Gently round the piece of dough without deflating it too much by pushing inward at the bottom with your flat upturned palms all around the piece of dough; the outside skin of the dough will tighten and become more spherical.

3 Slide the dough to a polenta-dusted peel or baking sheet and cover it with a tea towel or clingfilm. Let the dough rise until almost doubled in size, about 1 hour.

4 About 20 minutes before the dough is fully risen, set a rack in the centre of the oven and place the baking stone or inverted swiss roll tin on it (long side parallel to the oven door); preheat to 250°C (or the highest temperature on your oven). Place a spray bottle filled with water within reach.

5 Use a single-edged razor blade or X-Acto knife to slash the top of the loaf 4 times, overlapping the ends of the slashes to form a crosshatch pattern.

6 Open the oven and quickly slide the loaf from the peel to the baking stone or tin. Grab the bottle, generously spray inside the oven, and close the door.

7 Wait 5 minutes and spray again. Reduce oven temperature to 200°C/gas mark 6.

8 Bake the loaf until it is well risen and deep golden, and has an internal temperature of 93°C–99°C, about 50 minutes to 1 hour. Transfer to a wire rack to cool.

Serving: Use a sharp serrated knife to cut the cooled loaf into thick slices. This is a perfect bread to serve with cheese.

Storage: Keep the loaf uncovered on the day it is baked. If it's humid and the crust softens, crisp it in a 180°C/gas mark 4 oven for a few minutes and cool again before serving.

variation

Garlic Lovers' Bread: This is a fun bread to serve with casual food such as fried chicken, anything barbecued, or even a big substantial salad but it doesn't belong anywhere near delicately seasoned dishes. Many garlic breads use roasted garlic, but I'm borrowing a technique from Thai cooking and seasoning the bread with fried thin slices of garlic and some of the oil used to fry them.

6–8 large cloves garlic, peeled and thinly sliced lengthways

120ml olive oil

Combine the garlic and oil in a medium saucepan and place on a low heat. Have a plate covered with a double thickness of kitchen paper ready near the hob. Once the garlic starts to sizzle and take on a little colour, use a slotted spoon to stir it constantly or the sugars in the garlic will caramelise, causing all the slices to stick together. Once all the slices are an even light golden colour, pull the pan off the heat and continue stirring for 1 minute, then use the slotted spoon to remove the garlic to the plate. Pour a couple of tablespoons of the oil into a small cup and let the garlic and oil cool to room temperature. Refrigerate the leftover garlic oil in a small covered jar and use it in cooking or salad dressings. Substitute the garlic and the reserved oil for the olives.

08

flatbreads

These are some of my favourite breads to make, because they combine easy preparation with delicious results. They span the globe from the Middle East to Italy, moving right across the Atlantic to some contemporary versions I've tasted in New York City. After visiting Istanbul several years ago and enjoying the incredibly fine baked goods available even in the street, I resolved to make versions of what I had tasted after I returned home – and these are the results. To duplicate all of them would require an entire book... so I have included just a few of my favourites. I use a similar dough for a thin-crusted pizza (real Neapolitan pizza dough doesn't contain oil). My pizza crust is easy to press out thinly and always bakes to a delicate texture no matter what the toppings.

middle eastern flatbread dough

Makes 675g dough, enough for several flatbreads

390g bread flour

2 teaspoons salt

7g sachet active dried yeast

305ml warm tap water, about 43°C

2 tablespoons olive oil

essential tips for middle eastern flatbread dough

- This very soft dough needs to develop quite a lot of elasticity and smoothness or it won't rise well in the oven. Use bread flour for best results.

- Don't let the dough rise more than indicated in the recipe at any point or it might over-ferment slightly and not rise well in the oven.

- Make sure to have any ingredients necessary for topping or finishing the dough ready when you start to prepare it or the dough might over-ferment while waiting.

It would be entirely possible to write a very thick book only on the subject of Middle Eastern flatbreads, so this recipe just skims the surface. I'm happy with the results of using the same dough for both thick and thin flatbreads used respectively as table breads or as wraps for a variety of accompaniments.

1 Mix the flour and salt together and set aside.

2 Whisk the yeast into the water in the bowl of an electric mixer fitted with the dough hook. Wait 2 minutes, then whisk again to make sure it's completely dissolved. Whisk in the oil.

3 Stir in about half the flour mixture until smooth, then stir in the rest. Beat on a medium speed until fairly smooth, about 3 minutes. Stop the mixer and let the dough rest for 10 minutes.

4 Beat on a low speed until the dough is smoother and somewhat elastic, about 3 minutes more.

5 Scrape the dough into an oiled bowl and turn it over (it's very soft, so it's best to use a flexible scraper) so that the top is oiled. Cover the bowl with clingfilm. Let the dough rest until it starts to puff, 15 to 20 minutes.

6 Scrape the dough to a lightly floured work surface. Pat and stretch the dough into a rectangle 3 times longer than it is wide. Fold one third of the dough over the middle section, then fold the other side over that.

7 Turn the dough 90 degrees and repeat stretching and folding.

8 Return the dough to the bowl (it may be necessary to oil the bowl again) and turn it over so that the top is oiled. Cover with clingfilm and let the dough rise until it has doubled in size, about 30 minutes. Use the risen dough in any of the recipes on pages 90–91.

These recipes are but a few of the hundreds of slight variations possible in size, shape, dough and topping ingredients, and density of the finished bread. The soft dough might be difficult to shape, so flour the work surface well to prevent sticking. Form the larger variations on a rimless baking sheet, flexible chopping board, or piece of stiff cardboard to facilitate transfer to the baking tin.

ekmek
basic turkish flatbread

The Turkish name for this merely means 'bread', owing to the fact that this is so widely made. There are many variations of it too, some made with a sourdough starter instead of yeast.

Makes 1 loaf

1 batch Middle Eastern Flatbread Dough (page 88), fully risen

Polenta for the baking tin

Baking sheet or swiss roll tin sprinkled with a light dusting of polenta or lined with baking paper

Spray bottle filled with hot water

Serving: This is an excellent bread to serve with a meal. Cut into thick slices.

Storage: This bread is best on the day it's made. Wrap any leftovers and reheat them at 180°C/gas mark 4 for 10 minutes before serving; it's delicious warm.

A

D

1 Without folding over the dough, scrape it to a floured work surface. Turn the dough over so that the smooth top surface is uppermost. Round the dough by repeatedly pulling upward all around the perimeter and pushing and pinching those flaps of dough into the centre (A). Turn the dough over, cover it with a tea towel and let it rest for 5–10 minutes.

2 Without deflating the dough too much, stretch and pull it into an oval shape the length of your baking tin and half its width, about 12.5 x 38cm (B). Slide both hands, palms upright, under the dough and transfer it to the prepared tin (C and D). Cover the dough with oiled clingfilm.

3 Set a rack in the centre of the oven and preheat to 250°C (or the highest temperature on your oven). Have a spray bottle filled with hot water nearby.

4 Let the loaf rise until it just starts to puff, about 20 minutes (E).

5 Use a fingertip to dimple the top of the loaf gently at 2.5cm intervals without deflating it.

6 Place the tin in the oven, spray the inside of the oven all over with the water, and quickly close the oven door.

B

C

E

F

7 Wait 5 minutes and spray again. Reduce the heat to 200°C/gas mark 6 and continue to bake the bread until it is well risen, is deep golden, and has an internal temperature of 93°C–99°C, about 20 minutes. Slide the bread to a rack to cool.

variations

Seeded Flatbreads:

2 tablespoons white or black sesame seeds, or a combination

Divide the dough into 2 equal pieces. Round a piece by repeatedly pulling upward around the perimeter and pushing those flaps of dough into the centre. Repeat with the second piece. Invert both pieces of dough, cover with a tea towel, and let rest for 10 minutes. Preheat the oven and form the breads: gently press each piece of dough into a disk 20cm in diameter. Arrange on the prepared pan and cover. Let the dough rest until it starts to puff. Gently dimple the dough (F) and spray with a little water. Scatter seeds on each bread. Bake, cool, serve and store.

Za'tar Flatbreads: Za'tar is a blend of herbs, white sesame seeds, and salt popular in Middle Eastern cooking. Many regional variations exist, and packaged blends are easy to find. Just be sure not to buy the finely ground variety, which, when combined with the oil, will form a paste unsuitable for topping.

Makes 4 medium flatbreads

5 tablespoons za'tar

4 tablespoons olive oil

One batch Middle Eastern Flatbread Dough (page 88), fully risen

1 Stir the za'tar and oil together and set aside.

2 Divide the dough into four pieces, round and let rest as in Seeded Flatbreads, above.

3 After preheating the oven, shape into four 15cm discs, place on the prepared tin, cover, and allow to puff.

4 Dimple the formed loaves and spread each with a quarter of the topping. Bake, cool, serve, and store as on page 90.

focaccia dough

Makes about 1kg dough, enough for
1 large thick-crusted focaccia or
2 smaller ones

585g unbleached plain flour
or bread flour

2 teaspoons salt

7g sachet fast action dried yeast

420ml warm tap water, about 43°C

60ml olive oil

Focaccia, like pizza, means different things to different people. In a Roman pizzeria that makes typically Italian thin-crust pizza, it can be a similarly thin disc of the same dough brushed with olive oil and sprinkled with salt before it's baked for just a few minutes in a ferociously hot wood-burning oven. Thicker types of focacce (the plural) derive from the Italian region of Liguria, of which Genoa is the capital and typically have some fat added to the dough. The fat, usually olive oil or freshly rendered pork lard, adds flavour, tenderness and richness to the resulting focaccia. I like to use this version of the dough, which is more than easy to prepare, as a base for savoury toppings beyond the traditionally Italian.

1 Stir the flour and salt together and set aside.

2 In a large mixing bowl, whisk the yeast into the water. Wait 2 minutes and whisk again to make sure the yeast is completely dissolved. Whisk in the oil.

3 Use a large rubber spatula to smoothly stir half the flour mixture into the liquid. Stir in the remaining flour mixture, using the spatula to dig up any unmoistened flour from the bottom of the bowl.

4 After all the flour is moistened, scrape any dry bits from the side of the bowl and incorporate them into the dough. Use the spatula to beat the dough vigorously for about 15 seconds. Cover the bowl with clingfilm and let the dough rise until it has doubled in size, about 1 hour.

5 Use the dough with any of the seasoning and/or topping variations that follow.

essential tips for focaccia dough

- This dough is quickly made. For advance preparation, have all the ingredients ready, but make sure you'll be ready to follow through to the baking once you mix the dough. You may deflate and refrigerate the dough if you can't complete the process. Press it into the tin straight from the refrigerator. When cold it will take much longer to rise in the tin before baking, though.

- This soft dough is easy to mix, but not particularly easy to handle. If you have any difficulty turning the dough over once it's on the tin, just oil your hands to press the dough into the tin.

- Be creative about toppings and additions to the dough – just don't use too many different things at the same time or overload the top of the focaccia or it will not bake as well.

potato & gruyère focaccia

I first tasted a version of this made by my friend Amy Scherber, owner of Amy's Bread in New York. I liked it so much I developed a version of my own a few days later without ever finding out how she makes hers. Just recently Amy told me that for the topping she roasts the potatoes whole and unpeeled and then slices them once they're cold, another option you might want to try.

Makes one 30 x 46cm focaccia, 12 approximately 10cm squares

1 batch Focaccia Dough, left, completely risen

2 medium waxy potatoes, about 340g

Salt and freshly ground black pepper

55g coarsely grated Swiss Gruyère cheese

2 tablespoons olive oil

One 28 x 43cm or 30 x 46cm swiss roll tin, greased with 60ml olive oil

Serving: Slide the still-warm focaccia to a chopping board and use a sharp serrated knife to cut into 3 strips in the width and 4 in the length to make 10cm squares. To serve the focaccia as an hors d'oeuvre, cut it into 5cm squares.

Storage: Keep the focaccia on the rack until serving. Wrap leftovers in clingfilm and warm them in the oven before serving.

1 Scrape the dough into the tin, being careful not to fold the dough over on itself. Reach under it and flip it over – now the top is coated with oil. Use the palms of your hands to press the dough into the tin. If it resists, cover, and let rest for 10 minutes, then press again to cover the entire base of the tin. Cover with clingfilm and let rise until puffy, about 30 minutes.

2 Set a rack in the lowest level of the oven and preheat to 230°C/gas mark 8.

3 Peel the potatoes and cut them as thinly as you can; I use the little slicing blade on the side of a box grater. Slide into a saucepan, cover with water and bring to the boil over a medium heat. Drain, rinse and set aside in a colander.

4 Once the focaccia is risen, use your index finger to dimple the top all over at 2.5cm intervals. Cover with the potato slices, slightly overlapping them. Season with a little salt and pepper and evenly scatter on the cheese. Drizzle with the olive oil.

5 Place the focaccia in the oven and reduce the temperature to 220°C/gas mark 7. Bake until the dough is firm and the topping is golden, about 30 minutes. About halfway through the baking time, use a wide palette knife to lift the corner of the focaccia to check that the base is starting to colour. If it is colouring too quickly, slide another tin under the tin the focaccia is in to insulate it.

6 Slide the baked focaccia to a rack to cool so that the base doesn't become damp.

variation

Onion Focaccia: I know it doesn't sound very glamorous, but slowly cooked sliced onions are one of my favorite toppings for a focaccia. For a delicious variation, halve, seed, and thinly slice 450g red peppers and cook them along with the onions.

Makes one 30 x 46cm focaccia, 12 approximately 10cm squares

60ml olive oil

3 large white or yellow onions, about 650g, peeled, halved, and thinly sliced from stem to root end

1 batch Focaccia Dough, completely risen

Salt and freshly ground black pepper

1 Start cooking the onions before step 1 of the master dough recipe, left. Combine the oil and onions in a wide sauté pan that has a lid. Place on a medium heat and when the oil starts to sizzle, reduce to low, cover the pan, and cook, stirring occasionally, until the onions are soft and translucent, about 30 minutes. Uncover the pan, season with a little salt and increase the heat slightly. Cook until the liquid evaporates, 10–15 minutes. Scrape the onions into a thin layer on a baking sheet lined with clingfilm and cool quickly in the refrigerator or freezer.

2 Continue with the recipe above at step 4, substituting the cooled onions for the potatoes and cheese. Season with salt and pepper but do not drizzle with oil as there is plenty in the onions.

3 Bake, cool, serve and store as above.

sage & sundried tomato focaccia

Makes one 30 x 46cm focaccia,
12 approximately 10cm squares

Ingredients for Focaccia Dough (page 92)

**1 small bunch fresh sage, stemmed,
leaves stacked and cut into 5mm ribbons**

**55g sundried tomatoes, cut
into 1cm dice**

2 tablespoons olive oil

1 teaspoon coarse sea salt

One 28 x 43cm or 30 x 46cm swiss roll tin,
greased with 60ml olive oil

Sage and sundried tomatoes make a flavourful focaccia topping but if you like, add them directly to the dough as in the variation below. See the end of the recipe for suggestions on other additions to the dough. Don't be afraid to be creative. Other dry cheeses, cured meats, and fresh or dried herbs beyond the ones suggested are fine too, as long as you don't overdo it.

1 Mix and let the dough rise as on page 92.

2 Scrape the dough into the prepared tin, being careful not to fold the dough over on itself. After the dough is on the tin, reach under it and flip it over – now the top is coated with oil. Use the flat palms of your hands to press the dough into the tin. If it resists, cover and let rest for 10 minutes, then press again to cover the entire base of the tin. Cover with clingfilm and allow to rise until puffy, about 30 minutes.

3 Set a rack in the lowest level of the oven and preheat to 230°C/gas mark 8.

4 Once the focaccia is fully risen, use your index finger to dimple the top all over at 2.5cm intervals. Press pieces of the sage and tomato into the dough at about 2.5cm intervals all over the top. Drizzle with the oil and sprinkle with the salt.

5 Place the focaccia in the oven and reduce the temperature to 220°C/gas mark 7. Bake until the dough is firm and the topping is golden, about 30 minutes. About halfway through the baking time, use a wide palette knife to lift a corner of the focaccia to check that the base is starting to colour. If it is colouring too quickly, slide another tin under the tin the focaccia is in to insulate it.

6 Slide the baked focaccia to a rack to cool slightly so that the base doesn't become damp. Serve and store as for the Potato and Gruyère Focaccia, page 93.

variations

Instead of topping the focaccia with the sage and tomatoes, add them to the flour and salt when mixing the master recipe, then continue with step 1 above. Or use any of the following as additions to the dough instead of the sage and dried tomatoes: 4 tablespoons coarsely chopped fresh rosemary leaves, 2 tablespoons dried herbes de Provence or za'tar, 55g dry grating cheese such as Parmigiano-Reggiano (reserve a tablespoon to sprinkle on top with the salt before baking), 100g pitted and coarsely chopped oil-cured olives or 45g diced thinly-sliced mozzarella cheese and 55g diced thinly-sliced prosciutto.

thin-crusted pizza

Makes 1.1kg dough,
enough for four 30cm round pizzas
(see Note 1)

650g bread flour

2 teaspoons salt

2 teaspoons active dried yeast (see Note 2)

480ml warm water, about 43°C

5 tablespoons olive oil, divided

Note 1: You can divide the dough in thirds
or just in half to make three 25 x 38cm or
two 30 x 46cm rectangular pizzas.

Note 2: If you're preparing the dough
early in the day for the evening or even the
day before baking the pizzas, use only
1 teaspoon yeast.

essential tips for pizza

- Use a heavy-gauge tin with
  sides for baking the pizza. Thin
  tins don't hold enough heat to
  sufficiently colour and crisp the
  bottom of the pizza before the
  toppings dry out. And the tin
  has to have sides or oil might drip
  onto the bottom of the oven and
  create smoke or even flames.

- Don't overdo the pizza toppings;
  limit them to three or four.
  Otherwise they will begin
  cancelling each other out and
  you won't taste the crust at all.

- Serve the pizza immediately
  after baking for best results.

My quest for a thin-crusted pizza that's easy to prepare at home led me right to my friend Michael Ayoub, chef-owner of Fornino in Brooklyn, New York. Michael uses a long-rising dough made from a blend of different flours for his thin, delicate pizzas, but I wanted something that would work well if you decided you wanted to serve some pizza in a couple of hours. After a few false starts, including one that produced a perfect replica of a frozen pizza, I decided upon this dough, which is similar to a dough for a focaccia and is easy to press out thinly into a pizza tin. I decided on using an oiled tin for the pizza rather than a baking stone, another point that makes the process simpler to tackle. I like to proceed right from pressing the dough into the tin to adding the toppings and baking. Most domestic ovens won't hold two 25cm tins side by side but you can bake the pizzas in succession, which isn't that much of a problem since they bake quickly.

1 Stir the flour and salt together in a large mixing bowl.

2 Whisk the yeast into the water and whisk in 2 tablespoons of the oil.

3 Use a large rubber spatula to stir the liquid into the flour, continuously scraping the side of the bowl and folding up any unmixed flour from the bottom of the bowl.

4 Once most of the flour is moistened, repeatedly slide the spatula between the side of the bowl and the dough and fold the dough over on itself to make it smoother. Cover the bowl with clingfilm and set aside until doubled in size, about 1 hour.

5 Scrape the risen dough to a floured work surface and fold it over on itself several times to make it smoother. Use a dough scraper to divide the dough into equal pieces, depending on the size of the tins you're using (see Note 1, on the left).

6 Fold the sides of each piece of dough into the top centre to round it. Flip the pieces over so that the smooth sides are uppermost. Generously flour each piece and loosely wrap individually in clingfilm. They can be refrigerated for up to 24 hours.

7 About 20 minutes before forming and baking the pizzas, set a rack in the lowest level of the oven and preheat to your oven's highest setting (if possible, at least 285°C).

8 Use 2 more tablespoons of the oil to grease the base and sides of the tin and unwrap a piece of dough onto it (A). Turn the dough over so that the top is oiled too and press with the fingers of both hands to stretch the dough to fill the tin (B). If you're baking more than one pizza, repeat with the remaining pieces of dough. Only form as many crusts as you can bake immediately or the crusts that have to wait will rise on the tin and become thicker.

9 Spread and scatter the toppings on the crust to within 5mm of the edge and drizzle with the remaining tablespoon of olive oil (C through F). Bake the pizza until the topping is bubbling and lightly browned and the bottom is well baked through, about 10 minutes. After about 5 minutes, use a palette knife to lift the crust and check to see if the bottom is colouring.

A

B

C

D

E

F

10 Slide the pizza onto a chopping board and use a pizza wheel to cut into wedges. Serve immediately. Repeat for any remaining pizzas.

topping combinations for thin-crusted pizzas

The best advice I can give you is: don't overdo it! The first pizza I ever had in an actual pizzeria was in New Jersey where I grew up (my grandmother made thick-crusted pizza at home on special occasions). We ordered it with 'extra cheese'. What arrived at the table was a disc of dough that seemed to be topped with about a gallon of lava-like melted cheese, still seething from the oven – there was easily enough mozzarella on that pizza to top a dozen or more traditional Italian pizzas.

Please note that for the sake of clarity all the topping quantities are given for a single 30cm round pizza. A 25 x 38cm pizza needs $1\frac{1}{2}$ times the topping quantity to cover it and a 30 x 46cm pizza needs twice the quantity. The topping recipes and instructions make more than you need for a single batch of pizza dough; pack, cover, and freeze extras for future pizzas. Finally, avoid adding cheese to any pizza that contains anchovies.

Don't be afraid to be creative with your own ideas for pizza toppings, just remember a few simple rules: Limit your choices to 3 or 4 toppings per pizza. Use the quantities in the pizzas below as a guideline; toppings are meant to enhance, not overwhelm the crust. Blanch or cook vegetables before using. And use freshly prepared ingredients; a pizza isn't a vehicle for disposing of leftovers. **>**

Pizza Margherita: The queen of all pizzas and the most popular one at Michael's Fornino pizzeria, it's actually named in honour of Italy's Queen Margherita di Savoia. Devised by Neapolitan *pizzaiolo* Raffaele Esposito in 1889, the pizza's red (tomato), white (mozzarella), and green (basil) toppings mimic the colours of the newly united Kingdom of Italy's flag and the Margherita was so named after the queen chose it as her favourite among the ones Esposito prepared.

Thinly spread the crust with 70g Tomato Topping (right). Scatter on 8 large basil leaves that have been stacked and cut into 5mm shreds, followed by 55g grated low-moisture mozzarella or finely diced fresh mozzarella. Drizzle with olive oil (see the photos on page 97).

Variation: Don't tell the Neapolitan pizza mafia, but I like to scatter a large clove of garlic, cut into paper-thin slivers, on the tomato topping. The garlic melts to a mild and creamy flavour and texture while the pizza is baking.

Pizza di Patate: This potato pizza is different from the potato focaccia on page 93. Cover the pizza crust with thin slices of blanched potato (page 93) and lightly salt and pepper. Scatter on 2 teaspoons finely chopped fresh rosemary (or 1 teaspoon dried oregano) and 55g finely grated Parmigiano-Reggiano or Pecorino Romano. If using Romano, which is quite salty, omit the salt from the toppings. Drizzle with olive oil.

Pizza Salsiccia e Peperoni (sausage and pepper pizza): First mix together 55g Tomato Topping with 55g each Onion and Pepper toppings (right). Spread on the pizza. Scatter on thin slices of a cooked Italian sausage, sweet or hot as you wish, and 55g grated ricotta salata, mozzarella, Parmigiano or Pecorino cheese. Drizzle with olive oil.

Variations: Substitute 55g of soppressata, other dried sausage, or even prosciutto, thinly sliced, stacked and cut into 1cm shreds, for the freshly cooked sausage. Scatter the dried sausage on the pizza after removing it from the oven.

Pizza con le Alici (anchovy pizza): Drain and chop 30g anchovies packed in oil and stir them into 110g Tomato Topping (right). Evenly spread on the pizza crust and top with a large clove of garlic cut into paper-thin slivers, 1 teaspoon dried oregano and 2 tablespoons olive oil.

Pizza con le Cipolle: (onion pizza): Spread the crust with 70g Onion Topping (mix anchovies into it as above if you like). Top with 70g pitted and quartered Gaeta or Kalamata olives, 1 teaspoon dried oregano and 1 tablespoon olive oil. Scatter with 55g grated cheese of your choice if you haven't added anchovies.

Variation: Use 55g each of Onion Topping and Pepper Topping (below); omit the olives. Sprinkle with 55g grated cheese and 1/2 teaspoon dried oregano.

recipes & instructions for preparing pizza toppings

Each of the following makes enough for several pizzas. You needn't prepare all of them – look through the pizzas at left, select the ones you want to bake, and prepare the necessary toppings accordingly.

Tomato Topping: In Italy or any pizzeria elsewhere that has a woodburning oven, it's common to use fresh or canned chopped tomatoes as a pizza topping. In an oven that heats to close to 540°C, the excess water from the tomatoes easily evaporates. In a home oven, chopped tomatoes can produce a watery topping for a thin-crusted pizza, so I took Michael Ayoub's advice for a cooked puréed tomato topping.

Run a 785g tin of Italian San Marzano plum tomatoes through a food mill into a large saucepan. Add 4 large sprigs of basil tied together with kitchen twine and 3 cloves of garlic, peeled and halved. Bring to the boil, reduce heat to a very gentle simmer, place a lid partially over the pan and cook for 30 minutes. Cool, remove the garlic and basil and refrigerate covered if not using immediately. Makes about 400g.

Onion Topping: Peel, halve and thinly slice a large white onion (about 225–280g) from stem to root end. Pour 2 tablespoons olive oil into a wide sauté pan, add the onions, salt lightly and set over a high heat. When the onions begin to sizzle, reduce the heat to low and cook them slowly, stirring occasionally, until they are soft and light golden, about 20–30 minutes. Let cool.

Pepper Topping: Cut 2 red, green or yellow peppers, or a combination, by standing them up, stem upward and cutting away the four walls of the pepper. Slice away the bottom. Cut the pepper pieces in 7.5mm strips. Oil a swiss roll tin and add the pepper strips. Salt lightly. Bake in a preheated 190°C/gas mark 5 oven on the centre rack, stirring occasionally, until soft but not charred, about 20 minutes. If the pepper strips char at all while baking they'll turn to cinders on the pizza.

Potato Topping: Peel, slice and blanch 675g waxy potatoes according to the instructions on page 93. Only make as much as you need; this topping doesn't freeze well.

Cheese: Grate mozzarella or ricotta salata on the largest holes of a box grater. For harder cheese such as Parmigiano or Pecorino, use the smaller holes to make thin shreds.

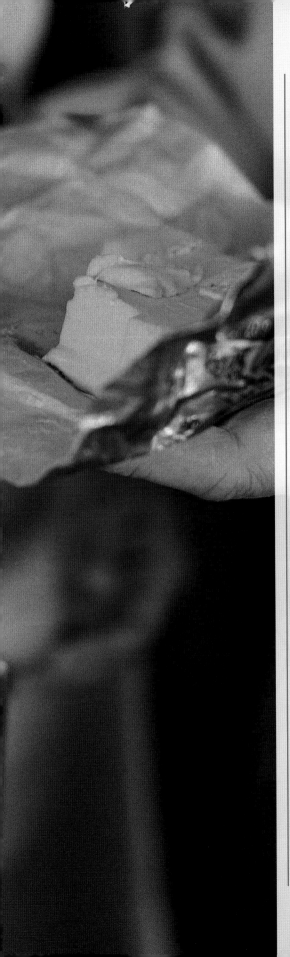

09

brioche

Tender, buttery and just slightly sweet, brioches are among the world's finest breakfast pastries. And yes, brioche is considered a pastry, not a bread. I have a special affection for brioche because the first class I ever taught, in February 1979, was on preparing brioche dough and making various buns and loaves from it. This chapter begins with some simply formed or adorned breakfast loaves and buns, then takes off to cover some fruited and other more elaborate ones, before finishing up with the world's most elegant pizza – a double-crusted affair created by a French chef for a Sicilian prince.

brioche dough

Makes about 800g dough

SPONGE

75ml milk

7g sachet active dried yeast

60ml warm tap water, about 43°C

100g bread flour

DOUGH

2 medium eggs, at room temperature

2 medium egg yolks, at room temperature

3 tablespoons sugar

All the sponge, above

260g bread flour

1 teaspoon salt

110g unsalted butter, softened

If you have an electric mixer to do all the work, brioche dough is as easy to prepare as the batter for a pound cake. This is a variation on the brioche dough I learned from my teacher Albert Kumin. His recipe called for starting with the butter and beating the other ingredients into it. I've revised the method to incorporate the butter at the end; the more traditional manner of preparing the dough.

1 For the sponge, warm the milk in a small saucepan over a low heat; pour it into a small bowl and allow it to cool to 38°C.

2 Whisk the yeast into the warm water in a medium bowl. Wait 2 minutes, then whisk again to make sure all the yeast has dissolved. Whisk in the cooled milk. Use a rubber spatula to stir the flour into the liquid. Cover the bowl with clingfilm and let the sponge ferment until more than doubled in size, about 30 minutes.

3 Once the sponge has risen, use a rubber spatula to break up the eggs and yolks in the bowl of an electric mixer fitted with the dough hook. Stir in the sugar. Scrape the risen sponge into the bowl and mix it into the eggs. Add the flour and salt to the bowl and stir in. Mix on medium speed until the dough comes away from the sides of the bowl, 3–4 minutes.

4 Add a third of the butter and continue mixing until the butter is completely absorbed. Repeat with the remaining two-thirds of the butter, mixing to incorporate after each addition.

5 Continue to mix until the dough is very smooth, elastic and shiny, 4–5 minutes more (A and B).

6 Scrape the dough into a buttered bowl and turn it over so that the top is buttered. Cover with clingfilm and let rise until doubled in size, about 30 minutes.

7 Scrape the dough to a lightly floured surface and press it into a square about 1cm thick. Use the dough immediately in any of the recipes that follow, except the pizza; wrap and chill it for easier handling if you wish, but it's not strictly necessary except for the pizza.

A

B

essential tips for brioche dough

- Be sure that both the milk and the water are just lukewarm (43°C maximum) or the yeast will not survive and the dough won't rise. Don't be afraid to use an instant-read thermometer to verify the temperature of the liquid.

- Don't let the sponge rise beyond a little more than doubled or it will lose some of its leavening power and also contribute a sour flavour to the dough.

- Make sure the butter is sufficiently soft or it will form lumps when added to the dough.

- Be careful that the dough doesn't get over-risen after mixing or after shaping or it might not retain an even shape during baking.

- After rising, brioche dough is pretty sticky, but it's still possible to form it into the shapes you need to make. For best results, flour your hands, rather than the work surface or the dough, for ease and accuracy in rounding and shaping the dough.

- If you're making any variation in which the dough needs to be rolled out, chill the dough thoroughly for several hours or it will be impossible to roll.

- For advance preparation, bake, cool, wrap and freeze brioches. Reheat them at 180°C/gas mark 4 for 10 minutes and cool before serving.

brioche breakfast loaf

Delicately sweet and buttery as is, slices of this loaf acquire an ethereal flavour when lightly toasted. It's a perfect backdrop for any jam or conserve. A day old or lightly toasted, it's an excellent sandwich bread for such delicate fillings as a tarragon-flavoured chicken salad or smoked salmon with chive-flavoured cream cheese. With cocktails or dinner it also makes a nice raft for a thick slice of a terrine of foie gras. The great American gastronome James Beard used to make exquisite onion sandwiches for tea or cocktails using buttered brioche and paper-thin slices of sweet onion.

Makes one 23 x 13 x 7cm loaf

1 batch Brioche Dough (page 102) prepared up to the end of step 7

Egg wash: 1 medium egg well beaten with a pinch of salt

One 23 x 13 x 7cm loaf tin, buttered

1 Scrape the risen dough from the bowl to a floured work surface. (If you're using chilled dough, let it soften at room temperature until it is no longer ice cold.) Flour your hands and gently round the dough without deflating it too much by pushing inward at the bottom with your flat upturned palms all around the piece of dough; the outside skin of the dough will tighten and become more spherical.

2 Stretch the rounded piece of dough into a rough rectangle and slide both hands under it, palms upward, and transfer it to the prepared tin.

3 Cover the tin with a piece of buttered clingfilm and let the dough rise until it comes about 3.75cm above the rim of the tin. Freshly made dough should rise within about 30 minutes and chilled dough will require 1 hour or more.

4 About 20 minutes before the loaf is completely risen, set a rack in the lower third of the oven and preheat to 190°C/gas mark 5.

5 Immediately before placing the risen loaf in the oven, brush the top with the egg wash, being careful not to drip any egg wash down the side of the tin. Use a single-edged razor or X-Acto knife to slash the top skin of the dough lengthways, down the centre of the loaf. Bake the loaf until it is well risen, is deep golden and has an internal temperature of 93°C–99°C.

6 Unmould the loaf to a rack and cool it on its side to prevent deflating.

Serving: Cool completely before slicing. Serve plain or toasted with any of your favourite spreads except butter, which it doesn't need.

Storage: Keep lightly covered at room temperature on the day it's baked. Wrap and chill or freeze leftovers.

variations

Raisin Brioche Loaf: Add 150g raisins or dried currants to the dough about 1 minute before the end of the mixing process when preparing Brioche Dough (step 5, page 102). After forming the loaf and transferring it to the tin (step 2 of Breakfast Brioche), pick off any raisins on the top that would burn during baking. If you can get some really delicious crystallised orange peel (avoid the supermarket variety), cut it into 1.5cm dice and use it to replace a third to all of the raisins.

Poppy or Almond Brioche Loaf: Before slashing the top of the loaf, sprinkle it generously with poppy seeds or crushed sliced almonds.

Chocolate Brioche Loaf: Whisk together 110g dark (not unsweetened) chocolate, melted and cooled, 3 tablespoons water, $1/2$ teaspoon bicarbonate of soda, and $1/8$ teaspoon ground cinnamon. Add the mixture to the Brioche Dough after it is completely mixed (step 5, page 100) and continue to mix until the chocolate mixture is fully incorporated, sprinkling in 65g flour as you do.

A

B

sugared brioche rolls

This is a popular use for brioche dough as a breakfast roll in France. The rolls are sprinkled with pearl sugar, large opaque sugar granules, right before baking. (The easiest place to find it is in a cake decorating shop or online.) This is the master recipe for the variations that follow, including my take on currant-studded Bath Buns, the Mexican Buns called *conchas* (shells), and Jam-Filled Crumb Buns.

Makes 12

1 batch Brioche Dough (page 102)

Egg wash: 1 egg well beaten with a pinch of salt

110g pearl sugar or other coarse clear or opaque (not coloured) sugar granules

Baking sheet or swiss roll tin lined with baking paper or foil

1   Divide the dough into 12 equal pieces. Round the pieces under the cupped palm of one hand, moving your hand in a small circle (A and B). If the dough is sticky, flour your hand, not the dough or the work surface or the dough will just slide around instead of rounding.

2   Place the rolls on the tin with 5cm between each roll and the sides of the tin.

3   Cover the rolls with buttered clingfilm and let rise until doubled in size, about 1 hour or longer depending on how cold the dough is.

4   About 20 minutes before the rolls are fully risen, set a rack in the centre of the oven and preheat to 190°C/gas mark 5.

5   Once the rolls have risen, neatly paint them with the egg wash, making sure to clean each side of the brush against the side of the egg wash container after each dip so that the brush is not too sodden. You don't want to leave puddles of egg wash under the rolls. Immediately sprinkle with the pearl sugar.

6   Bake the rolls until they are well risen and deep golden, about 20 minutes.

7   Cool the rolls on a rack and serve them soon after they are baked.

Serving: These really don't need an accompaniment but you might like jam or marmalade.

Storage: Keep the rolls loosely covered at room temperature until serving. Bag and freeze for longer storage. Defrost and bring to room temperature before serving.

variations

Bath Buns Many different version of these exist, some of which are almost indistinguishable from the sugared brioche rolls above. My favourite version incorporates some dried currants in the dough and on the outside of each bun.

When preparing the master recipe for Brioche Dough, add 150g dried currants right before completing the mixing process (step 5, page 102). Prepare exactly as for sugared brioche rolls, above, adding a pinch of currants on top of each bun in the centre before sprinkling on the pearl sugar. Let rise, bake, cool, serve and store as above. **>**

A

topping into a fat cylinder and divide it in half. Knead the cocoa powder into one half to colour it (it's light coloured, but will darken as it bakes).

2 Roll each batch of topping into a cylinder again and cut each cylinder into 6 equal pieces. Cover with clingfilm and set aside at room temperature until needed.

3 Form the dough into 12 buns as in step 1 of the Sugared Brioche Rolls recipe (page 103). Arrange the buns on the prepared tin and cover them with a tea towel; let rest until they start to puff slightly, 10–30 minutes, depending on the starting temperature of the dough. While the buns are resting, form each piece of the topping into a flat 6cm disc, pressing it with the palm of one hand to shape.

4 Once the buns have risen a little, flatten each one and press a disc of the topping against it. Use a paring knife with the blade perpendicular to the topping to press 5 equidistant lines through only the topping (A). Press in 5 more lines at a 45 or 90 degree angle to the first set of lines. Cover the buns with a tea towel or clingfilm and let rise until doubled in size. Bake, cool, serve and store as for the Sugared Brioche Rolls. In Mexico these are always eaten with hot chocolate.

Jam-Filled Crumb Buns Vary these by using any type of jam or conserve you like. They're also great with the prune or apricot filling in Chapter 10, Danish Pastry.

180g strawberry or seedless raspberry jam, or any other jam of your choice

Egg wash: 1 egg well beaten with a pinch of salt

Crumb Topping (page 45), unbaked

Form the dough into 12 buns as in the Sugared Brioche Rolls (page 105). Arrange the buns on the work surface and cover them with a clean tea towel; let them rest until they start to puff slightly, 10–30 minutes, depending on the starting temperature of the dough. Pick up and invert one of the buns; supporting the rounded (top) side with your fingers, use your thumbs to make a 1cm depression. Drop in about $1^1/_2$ teaspoons of jam, then pinch the dough to enclose the jam and seal the bottom of the bun. Arrange the buns on the tin, rounded side up, as they are formed. Cover the buns with a tea towel and let rest again until they begin to puff slightly, 10–30 minutes. Flatten each bun, paint with egg wash and cover with the crumb topping, pressing it on. Cover the tin and let the buns rise until they are doubled in size. Bake, cool, serve and store as above.

Mexican Buns Called *conchas* or shells, because of the traditional pattern pressed into the topping with a round tool like a biscuit cutter, these are not only delicious but also quite slick looking. The topping recipe is meant to be divided in half so that you can make half vanilla and half chocolate-topped buns. For all vanilla, omit the cocoa; for all chocolate double it.

CONCHA TOPPING

85g unsalted butter, softened

85g icing sugar

85g plain flour

1 teaspoon vanilla extract

2 teaspoons cocoa powder, sifted after measuring

1 Before beginning with step 1 on page 103, make the topping. Beat the butter in an electric mixer fitted with the paddle attachment on medium speed. Decrease the speed to low and beat in the icing sugar and flour. Mix until smooth, then scrape the bowl and beater. Increase the speed to medium and beat in the vanilla extract. Beat for a few seconds longer, then scrape the topping, which should have the consistency of a soft dough, to a lightly floured work surface. Roll the

pizza alla campofranco

Makes one 30cm pizza, about
8 generous servings

2 tablespoons olive oil

900g plum tomatoes, skinned,
quartered, and seeded (see Note)

One batch Brioche Dough (page 102),
pressed flat on a floured baking sheet,
covered with clingfilm and chilled
in the refrigerator until firm, at least
2 hours or up to 18 hours

Freshly ground black pepper

50g grated Parmigiano-Reggiano

10g torn basil leaves

350g fresh mozzarella cheese, thinly sliced

100g prosciutto, thinly sliced and
shredded

One loose-based 30cm flan tin

The town for which this unusual pizza is named is in Sicily. Pizza alla Campofranco was probably invented by a *monzù* (the *monzù* were French-trained chefs who worked for the nobility in Sicily and Naples) in the home of Don Antonio Lucchesi Palli, Prince of Campofranco. During the prince's life he was a right-hand man to King Ferdinand of the Kingdom of the Two Sicilies. Naples was also a part of the kingdom, which explains why they were making pizza – a Neapolitan speciality – in Campofranco. The Kingdom of the Two Sicilies ceased to exist when Garibaldi conquered both Sicily and Naples in 1860 and the Kingdom of Italy was established in early 1861, but this unusual pizza with its brioche crust (much used by the *monzù*) has survived. After the shallow bottom crust is filled with some typical pizza topping ingredients, including some thinly sliced prosciutto, a top crust seals them in and the pizza is baked without allowing the dough to rise again, as in a typical pizza.

1 For the filling, heat the oil in a sauté pan and add the tomato quarters. Cook quickly over high heat to evaporate some moisture from them, but not until they disintegrate. Cool the tomatoes.

2 When you are ready to assemble the pizza, set a rack in the lowest level of the oven and preheat to 200°C/gas mark 6.

3 Remove the dough from the refrigerator and divide it into two pieces, one slightly larger than the other. Roll the larger piece of dough to line the tin, letting the excess dough hang over the edge.

4 Arrange the tomatoes on the crust, then grind pepper over them (no salt is necessary because of the grated cheese and prosciutto); scatter over the grated cheese, then the basil. Cover with the mozzarella cheese, then the prosciutto.

5 Roll the remaining dough for the top crust and put it in place. Press the edges of the top and bottom crust together and remove the excess dough at the rim of the tin.

6 Bake the pizza until the crust is deep golden and baked through, about 30 minutes. Unmould and slide to a serving plate; serve immediately.

Serving: Cut into wedges at the table and serve as a first course, or as the main course of a light meal.

Storage: You may refrigerate the pizza after it is assembled, but bake and serve it on the day it is assembled.

Note: If you only have under-ripe, out of season tomatoes, don't bother to skin them. Use 1.35kg of tomatoes, halve and seed them, and place them on a tin covered with oiled foil. Sprinkle the tomatoes with sugar and bake them at 180°C/gas mark 4 for 30 minutes to concentrate their flavour. Cool and arrange them on the crust as above.

10

danish pastry

Good Danish pastry isn't easy to find. Most of what's available isn't even made using the traditional method of rolling layers of butter into the dough. Though I've been making Danish pastry for years, I only recently tried a quick method – similar to the puff pastry in Chapter 4. After this yeasted Danish recipe, there's an even quicker one that is leavened with baking powder. Each recipe in this chapter is for individual Danish pastries, with plenty of variations on the fillings and toppings and each recipe calls for a half batch of the dough (the baking powder version makes the same amount of dough) so that you can try a couple of different pastries at the same time.

quick danish pastry dough

What we know as Danish pastry probably originated in Vienna, though it's not much in evidence there today. In Denmark, these pastries are referred to as *wienerbrod,* which in English translates literally as 'Vienna bread', pointing to their origin in Austria. No matter what you call it, homemade Danish is exquisite and nothing like what comes from a bakery, unless you happen to live in Scandinavia. The following method is similar to the food processor variation for puff pastry in Chapter 4. The non-yeasted variation that follows is made the same way.

Makes about 1kg dough

10g (1½ sachets) active dried yeast

60ml warm tap water, about 43°C

60ml milk, heated and cooled to 38°C

390g plain flour

55g sugar

¾ teaspoon salt

340g unsalted butter, cold

2 medium eggs, at room temperature

1   Whisk the yeast into the warm water. Wait a minute or two, then whisk again to make sure that all the yeast has dissolved. Whisk in the milk.

2   Combine the flour, sugar and salt in the bowl of a food processor fitted with the metal blade. Pulse a few times to mix.

3   Cut 55g of the butter into thin slices and add to the bowl. Pulse to a fine texture, but don't let the mixture become pasty.

4   Cut the remaining butter into 1cm cubes and add to the bowl. Pulse exactly twice for 1 second at a time to combine very roughly.

5   Transfer to a mixing bowl (A). Whisk the eggs into the yeast mixture and add it to the mixing bowl. To mix in the liquid, position a rubber spatula so its blade is flat and parallel with the bottom of the bowl and repeatedly dig down to the bottom of the bowl while turning the bowl (B). Mix until the dough comes together; it will be soft and sticky.

6   Press clingfilm against the dough and refrigerate for 1–2 hours.

7   Scrape the chilled dough to a floured surface and flour the dough. Use the palms of your hands to press the dough into a rectangle about twice as long as it is wide.

8   Starting at the narrow end of the rectangle furthest from you, use a rolling pin to firmly press the dough in parallel strokes close to each other. If there are sticky pieces of butter on the surface of the dough, seal them with a large pinch of flour, making sure to clean the rolling pin of anything stuck to it before continuing. Repeat the pressing motion from the nearest to furthest narrow end of the dough.

9   Press the dough once in the width – it should now be a rectangle about 1cm thick. Once again, flour under and on top of the dough and roll the dough away and back toward you in the length and once in the width, without rolling over the ends, to make a rectangle about 46cm long and 20cm wide.

10   Fold the two 20cm ends of the dough in toward the middle of the rectangle, leaving a 2.5cm space in the centre. Fold the top down to the bottom to form 4 layers of dough. Reposition the dough so that the folded edge that resembles the spine of a book is on your left. Rolling and folding the dough is known as 'giving the dough a turn'.

11   Give the dough another full turn of rolling and folding.

12   Wrap the folded dough in clingfilm and chill for at least 2 hours or up to 12 hours before using it to prepare one of the pastries that follow.

A

B

christel's danish pastry dough

Thanks to my friend Kyra Blumberg Effren for sharing this family recipe. Named for the Blumberg family's German cook, who worked for them first in London, then outside Cape Town, this is an unsweetened version of Danish pastry that is leavened with baking powder. You may substitute an equal quantity of this dough in any of the Danish pastry recipes in this chapter; the technique is less fussy. Unlike the yeasted danish pastry dough at left, this one may be entirely mixed in a food processor.

Makes about 1kg dough

240g full fat ricotta cheese

2 medium egg yolks, at room temperature

375g plain flour

2½ teaspoons baking powder

¾ teaspoon salt

340g unsalted butter, cold, cut into 20 pieces

1   Stir the ricotta cheese and egg yolks together and set aside.

2   Combine the flour, baking powder and salt in the bowl of a food processor fitted with the metal blade. Pulse several times to mix.

3   Add the butter to the bowl and pulse repeatedly until it is finely mixed into the dry ingredients. No visible pieces of butter should remain.

4   Scrape in the ricotta mixture and pulse at 1 second intervals until the dough forms a ball.

5   Turn the dough out onto a floured work surface and carefully remove the blade. Lightly flour the dough and form it into a rectangle about 1cm thick. Wrap and refrigerate the dough until firm, about 1 hour.

essential tips for danish

• If the dough is very soft after mixing, develop some elasticity by pressing the dough into a rectangle on a floured surface and folding one third over the middle section and the other third over them, as in the American 'biscuit' recipe on page 180. Turn the dough 90 degrees and repeat before wrapping and chilling.

• See Essentials for Puff Pastry on page 52 for information on the rolling and folding process.

• Use the yeasted dough within 12 hours for best flavour, and let rise after pastries are formed and baked.

• Freeze the dough, double wrapped in clingfilm, for up to several weeks after the rolling and folding process. Defrost the dough in the refrigerator before using it.

danish cheese pockets

This versatile Danish shape may be made with any filling that isn't runny when heated. See the variations at the end of the recipe for ideas.

Makes twelve 10cm square pastries

½ batch Quick Danish Pastry Dough (page 110) or Christel's Danish Pastry Dough (page 111), chilled

CHEESE FILLING

225g cream cheese, softened

3 tablespoons sugar

1 medium egg yolk, at room temperature

½ teaspoon vanilla extract

Egg wash: 1 egg well beaten with a pinch of salt

55g flaked almonds

WATER ICING

85g icing sugar, sifted

1 tablespoon water

½ teaspoon vanilla extract

Large baking sheet or swiss roll tin lined with baking paper or foil

Serving: Serve the pastries from a platter rather than a bread basket for breakfast or brunch.

Storage: Keep the pastries at room temperature, loosely covered with clingfilm on the day they are baked. Wrap leftovers or keep them under a cake dome.

1 For the filling, combine the cream cheese, sugar, egg yolk and vanilla in a small bowl and use a small rubber spatula to beat them together.

2 Place the dough on a floured surface and lightly flour the dough. Use your rolling pin to press the dough in firm parallel strokes in both directions to soften it slightly. Flour the surface and the dough again if necessary and roll the dough to a 30 x 43cm rectangle. Slide the dough to a baking sheet or flexible chopping board and refrigerate it until firm, about 10 minutes.

3 Use a sharp pizza wheel to cut away a 2.5cm strip of dough from one of the 30cm sides and reserve it. Cut the remaining dough into twelve 10cm squares.

4 Leave the squares of dough in place on the work surface and drop a heaped teaspoon of the filling in the centre of each. Fold the 4 corners of the square to meet in the centre over the filling, only overlapping them about 5mm. Place the pastries on the prepared tin.

5 Cut the reserved strip of dough into twelve 2.5cm squares. Brush a little egg wash in the centre of each pastry; centre one of the squares of dough on each so that the sides align with the open areas of the folded-in dough. Cover the tin with a tea towel and let the pastries rise until they just start to puff, 20–30 minutes.

6 Set a rack in the centre of the oven and preheat to 200°C/gas mark 6.

7 Once the pastries have risen, brush them with the egg wash and sprinkle with the flaked almonds. Bake until they are deep golden and the filling is set, about 20 minutes. Transfer to a rack to cool.

8 While the pastries are cooling, prepare the water icing. Combine all ingredients in a small saucepan and stir well to mix. Place over a low heat and cook until just lukewarm, about 43°C. Use a spoon to drizzle the icing in parallel lines on each pastry. Let the icing dry before serving.

variations:

Danish Poppy Seed or Walnut Pockets: Substitute the filling from Danish Poppy Seed Crescents (or the walnut variation) on page 118 for the cheese filling. Omit the flaked almonds and brush with the water icing instead of streaking it and immediately sprinkle each pastry with a pinch of poppy seeds or chopped toasted walnuts.

Danish Apricot or Prune Pockets: Use the filling from Danish Apricot Crescents (or the prune variation) on page 119, for the cheese filling above. Omit the flaked almonds and brush with Danish Apricot Glaze (see page 116) instead of the water icing.

Danish Envelopes: This is a shape variation. Only roll the dough to 30 x 40cm. Cut into 10cm squares and fill as above. Overlap one corner of the dough over your index finger about 1cm over the filling. Overlap the opposite corner about 1cm over the first. Firmly pinch the two corners together and remove your finger so that the sealed dough is centred on the filling. Bake and finish as above.

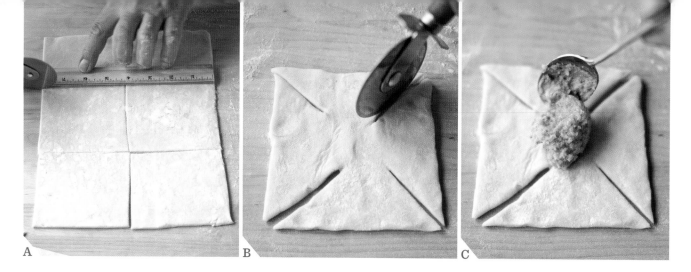

A   B   C

danish apricot pinwheels

Makes twelve 10cm pastries

ALMOND FILLING

55g whole almonds, with or without skin, finely ground in the food processor

55g unsalted butter, softened

70g sugar

2 medium egg yolks, at room temperature

1 teaspoon finely grated lemon zest

½ teaspoon vanilla extract

3 tablespoons plain flour

½ batch Quick Danish Pastry Dough (page 110) or Christel's Danish Pastry Dough (page 111)

6 fresh apricots, rinsed, halved and stoned

Egg wash: 1 egg well beaten with a pinch of salt

Icing sugar for finishing

Large baking sheet or swiss roll tin lined with baking paper or foil

Possibly the most attractive Danish pastry, pinwheels are the best shape for fresh fruit Danish. If you cannot find fresh apricots, drained tinned ones, especially those that are not overly sugared, make an adequate substitute. See the end of the recipe for ideas using other fruit. Normally this type of Danish pastry has some crème pâtissière under the fruit; if you intend to assemble and bake the pastries shortly before serving them and use all of them and not have leftovers, see the end of the recipe for the crème pâtissière filling. Don't use crème pâtissière if you're preparing them any more than a few hours in advance, or it might spoil. In this recipe I've substituted an almond filling that harmonises well with the apricots.

1   For the filling, combine the almonds, butter and sugar in a medium bowl and use a small rubber spatula to beat them together. Beat in the egg yolks, one at a time, followed by the lemon zest and vanilla. Stir in the flour.

2   Place the dough on a floured surface and lightly flour the dough. Use your rolling pin to press the dough in firm parallel strokes in both directions to soften it slightly. Flour the surface and the dough again, if necessary, and roll the dough to a 30 x 43cm rectangle. Slide the dough to a baking sheet or flexible chopping board and refrigerate until firm, about 10 minutes.

3   Use a pizza wheel to cut away a 2.5cm wide strip of dough from one of the 30cm sides and reserve it. Cut the remaining dough into twelve 10cm squares (A). Make a 5cm diagonal cut from each corner toward the centre of the square (B).

4   Leave the squares of dough in place on the work surface and drop 1 heaped teaspoon of the almond filling in the centre of each (C). Place one of the apricot halves cut side down on the filling.

5   Starting with the top left point, move clockwise to fold every other point into the centre over the apricot (D through F). Repeat with the remaining pieces of dough. Place them on the prepared pan.

6   Use a 2.5cm round cutter to cut the reserved piece of dough into 12 discs. Brush a little egg wash in the centre of each pastry and put one little disc of dough on top of

D   E   F   G

each (G). Cover the pastries with a clean tea towel and let rise until they just start to puff, 20–30 minutes.

7 Set a rack in the centre of the oven and preheat to 200°C/gas mark 6. Bake the pastries until they are deep golden and the filling is set, about 20 minutes. Transfer to a rack to cool.

8 Immediately before serving, generously dust the pastries with icing sugar.

Serving: Serve the pastries from a platter rather than a bread basket for breakfast or brunch.

Storage: Keep the pastries at room temperature, loosely covered with clingfilm on the day they are baked. Wrap leftovers or keep them under a cake dome.

variations

Small prunes or red plums may be substituted for the apricots. If they are very small, use two halves in each pastry.

For apple, use a tablespoon of the apple filling on page 116 in each pastry.

For pineapple, choose a small ripe pineapple and peel, halve and core it. Cut one of the pineapple halves into 1cm thick slices and arrange them in a shallow ovenproof pan. Bake uncovered at 200°C/gas mark 6 until slightly dry, about 30 minutes, sprinkling the slices with a couple of teaspoons of sugar during the last 10 minutes. Cool, cut the half rings in half again, and use 2 quarter rings in each of the pastries.

For crème patissière, stir 2 tablespoons cornflour and 3 tablespoons sugar together in a small saucepan and whisk in 180ml milk. Whisk in 2 medium egg yolks and then place over a medium heat. Cook, whisking constantly, until the cream thickens and comes to the boil. Off heat, whisk in 1 teaspoon vanilla essence and then scrape into a shallow bowl. Press clingfilm against the surface and chill until cold, 1 hour.

A   B   C

individual danish apple strudels

Makes eight 10cm strudels

APPLE FILLING

30g unsalted butter

1.35kg tart apples, such as Granny Smith

70g sugar

¼ teaspoon ground cinnamon

75g dried currants

½ batch Christel's Danish Pastry Dough (page 111), chilled

Egg wash: 1 egg well beaten with a pinch of salt

Granulated sugar for finishing

Baking sheet or swiss roll tin lined with a double thickness of baking paper or heavy-duty foil

Serving: Serve the strudels for breakfast, brunch or tea. They need no accompaniment.

Storage: Keep the strudels loosely covered at room temperature before and after serving.

This has nothing to do with the typical Viennese strudel made from dough that's stretched paper-thin, though in Vienna strudels are made from many kinds of dough, including Danish pastry dough. The apple filling here is cooked in advance and cooled in order to prevent a soggy bottom.

1 For the apple filling, melt the butter in a large sauté pan with a lid or a large casserole. Pare, halve and core the apples and cut the apple halves into 1cm dice. Add the diced apples to the pan as they are cut.

2 When all the apples have been diced, sprinkle them with the sugar and cinnamon.

3 Place the pan on a high heat and wait until the butter begins to sizzle. Use a wooden spoon or silicone spatula to stir everything together. Decrease the heat to low and cover the pan. Let the apples steam and exude their liquid for 5 minutes. Uncover the pan, turn the heat to low and stir in the dried currants. Continue cooking until the liquid has evaporated and the apples are tender and sizzling again. Scrape the cooked filling into a shallow bowl and allow it to cool to room temperature. To hasten cooling, place the bowl in the refrigerator or freezer and stir the filling occasionally.

4 Place the dough on a floured surface and lightly flour the dough. Use your rolling pin to press the dough in firm parallel strokes in both directions to soften it slightly. Flour the surface and the dough again, if necessary and roll the dough to a 30 x 46cm rectangle. Slide the dough to a baking sheet or flexible chopping board and refrigerate it until firm, about 10 minutes.

5 Remove the dough from the refrigerator and cut it into two strips, each 15 x 46cm. Arrange each piece of dough on a piece of baking paper for easy transfer to the baking tin. Brush the long ends of both strips with egg wash and divide the filling equally between the two strips, spooning it down the centre of the length (A and B). Bring the uncovered side of the dough closest to you over the filling and then bring the opposite dough over the filling to meet and slightly overlap the first piece of dough (C and D). Quickly flip the strudel onto the pan so that the seam is underneath (E). Don't be afraid; it's easy! Repeat with the second piece of dough. Chill or freeze the strudels for 1 hour before baking them.

D   E   F   G

6 About 15 minutes before the end of the hour, set a rack in the centre of the oven and preheat to 200°C/gas mark 6.

7 Brush the outside of the strudel with egg wash and sprinkle generously with granulated sugar (F). Use a paring knife to make a series of 1cm diagonal slashes every couple of centimetres or so along the top of each strudel (F).

8 Bake the strudels until they are deep golden and the pastry feels firm, about 20 minutes.

9 Cool the strudels on the pan. Trim the ends and cut each pastry into quarters.

danish poppy seed crescents

Makes twelve 10cm pastries

½ batch Quick Danish Pastry Dough
(page 110) or Christel's Danish Pastry
Dough (page 111)

POPPY SEED FILLING

120ml milk

55g sugar

1 tablespoon honey

140g ground poppy seeds (see recipe
introduction)

55g fresh breadcrumbs made from
firm white bread

40g raisins

1 teaspoon finely grated lemon zest

⅛ teaspoon ground cinnamon

Egg wash: 1 egg well beaten with
a pinch of salt

DANISH APRICOT GLAZE

275g apricot jam

1 tablespoon water

1 tablespoon dark rum

Whole poppy seeds for finishing

Large baking sheet or swiss roll tin
lined with baking paper or foil

Unlike croissants, which are often plain, Danish crescents always have a filling. Poppy seed filling is one of the most popular in Vienna, where Danish pastry originated. There are also variations with walnut, apricot and prune fillings, as well as several variations on the shape of the crescents. Before poppy seeds can be used in a filling, they must be ground. Eastern European shops sell the seeds already ground, or you may grind them yourself in a spice grinder, but the seeds are quite hard and it takes a bit of time and a sharp blade to grind them. Note that poppy seeds and poppy seed filling do not appeal to everyone. It's an acquired taste and people who are squeamish about things with 'texture' don't necessarily like poppy seed pastries. The filling below makes about twice as much as you need, but you can wrap the extra filling and freeze it for a later use.

1   For the filling, bring the milk, sugar and honey to the simmer in a medium saucepan. Add the ground poppy seeds and breadcrumbs and stir until smooth. Cook, stirring constantly, until the mixture thickens, 1–2 minutes. Remove from the heat and stir in the raisins, lemon zest and cinnamon. Scrape the filling into a bowl and let cool to room temperature.

2   Place the dough on a floured surface and lightly flour the dough. Use your rolling pin to press the dough in firm parallel strokes in both directions to soften it slightly. Flour the surface and the dough again if necessary and roll the dough to a 30cm square. Use a sharp pizza wheel to cut the dough into two 15 x 30cm rectangles. Slide the strips of dough to a baking sheet or a flexible chopping board. Using a ruler, make a shallow mark along the bottom of each strip with your fingertip every 4 inches. Pull the top right corner and the bottom left corner of each strip at the same time to slant them slightly in opposite directions. Then mark the top of each strip every 4 inches. Use the edge of a plastic scraper or bench scraper to imprint shallow lines (do not cut through the dough) that connect the marks top to bottom on the diagonal so that each strip is marked with 6 equal triangles. Refrigerate the marked strips of dough until firm, about 10 minutes.

3   Remove the dough from the refrigerator and use a sharp pizza wheel to cut through the shallow marked lines to make 12 equal triangles. Place a heaped tablespoon of the poppy seed filling at the long base of each triangle.

4   To form a crescent, gently pull on the side corners of the base to widen it slightly, then fold and press about 2.5cm of the base up over the filling. Roll up the base of the triangle of dough toward the point while gently pulling on the point to increase the height of the triangle. Pinch the point in place and position it under the formed pastry. Place each pastry as it is formed on the prepared tin, curving them into a crescent shape as you set them down.

5   Cover the tin with a clean tea towel and let the pastries rise until they just start to puff, 20–30 minutes.

6　Set a rack in the centre of the oven and preheat to 200°C/gas mark 6.

7　Once the pastries have risen, brush them with the egg wash and bake until they are deep golden, about 20 minutes. Transfer to a rack to cool.

8　While the pastries are cooling, prepare the apricot glaze. Combine all ingredients in a small saucepan and stir well to mix. Place on a low heat and bring to the simmer. Strain into a bowl, rinse the pan, return the glaze to the pan and bring the glaze back to the simmer. Cook until slightly thickened, about 5 minutes.

9　Brush the pastries with the glaze while it is still liquid. Sprinkle each pastry with a pinch of poppy seeds.

Serving: Serve the pastries from a platter rather than a bread basket for breakfast or brunch.

Storage: Keep the pastries at room temperature, loosely covered with clingfilm on the day they are baked. Wrap leftovers or keep them under a cake dome.

variations

Danish Walnut Crescents: Substitute 170g walnut pieces, finely ground in a food processor fitted with the metal blade, for the ground poppy seeds in the filling above. Decrease the milk to 75ml and add 30g unsalted butter to the milk mixture when heating it. Omit the raisins and stir 1 teaspoon each vanilla essence and dark rum into the cooled filling. Sprinkle the glazed pastries with a pinch of chopped toasted walnuts.

Danish Apricot or Prune Crescents: Combine 130g diced dried apricots or pitted prunes and 300ml water in a saucepan. Bring to the boil, remove from the heat, and allow to soak for 1 hour. Purée the mixture in a food processor or blender. Return the purée to the pan and add 2 tablespoons sugar. Bring to the simmer and cook, stirring frequently, until thickened to the consistency of jam, about 10 minutes. Cool the filling and stir in 1 teaspoon finely grated lemon zest. Add 1/4 teaspoon ground cinnamon to prune filling only. Substitute the apricot or prune filling for the poppy seed filling above. Omit the sprinkling of poppy seeds after the egg wash. Brush the cooled pastries with apricot glaze (see page 118) and sprinkle with a pinch of toasted sliced almonds.

essential tips for finishing danish pastries

- Real Danish pastries, whether they're made in Copenhagen or Vienna are usually finished on the outside with a brushing of apricot glaze (see page 118) and another of thin water icing (see page 113). All the Danish pastries in this chapter may be finished that way, though I've detailed specific finishes in each recipe, too. The double brushing is especially useful if you decide to substitute Christel's Danish Pastry Dough (page 111) for the yeast-risen variety, since the non-yeasted dough contains no sugar. Remember to wait a few minutes for the coat of apricot glaze to dry before applying the sugar icing. In fact, if you brush the pastries with the apricot glaze then make the water icing afterwards, your timing will be perfect.

- If you like you can add a pinch of cinnamon or cocoa powder to either a brushing or drizzling glaze. Add just enough to impart a subtle flavour but not to colour the glaze too deeply.

- If the recipe calls for sprinkling on flaked almonds or other chopped nuts, make sure to do so one at a time so that you brush the sugar glaze on one pastry and sprinkle and move on to the next. If you glaze all of them first, the glaze will harden and you won't be able to sprinkle.

11
butter cakes

Aside from contributing an exquisitely delicate flavour to cake layers, butter also enhances a cake's tenderness, moisture, and keeping qualities. The recipes in this chapter follow a batter-mixing method known as the 'creaming' method, named for the technique of beating (creaming) butter and sugar together until soft and light, which is the first step in the recipe. The term 'creaming' has pretty much fallen from use because of the ambiguity of the phrase 'combine the butter and sugar and cream until light', which sent everyone to the phone to ask how much cream to use. I refer to it as the 'butter-cake method'. Most butter-cake layers call for a good amount of sugar and use baking powder. Since the baking powder makes the layers rise during baking, I've eliminated folding whisked egg whites into the batter. The extra leavening from the egg whites is adequately replaced by beating the batter for a few minutes for smoothness.

white butter cake

A quintessentially American cake layer, this deserves to be better known by a wider audience. More than easy to prepare, a good butter cake is the perfect foundation for fillings and frostings, whether light or rich. And butter cake layers can't be beaten if you need to mix up a birthday cake in a hurry.

Makes two 23cm round layers, each 5cm high

300g plain flour

2 teaspoons baking powder

¼ teaspoon salt

300ml full fat milk, at room temperature

4 medium egg whites, at room temperature

170g unsalted butter, softened

340g sugar

2 teaspoons vanilla extract

Two 23 x 5cm round cake tins, buttered and the bases lined with discs of buttered baking paper cut to fit

A

1   Set a rack in the centre of the oven and preheat to 180°C/gas mark 4.

2   Use a small whisk to stir together the flour, baking powder and salt; set aside.

3   Thoroughly whisk the milk and egg whites together, then transfer to a 500ml jug (you won't have enough room to whisk them properly in the measuring jug); set aside.

4   Combine the butter and sugar in the bowl of an electric mixer fitted with the paddle attachment. Beat on a low speed until well mixed, then increase the speed to medium and beat the mixture until very light and pale in colour (A), about 5 minutes. Beat in the vanilla extract.

5   Use a rubber spatula to scrape the bowl and beater. Restart the mixer on low speed and add about one quarter of the flour mixture until it is absorbed (B). Increase the speed to medium low and beat in one third of the milk mixture.

6   Repeat step 5, including the change of speed, twice more.

7   Stop and scrape and beat in the remaining quarter of the flour mixture. Scrape again (C). Increase the mixer's speed to medium and continuously beat the batter for 3 minutes.

8   Divide the batter equally between the prepared tins (D) and smooth the tops. Bake the layers until they are well risen, firm in the centre to the touch, and lightly coloured, 20–25 minutes.

9   Cool the baked layers in the tins on racks for 5 minutes. If necessary, use a small paring knife to loosen the layers from the side of the tins. Invert one layer to a rack or cake board (don't remove the paper under the layer) and quickly invert again onto a rack. Repeat with the other layer. Cool the layers completely. Use the layers for one of the sandwich cakes in Chapter 15.

Storage: Wrap cooled layers in clingfilm and keep them at room temperature if finishing the cake on the same day. Store wrapped layers in the refrigerator for up to 3 days or freeze them for up to 3 months.

essential tips for the butter-cake method

- Have all your ingredients at room temperature before beginning to mix the batter. This isn't optional; it's the difference between a cake with excellent texture and a coarse-textured one.

- If you are ready to make the cake and realise you've neglected to bring the butter to room temperature, cut it into thin pats and put them on a plate. They should soften in 5 minutes or so.

- If the milk (or other liquid in different recipes) and egg whites (or whole eggs or yolks) are cold, after whisking them together, stand the bowl containing them in a larger bowl of hot water in the sink. Make sure the level of the water in the lower bowl doesn't exceed the level of the milk mixture or the smaller bowl will capsize. Whisk occasionally until warmed just to room temperature, no more than 24°C.

- Alternating the flour and liquid as you add them to the batter keeps the batter smooth, resulting in a fine-textured cake. Adding too much liquid at once can make the batter separate and bake up with a coarse texture.

- When unmoulding the layers, press the paring knife against the pan, not into the cake layer, or the side of the cake will tear. Use a clean sweeping motion rather than an up-and-down one, which can cut diagonally into the side of the layer and make it uneven.

- Sprinkle a large pinch of sugar on the top of the layer before inverting it to a cake board to keep it from sticking. You may brush away the excess sugar after the layer has cooled.

- Leaving the paper stuck to the bottom of the layer makes it easy to pick up the layer once it has cooled without the danger of having it break apart. Just remember to remove the paper before assembling and filling the final cake.

- To defrost layers, unwrap them and place them back on a rack. Cover with a clean tea towel and defrost at room temperature. Leaving the layers in the clingfilm as they defrost may result in condensation forming inside the package, which will make the cake's crust stick to the clingfilm.

moist yellow cake layers

So called because of the light yellow colour whole eggs impart to the baked cake, yellow cake is an essential part of any baking repertoire. Add a simple chocolate ganache filling and frosting and you have a classic chocolate sandwich cake, or add whipped cream and sliced sweetened berries and you have what most American retail bakeries used to call 'strawberry shortcake'. Many yellow cake recipes suffer from the dryness so characteristic of overly lean butter cake layers, but this one is moist and tender.

Makes two 23cm round layers, 5cm high

260g plain flour

1½ teaspoons baking powder

¼ teaspoon salt

3 medium eggs, at room temperature

180ml full fat milk

170g unsalted butter, softened

340g sugar

2 teaspoons vanilla extract

Two 23 x 5cm round cake tins, buttered and the bases lined with discs of buttered baking paper cut to fit

Prepare the batter according to the master recipe for White Butter Cake on page 122, whisking the whole eggs and milk together in step 3. Mix, bake, cool and store the same way.

chocolate butter cake layers

The rich chocolate flavour of these layers derives from unsweetened chocolate, which transforms what is basically a yellow cake batter into a chocolate one. To further enhance the flavour of the chocolate, add ¼ teaspoon cinnamon, 2 teaspoons instant coffee granules dissolved in the milk, or the grated zest of a lemon or orange.

Makes two 23cm round layers, 5cm high

260g plain flour

1 tablespoon baking powder

¼ teaspoon salt

170g unsalted butter, softened

340g sugar

2 teaspoons vanilla extract

3 medium eggs, at room temperature

85g unsweetened chocolate, melted and cooled

180ml full fat milk, at room temperature

Two 23 x 5cm round cake tins, buttered and the bases lined with discs of buttered baking paper cut to fit

Prepare the batter according to the master recipe for White Butter Cake on page 122, starting with step 1, using the ingredients above and skipping step 3. At the end of step 4, beat in the eggs one at a time, beating smooth after each addition, then beat in the melted chocolate. Finish mixing, bake, cool, and store as in the master recipe.

golden soured cream layers

Golden butter method cakes are made with egg yolks only and are the richest and most tender of all cakes of this type. Just be careful with the baked layers; they are more fragile than the others, which have more firmness and elasticity due to the presence of egg whites.

Makes two 23cm round layers, 5cm high

390g plain flour

1 tablespoon baking powder

¼ teaspoon salt

8 medium egg yolks, at room temperature

140g soured cream, at room temperature (if some whey drains from the cream, just whisk it back in)

170g unsalted butter, softened

280g sugar

2 teaspoons vanilla extract

Two 23 x 5cm round cake tins, buttered and the bases lined with discs of buttered baking paper cut to fit

Prepare the batter according to the master recipe for White Butter Cake on page 122, whisking the egg yolks and soured cream together in step 3. Mix, bake, cool and store the same way.

butter-cake cupcakes

Butter cake layers also make excellent cupcakes. In general, richer batters will make cupcakes with well-risen domed tops, while leaner ones tend to result in cupcakes that are more flat-topped. A standard 12-hole muffin tin used for baking cupcakes holds a little less than 120ml batter. Even if you think you have standard tins, please check by measuring 120ml water and pouring it into one of the holes. You may certainly use any size tin you wish. If your tin has holes that are larger or smaller, do a test run of the batter, filling one or two paper-lined holes to within 1.5cm of the top and seeing how they bake. Then you can adjust the amount of batter accordingly. These rich batters are not meant to be baked in free-standing aluminium foil cases, which would flatten from the weight of the batter. Since all the cake recipes in this chapter make approximately the same volume of batter, each one will make 18–20 individual standard-size cupcakes. When baking cupcakes, remember to spray the top of the tin with vegetable cooking spray or to brush it with some very soft butter; this will prevent cupcakes with large domed tops from sticking to the top of the tin and breaking apart when you try to unmould them. Look for signs of doneness 7–10 minutes before the time indicated in the cake recipe and if you're not sure, use a cake tester or the point of a paring knife to test the centre of one of the cupcakes for still unbaked batter.

oil-based cakes

Confirmed butter addict that I am, it took me a long time to warm up to the idea of oil-based cakes. Every time I came across a recipe that seemed interesting, I would substitute melted butter with about a 50 per cent rate of success. Then I tasted a wonderful cake at a restaurant in Atlanta years ago and when I received the requested recipe I was surprised to see that the really delicious cake had been made with oil. I became a convert, but one with reservations. I still don't use oils that have been chemically extracted from their sources. I like safflower oil because it has a neutral flavour and it's also fairly light. The one I use is expeller pressed, which means that the oil is extracted by means of pressure, not chemical processes. I've already published that original oil-based chocolate cake in another book, but I've varied that recipe to develop a few more for cakes that are just as good – devil's food, carrot, apple, pear and ginger and pumpkin among them.

oil-based devil's food cake batter

Makes two 23cm round layers, 5cm high

110g unsweetened chocolate, cut into 5mm pieces

240ml boiling water (boil, then measure)

225g granulated sugar

195g plain flour

½ teaspoon salt

¾ teaspoon bicarbonate of soda

225g light brown sugar

120ml vegetable oil, such as safflower

110g soured cream

2 medium eggs, at room temperature

1½ teaspoons vanilla extract

Two 23 x 5cm round cake tins, buttered and the bases lined with discs of buttered baking paper

A

Using vegetable oil in a cake works well when the batter contains strong-flavoured ingredients that would mask the flavour of butter. See the Essential Tips on page 129 if you would like to substitute butter anyway.

1 Set a rack in the centre of the oven and preheat to 180°C/gas mark 4.

2 Place the chocolate in a large mixing bowl and pour the hot water over it. Shake the bowl to make sure all the chocolate is submerged, then let stand for a few minutes to melt the chocolate.

3 In a mixing bowl, stir together the sugar, flour, salt and bicarbonate of soda and set aside.

4 Whisk the chocolate and water smooth, then whisk in the brown sugar, oil, soured cream, eggs and vanilla one at a time, whisking smooth after each addition.

5 Whisk in the flour mixture about one third at a time (A). The batter will be very liquid.

6 Divide the batter between the prepared tins (B). Bake until risen and firm, 30–35 minutes.

7 Let the cakes stand in the tins for 5 minutes, then unmould to racks, turn right side up and cool completely. To finish as a sandwich cake, see Chapter 15 and use boiled icing, whipped cream, ganache or buttercream to fill and cover the cake.

Storage: Wrap and freeze the layers for up to one month if you don't intend to use them immediately.

B

essential tips for oil-based cake batters

- The basic method for mixing these batters is to combine all the liquid ingredients and all the dry ingredients separately, then gradually whisk the dry ingredients into the liquid.

- In the batter, left, the brown sugar is added with the liquid to prevent lumps of brown sugar from forming in the baked cake.

- To substitute butter, melt about $1\frac{1}{2}$ times the equivalent of the quantity of oil in the recipe, then skim any foam from the top and discard. Pour off and measure just the clear butterfat that remains (clarified butter), leaving the watery milk solids behind.

- Alternatively, continue cooking the butter after it melts until it colours to a light brown and all the water has evaporated. Quickly pour the brown butter into a small heat-proof bowl to arrest the cooking and stop any further colouring and allow the butter to cool before measuring and adding to the batter. This is a little more difficult, but it results in butter with more flavour.

- Oil-based cakes can have a sticky top surface, which makes them a little tricky to unmould. Work quickly and sprinkle the top surface of the cake with a teaspoon of sugar to prevent sticking when inverting the cake from the tin. It will turn right side up without sticking to the cake board or rack.

best & easiest carrot cake

Makes two 23cm round layers,
5cm high

325g plain flour

225g granulated sugar

1 teaspoon baking powder

1 teaspoon bicarbonate of soda

¾ teaspoon salt

1 tablespoon ground cinnamon

225g dark brown sugar

4 medium eggs, at room temperature

300ml vegetable oil, such as safflower

450g carrots, rinsed, trimmed, peeled and grated in the food processor or on the largest holes of a box grater

85g walnut or pecan pieces, coarsely chopped

Two 23 x 5cm round cake tins, buttered and the bases lined with discs of buttered baking paper

No cake is more casual or old-fashioned than a carrot cake, especially a carrot cake with a cream cheese filling or topping. This is loosely adapted from a recipe by Maida Heatter in her landmark _Book of Great American Desserts_.

1   Set a rack in the centre of the oven and preheat to 190°C/gas mark 5.

2   Combine the flour, granulated sugar, baking powder, bicarbonate of soda, salt, and cinnamon in a medium bowl and whisk to mix; set aside.

3   Place the brown sugar in a mixing bowl and use a large rubber spatula to work in the eggs, one at a time. Whisk in the oil.

4   Whisk in the dry ingredients about one third at a time. Use a large rubber spatula to fold in the carrots and nuts.

5   Divide the batter between the prepared tins. Bake until risen and firm, 40–45 minutes.

6   Let the cakes stand for 5 minutes in the tins, then unmould to racks, turn right side up and cool completely. To finish as a sandwich cake, see Chapter 15 and use Cream Cheese Frosting (page 159) to fill and cover the cake.

Storage: Wrap and freeze the layers for up to one month if you don't intend to use them immediately.

Variation: Bake the batter in a 23 x 33 x 5cm tin, prepared as above, for 45–50 minutes. Use a half batch of Cream Cheese Frosting to cover the top of the cake only.

spiced pumpkin cake

Makes two 23cm round layers,
5cm high

390g plain flour

225g granulated sugar

2 teaspoons baking powder

2 teaspoons bicarbonate of soda

¾ teaspoon salt

1 tablespoon ground cinnamon

2 teaspoons ground ginger

2 teaspoons freshly grated nutmeg

225g light brown sugar

450g tinned pumpkin purée

5 medium eggs, at room temperature

300ml vegetable oil, such as safflower

Two 23 x 5cm round cake tins, buttered
and the bases lined with discs of buttered
baking paper

Puréed pumpkin makes a wonderfully moist cake and I particularly love this version of pumpkin cake because it echoes the flavours of a pumpkin pie, near the top of my list of favourite desserts. It has become stylish to use fresh pumpkin for pies and cakes, but unless you use an orange-fleshed pie pumpkin, you'll get a watery purée that's low in pumpkin flavour. For this reason I prefer to use tinned pumpkin, which also makes it possible to prepare this cake when fresh pumpkins aren't in season. If you absolutely have to use a fresh vegetable, then use cooked, puréed winter squash (but not spaghetti squash) or cooked sweet potatoes as on page 19. Thanks to my dear friend, baking teacher and author Carole Walter, for allowing me to adapt this recipe from her book *Great Cakes*, for which I wrote the preface.

1 Set a rack in the centre of the oven and preheat to 180°C/gas mark 4.

2 Combine the flour, granulated sugar, baking powder, bicarbonate of soda, salt and spices in a medium bowl and whisk to mix; set aside.

3 Place the brown sugar in a mixing bowl and use a large rubber spatula to work in about one third of the pumpkin a little at a time, until there are no lumps of brown sugar. Use a whisk to incorporate the remaining pumpkin, the eggs and the oil, adding them one at a time and stirring to combine between additions.

4 Whisk in the dry ingredients one third at a time.

5 Divide the batter between the prepared tins. Bake until risen and firm, 40–45 minutes.

6 Let the cakes stand in the tins for 5 minutes, then unmould to racks, turn right side up and cool completely. To finish as a sandwich cake, see Chapter 15 and use the larger amount of Cream Cheese Frosting (page 159) to fill and cover the cake.

Storage: Wrap and freeze the layers for up to one month if you don't intend to use them immediately.

variations

Bake the batter in a 23 x 33 x 5cm tin, prepared as above, for 45–50 minutes.
Use the lesser amount of Cream Cheese Frosting to cover the top of the cake only.

Add 170g coarsely chopped walnut or pecan pieces and/or 145g raisins or sultanas (or a combination of the two) to the batter after the dry ingredients, if you wish.

pear & ginger cake

Makes one 25cm tube or Bundt cake, about 16 servings

390g plain flour

340g sugar

1½ teaspoons bicarbonate of soda

½ teaspoon salt

2 teaspoons ground ginger

1 teaspoon ground cinnamon

½ teaspoon freshly grated nutmeg

¼ teaspoon ground cloves

5 medium eggs, at room temperature

1 tablespoon vanilla extract

1½ cups vegetable oil (see Note)

55g finely chopped crystallised ginger

900g pared and chopped or grated williams pears, about 4 medium pears

One 25cm (3.85litre capacity) tube or Bundt pan, buttered, coated with fine dry breadcrumbs and sprayed with vegetable cooking spray

Use firm-ripe Williams pears for this cake. When you press the blossom end of the pear with your thumb, it should yield to gentle pressure. Softer pears will immediately turn to a watery purée if you try to grate them. This cake, and the apple variation that follows it, utilise the grated fruit as a means of retaining moisture in the baked cake. While each contributes a dimension of flavour to the cake, it's one that successfully blends with the seasonings to create a moist harmonious finished product. Neither is anything like biting into a ripe pear or apple.

1 Set a rack in the lower third of the oven and preheat to 180°C/gas mark 4.

2 In a medium bowl, combine the flour, sugar, bicarbonate of soda, salt and spices and whisk well to combine.

3 In a large mixing bowl, whisk the eggs with the vanilla. Whisk in the oil followed by the crystallised ginger.

4 Use a large rubber spatula to stir in all the grated pears, followed by the dry ingredients, one third at a time.

5 Pour the batter into the prepared tin and bake the cake until it is well risen and firm and the point of a paring knife inserted halfway between the side of the tin and the central tube emerges clean, about 65–75 minutes.

6 Cool the cake in the pan for 5 minutes, then invert it to a rack to cool completely.

Serving: Serve the cake with some lightly sweetened whipped cream.

Storage: Keep the cake under a cake dome or covered with clingfilm at room temperature. Double wrap and freeze for longer storage. Defrost and bring to room temperature before serving.

Note: You may replace half of the vegetable oil with melted butter for both this recipe and the apple variation that follows.

variation

Apple Spice Cake: Replace the pears with peeled and grated Granny Smith apples. Omit the ginger and crystallised ginger and fold in 110g coarsely chopped walnut or pecan pieces and 145g raisins or sultanas after the last of the dry ingredients.

individual coconut cakes

Makes 24 individual cakes

170g sugar

65g plain flour

110g unsweetened desiccated coconut

4 medium egg whites, at room temperature

Pinch of salt

2 teaspoons finely grated lemon zest

110g unsalted butter, melted and slightly cooled

2 tablespoons sweetened flaked coconut or unsweetened ground or flaked coconut, for topping the cakes before baking

Two 12-hole mini muffin tins, buttered and floured

These snow-white little cakes are as delicious as any coconut confection I've ever tasted. It's not necessary to clarify the butter for these. Unsweetened coconut is available both flaked or more finely ground. The flakes retain more moisture than the desiccated coconut does. Either may be used in this recipe, but if you use the flaked variety, pulse it in the food processor half a dozen times, not to grind it to a powder, but to reduce the flakes in size to about 3mm. Obviously this isn't an oil-based batter but it's grouped here because it's mixed the same way.

1 Set a rack in the centre of the oven and preheat to 190°C/gas mark 5.

2 In a medium mixing bowl, combine the sugar, flour and unsweetened desiccated coconut; set aside.

3 In another bowl, whisk the egg whites with the salt until smooth, then whisk in the lemon zest and butter. Whisk in about half the dry ingredients, then use a rubber spatula to fold in the remainder.

4 Spoon the batter into the prepared tins, filling them about two-thirds full. Sprinkle the top of each cake with a pinch of flaked coconut.

5 Bake the cakes until they are well risen and deep golden and they are firm when pressed with a fingertip, about 15 minutes. Invert them to a rack, then immediately turn them right side up and let them cool completely.

Serving: Serve these after dessert with coffee, or as part of an assortment of desserts.

Storage: Keep the cakes loosely covered with clingfilm on the day they are made. Arrange them in a tin or plastic container with a tight-fitting lid in one layer and refrigerate them for longer storage. Bring to room temperature before serving.

variations

Substitute ground blanched almonds or a combination of ground hazelnuts and ground almonds for the coconut.

Before baking, sprinkle the top of each little cake with a pinch of chopped almonds or hazelnuts.

Bake the batter in a buttered and paper-lined 20 x 5cm round cake tin. It will take about 5 minutes longer to bake; test for doneness with the point of a paring knife in the centre of the cake. Unmould, cool, and serve in wedges.

13

pound cakes & 'plain' cakes

Though there isn't anything uninteresting about this type of cake, it is frequently referred to as a 'plain' cake. Pound cakes and 'plain' cakes are usually not iced, except for perhaps a drizzle of glaze, so they depend on their intrinsic flavour and texture rather than on a rich accompaniment such as ganache or buttercream. The cakes in this chapter are all mixed according to a fairly recent innovation called the high-ratio method. The name refers to the high ratio of sugar to flour. Developed in the late 1940s by American food chemists for commercial and industrial bakeries, the method ensures a perfectly smooth and emulsified batter – essential when hundreds or thousands of pounds of batter are being mixed at the same time. Fortunately, the method works well even in a recipe for a single cake and results in a moist and tender crumb.

A   B

high-ratio pound cake

Makes one 23 x 13 x 7cm cake, about 16 slices

260g plain flour

225g sugar

1 teaspoon baking powder

¼ teaspoon salt

225g unsalted butter, very soft

5 medium eggs, at room temperature

2 teaspoons vanilla extract

2 teaspoons finely grated lemon zest, optional

One 23 x 13 x 7cm loaf tin, buttered and the base lined with a rectangle of baking paper

The 'pound' in the title refers to the quantity of the three main ingredients in the batter. There are also many variations on the original recipe that include milk or another dairy product such as soured cream. See the variations at the end of the recipe for some of the more popular twists on the classic pound cake.

1   Set a rack in the centre of the oven and preheat to 160°C/gas mark 3.

2   Combine the flour, sugar, baking powder and salt in the bowl of an electric mixer fitted with the paddle attachment. Mix on the lowest speed for 30 seconds.

3   Stop the mixer, add the butter and continue mixing on the lowest speed until the butter is absorbed and no visible pieces remain (A). Stop the mixer and use a rubber spatula to scrape down the bowl and beater.

4   In a small bowl, whisk the eggs with the vanilla and lemon zest, if using.

5   Start the mixer on the lowest speed and add about one third of the egg mixture to the bowl. Beat for 1 minute on medium speed; stop and scrape the bowl and beater (B). Repeat two more times. Then beat the batter for 2 minutes continuously on medium speed (C).

6   Scrape the batter into the prepared tin (D) and smooth the top.

7   Bake the cake until it is well risen and deep golden and the point of a paring knife inserted in the centre emerges clean, about 60 minutes.

8   Cool the cake on a rack for 10 minutes. Unmould and cool completely right side up.

Serving: Serve slices of the cake with coffee or tea, or use a slice of pound cake as the base for a simple dessert, topping it with some whipped cream and lightly sweetened berries or soft fruit.

Storage: Keep the baked cake under a cake dome or wrapped in clingfilm at room temperature. Double wrap and freeze for longer storage. Defrost and bring back to room temperature before serving.

C   D

variations

Vanilla Pod Pound Cake: Split a plump vanilla pod and scrape the seeds from the inside instead of using vanilla extract in the cake batter.

New Orleans Praline Pound Cake: Use light brown sugar for half the sugar; add ¼ teaspoon ground cinnamon along with the other dry ingredients. Add 2 tablespoons dark rum or bourbon to the egg mixture. Fold in 110g coarsely chopped pecan pieces tossed with 1 tablespoon flour after taking the batter off the mixer.

Chocolate Chip Pound Cake: Add 170g dark or milk chocolate chips, or a combination, using a rubber spatula to fold them in after taking the batter off the mixer.

Lemon Pound Cake: Increase the lemon zest to 4 teaspoons and add 2 tablespoons lemon juice, strained before measuring, to the batter.

'Le Cake' (French Pound Cake): Fold in 55g each of 5mm diced candied orange peel and quartered glacé cherries after taking the batter off the mixer.

'Le Weekend' (French Lemon Pound Cake): Prepare Lemon Pound Cake. While the cake is baking, bring 120ml water and 70g sugar to the boil, stirring to dissolve the sugar. Cool and stir in 2 tablespoons strained lemon juice. After unmoulding the cake, place the rack over a serving plate or swiss roll tin and paint the warm cake repeatedly with the cooled syrup, using all of it and scooping up and reusing any that drips off the cake, until all the syrup is absorbed.

essential tips for high-ratio cakes

- Make sure the butter is as soft as mayonnaise or it will not be easily absorbed by the batter.

- Make sure the eggs and any liquid are both at room temperature – not cold – or they will make the batter separate.

- Follow the timing instructions exactly when mixing, or the batter will not be as smooth as necessary. If adding liquid of any kind as a flavouring, as in the lemon pound cake, be sure to whisk it into the eggs so that they are added together.

- Try using a 1.75–2 litre capacity tube tin instead of the loaf tin. The baking time will be about 10 minutes shorter.

- The pound cake and the almond cake in this chapter are better when served the day after they are baked. Freshly baked and cooled, they can sometimes have a slightly rubbery texture.

torta di mandorle: ligurian almond cake

Makes one 23cm tube or Bundt cake, about 16 slices

280g blanched almonds, very lightly toasted

340g sugar

290g plain flour

1 teaspoon baking powder

¼ teaspoon ground cinnamon

340g unsalted butter, very soft

1 tablespoon grated lemon zest

5 medium eggs, at room temperature

One 23cm (2.5litre capacity) tube or Bundt tin, buttered, coated with fine dry breadcrumbs and sprayed with vegetable cooking spray

In the Italian region of Liguria, of which Genoa is the capital, almond trees thrive, though Sicily is the largest almond-growing area of the country. The cooking of the two regions is even similar, due to the fact that they are separated only by the Tyrrhenian Sea. Though they may look far apart on a map, when travel by boat was easier than overland travel, there was frequent contact between the two areas. Slightly reminiscent of a French *gâteau breton*, this dense cake is perfect with a glass of sweet wine or a cup of tea. As a dessert, it would need to be dressed up with some fruit or berries.

1 Set a rack in the centre of the oven and preheat to 160°C/gas mark 3.

2 Combine the almonds and sugar in the bowl of a food processor fitted with the metal blade and pulse repeatedly until the mixture is a fine powder. Invert the work bowl to the bowl of an electric mixer fitted with the paddle attachment.

3 Add the flour, baking powder and cinnamon and mix on the lowest speed for 1 minute.

4 Add the butter and mix until absorbed.

5 Add the lemon zest and 2 eggs and mix until absorbed. Increase the speed to medium and beat for 1 minute. Add another 2 eggs and repeat, beating for 1 minute after they are absorbed. Add the last egg and repeat.

6 Scrape the batter into the prepared tin and bake the cake until it is well risen and deep golden and the point of a thin knife inserted midway between the side of the pan and the central tube emerges clean, 45–50 minutes.

7 Cool the cake in the tin for 5 minutes, then unmould and cool completely.

Serving: This is best as a tea cake. Serve thin slices; a spoonful of lemon curd to accompany it wouldn't be bad, either.

Storage: Keep the baked cake under a cake dome or wrapped in clingfilm at room temperature. Double wrap and freeze for longer storage. Defrost and bring back to room temperature before serving.

maida's chocolate bourbon pound cake

Makes one short 23cm tube or Bundt cake, about 16 slices

140g unsweetened chocolate, cut into 5mm pieces

360ml hot brewed coffee

120ml best bourbon whiskey

260g plain flour

450g sugar

1 teaspoon bicarbonate of soda

¼ teaspoon salt

225g unsalted butter, softened

3 medium eggs, at room temperature

2 teaspoons vanilla extract

One 23cm (2.5litre capacity) tube or Bundt tin, buttered, coated with fine dry breadcrumbs and sprayed with vegetable cooking spray

This recipe from my friend and mentor Maida Heatter is adapted from one called 86-Proof Chocolate Cake in her *Book of Great Chocolate Desserts*. The original recipe calls for dissolving 60ml instant espresso or regular instant coffee granules in boiling water before proceeding. I prefer to use strong brewed coffee.

1 Set a rack in the lower third of the oven and preheat to 160°C/gas mark 3.

2 Place the chocolate in a medium mixing bowl and pour the hot coffee over. Gently shake the bowl a couple of times to immerse the chocolate, then wait 1–2 minutes; whisk smooth.

3 Whisk in the bourbon whiskey.

4 Combine the flour, sugar, bicarbonate of soda and salt in the bowl of an electric mixer fitted with the paddle attachment. Mix on the lowest speed for 30 seconds.

5 Stop the mixer, add the butter and continue mixing on the lowest speed until no visible pieces of butter remain. Stop the mixer and use a rubber spatula to scrape down the bowl and beater.

6 Start the mixer on the lowest speed and add the eggs and vanilla. Beat for 1 minute on medium speed; stop and scrape the bowl and beater. Add half the chocolate mixture and beat 1 minute. Add the remaining chocolate mixture and beat on medium speed for 2 minutes. The batter will be very liquid.

7 Pour the batter into the prepared tin and bake the cake until it is well risen and firm and the point of a thin knife inserted midway between the side of the tin and the central tube emerges clean, 60–70 minutes.

8 Cool the cake in the tin for 15 minutes, then unmould and cool completely.

Serving: Serve thick slices with some lightly sweetened whipped cream.

Storage: Keep the baked cake under a cake dome or wrapped in clingfilm at room temperature. Double wrap and freeze for longer storage. Defrost and bring back to room temperature before serving.

banana coconut crumb cake

Makes one 23cm cake, 8–10 servings

160g plain flour

170g sugar

½ teaspoon baking powder

¼ teaspoon salt

110g unsalted butter, softened

2 medum eggs, at room temperature

1 medium egg yolk, at room temperature

1 teaspoon vanilla extract

500g bananas, peeled and sliced about 1cm thick

Almond Crumb Topping (see page 45), unbaked, substitute 40g sweetened flaked coconut for the almonds

One 23cm springform tin, buttered and the base lined with a disc of baking paper

Sliced bananas make a perfect crumb cake because they're safely insulated between the cake batter and crumb topping and baked to a moist jam-like consistency. See the Variations for suggestions for using other fruit in this cake or other nuts in the crumb topping.

1 Set a rack in the centre of the oven and preheat to 180°C/gas mark 4.

2 For the batter, combine the flour, sugar, baking powder and salt in the bowl of an electric mixer fitted with the paddle attachment. Mix on the lowest speed for 30 seconds.

3 Stop the mixer, add the butter and continue mixing on the lowest speed until no visible pieces of butter remain. Stop the mixer and use a rubber spatula to scrape down the bowl and beater.

4 In a small bowl, whisk the eggs, yolk and vanilla together.

5 Start the mixer on the lowest speed and add about one third of the egg mixture to the bowl. Beat for 1 minute on medium speed; stop and scrape the bowl and beater. Repeat two times. Then beat the batter for 2 minutes continuously on medium speed.

6 Scrape the batter into the prepared tin and smooth the top. Arrange the banana slices on top of the batter, leaving a clear 5mm margin near the side of the tin. Evenly scatter on the crumb topping.

7 Bake the cake until it is well risen and deep golden and the point of a paring knife inserted in the centre of the cake emerges clean, about 50–60 minutes.

8 Cool the cake on a rack for 10 minutes. Unbuckle the side of the tin and let the cake cool on the springform base. Once the cake has cooled completely, use a wide palette knife slipped between the cake and the paper to ease it off the tin base and transfer it to a serving plate.

Serving: Serve wedges of this cake for tea or brunch or as dessert after a light meal.

Storage: Keep the baked cake under a cake dome or wrapped in clingfilm at room temperature. Double wrap and freeze for longer storage. Defrost and bring back to room temperature before serving.

variations

Use 500g of fruit, such as peeled, cored and sliced pineapple, pitted prunes, stoned fresh apricots, stoned sour cherries or blueberries in place of the bananas.

Substitute any nut you wish for the almonds in the Almond Crumb Topping recipe on page 45 instead of adding the coconut. Or omit any nuts or coconut from the crumb topping.

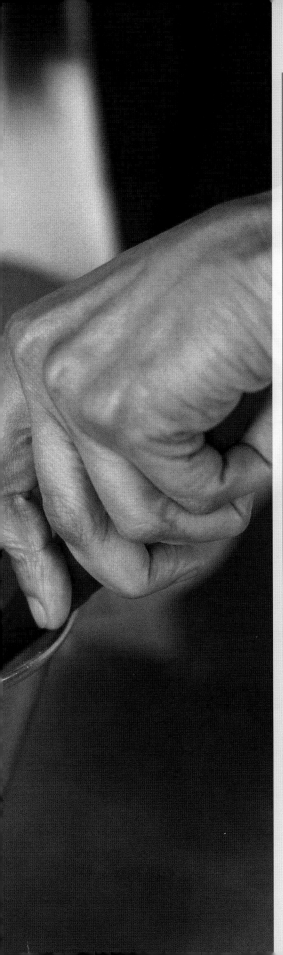

14

sponge &
meringue
layers

This chapter is about how eggs, or just egg whites, can absorb and trap air and use steam during baking to create leavening. Genoise is the classic French sponge cake, made with whole eggs, enriched with extra yolks, warmed with sugar, and whisked to a dramatic increase in volume before the dry ingredients are added. Nut sponge cakes are made with separated eggs and a portion of the sugar is separately whisked with the yolks and whites before they're combined and the ground nuts and flour are added. Finally, meringue layers are made from egg whites warmed with part of the sugar, the rest being incorporated later – my new technique that guarantees crisp, but never hard, results.

A   B

genoise sponge cake

Makes one 23cm layer about
6cm high

4 medium eggs

**2 medium egg yolks (save the whites
for buttercream or meringue)**

140g sugar

Pinch of salt

2 teaspoons vanilla extract

100g plain flour

40g cornflour

One 6–7.5cm deep x 23cm round
springform tin or one 7.5cm deep x 23cm
round cake tin, buttered and the base
lined with a disc of baking paper

1 Set a rack in the centre of the oven and preheat to 180°C/gas mark 4.

2 Whisk the eggs, yolks, sugar, salt and vanilla together by hand in the bowl of an
electric mixer.

3 Set the bowl over a saucepan of gently boiling water and slowly whisk until the egg
mixture is warm, around 49°C, about 30 seconds. Don't overheat or the eggs won't
whisk well.

4 Place the bowl on a mixer fitted with the whisk attachment and whisk on medium-
high speed until the egg foam is light in colour and increased in volume and the
bowl no longer feels warm, about 3 minutes. When the eggs are ready, they'll hold
their shape on the whisk and you'll be able to draw a line through them (A and B).

5 While the eggs are whisking, stir the flour and cornflour together. Use a sieve with
open mesh to sift the flour mixture once onto a piece of paper.

6 Remove the bowl from the mixer and sift about one third of the flour mixture over
the egg foam, using a large rubber spatula to fold it in (C). Dig down to the bottom
of the bowl and cut through the batter with the flat side of the spatula parallel to the
bottom of the bowl to prevent the flour from accumulating there. Repeat with the
last two batches of the flour.

7 Scrape the batter into the prepared tin (D). Tilt the tin in a circular motion to bring
the batter about 2cm from the top of the tin; this prevents the batter from doming
in the centre so that the baked layer has a flat, even top. Bake until it is well risen
and firm in the centre and the point of a paring knife inserted in the centre of the
cake emerges clean, about 30 minutes.

8 Immediately use a small paring knife to loosen the cake from the side of the tin if it
is at all stuck and invert it to a rack. Remove the tin, but leave the paper on the cake

C

D

layer. Cover with another rack and invert the stack, removing the top rack. Cool the cake completely on the rack.

Storage: Wrap the cooled cake in clingfilm and refrigerate it for 3 days, or double wrap and freeze for up to a month. Unwrap and defrost before using.

variation

For cocoa genoise, use 85g flour, 35g cornflour and 3 tablespoons akalised (Dutch process) cocoa powder. After measuring the cocoa, force it through a fine mesh sieve to eliminate any lumps. Then mix it with the flour and cornflour, but use a sieve with larger mesh to sift the mixture into the batter, as it will go more quickly.

essential tips for genoise

- Fill a saucepan halfway with water and begin to heat it as soon as you start measuring the ingredients.

- It's not necessary to whisk the egg mixture furiously while it's heating; just keep it in motion so it doesn't begin to set in the bottom of the bowl.

- Don't overheat the eggs; they won't whisk up to the necessary volume afterward if you do.

- You can test the egg foam for the right degree of expansion by drawing a line about 5mm deep on top of it with a fingertip. If the line holds and the two sides don't flow back together, the egg foam is ready.

- You can decrease the speed on a stand mixer to lowest once the egg foam is ready, sift the flour onto a piece of paper, and then slowly shake the flour over the egg foam. After you take the bowl off, use a large rubber spatula to dig down to the bottom to make sure there is no flour hiding there. This only works in a stand mixer.

- Unmould the genoise immediately or it will shrink and fall if left in the tin. Work quickly once you have inverted the layer to the first rack or it will stick there.

- Always chill the genoise overnight before cutting if possible; it makes cutting through it easier.

kyra's
hot milk
sponge cake

Makes two 23cm round layers, each about
3.75cm high

55g unsalted butter

120ml full fat milk

195g plain flour

2 teaspoons baking powder

3 medium eggs, at room temperature

¼ teaspoon salt

225g sugar

1 teaspoon vanilla extract

Two 3.75–5cm deep x 23cm round cake
tins, buttered and the bases lined with
discs of baking paper

This is the easiest and best-tasting sponge layer you can imagine, and since it's baked in two tins, you won't need to slice through it to make a sandwich cake. Thanks to my friend Kyra Effren, one of the world's great bakers, for sharing this recipe. Kyra often serves this as a tea cake with a thin layer of raspberry jam between the layers and a light dusting of icing sugar on top; it is elegant simplicity at its best. Though a hot milk sponge is not quite as light and delicate as a genoise layer, you may easily substitute these layers in recipes that call for genoise. In fact, they can often substitute for white or yellow cake layers, too.

1   Set a rack in the centre of the oven and preheat to 180°C/gas mark 4.

2   Combine the butter and milk in a small saucepan and cook over a low heat until the butter is completely melted. Set aside in the pan.

3   Stir the flour and baking powder together and sift onto a piece of baking paper.

4   In the bowl of an electric mixer, whisk the eggs by hand to break them up, then whisk in the salt. Whisk in the sugar in a stream, then whisk in the vanilla. Place on the mixer fitted with the whisk attachment and whisk on medium-high speed until very light, about 3 minutes.

5   Gently whisk in the warm milk mixture by hand. Use the whisk to fold the flour mixture into the liquid in 4 additions, again gently whisking to incorporate between additions. Using the whisk helps to prevent lumps from forming. Handle the whisk exactly as though you were using a rubber spatula for the folding.

6   Evenly divide the batter between the prepared tins and smooth the tops.

7   Bake the layers until they are well risen and golden and feel firm when touched in the centre with a fingertip, about 20 minutes.

8   Use a sharp paring knife to loosen the layers from the sides of the tins, then invert to racks. Immediately re-invert the layers so that they cool with the paper on the bottom. Cool completely.

Storage: Wrap and store as for Genoise Sponge Cake (page 146).

almond sponge cake layer

Makes one 23cm round layer, 5cm high

85g whole or flaked blanched almonds, lightly toasted

170g sugar, divided

5 medium eggs, at room temperature, separated

1 teaspoon finely grated lemon zest

¼ teaspoon almond extract

Pinch of salt

130g plain flour

One 6–7.5cm deep x 23cm round springform tin or one 7.5cm deep x 23cm round cake tin, buttered and the base lined with a disc of baking paper, see Note below

Storage: Wrap the layer in clingfilm and keep at room temperature until needed, up to 24 hours. Double wrap and freeze for longer storage. Defrost at room temperature for several hours before using.

Note: If you prefer to bake the cake in two tins, use two 2.5–3.75cm deep x 23cm round cake tins, prepared as above. Check for doneness after about 20 minutes.

Use this as a model for all sponge cake layers made with the addition of ground nuts. Quantities for different kinds of nuts follow in the variations. I like to bake this as a single layer and split it afterward (instructions are in the cake recipes that use the layer), but you may also bake it in two separate tins; see the Note at bottom left.

1   Set a rack in the centre of the oven and preheat to 180°C/gas mark 4.

2   Combine the almonds and 1 tablespoon of the sugar in the bowl of a food processor fitted with the metal blade and pulse repeatedly until the mixture is finely ground. Use a thin palette knife to scrape away any of the mixture caked up in the corner where the bottom meets the side of the bowl. Set aside.

3   Whisk half the remaining sugar into the egg yolks in the bowl of an electric mixer fitted with the whisk attachment. Whisk the yolk mixture on medium speed until lightened, about 3 minutes. Whisk in the lemon zest and almond extract.

4   In a clean dry mixer bowl (if you only have one bowl and whisk attachment, scrape the yolk mixture into a mixing bowl and wash the bowl and whisk attachment in hot soapy water, rinse well, and dry) combine the egg whites and salt. Whisk on medium speed until white and beginning to hold their shape. Increase speed to medium-high and whisk in the remaining sugar 1 tablespoon at a time, continuing to whisk until the egg whites hold a firm peak (A).

5   Use a large rubber spatula to fold the yolk mixture into the whisked whites (B). Then scatter the ground almond mixture over the egg mixture and sift the flour over. Use a large rubber spatula to fold everything together (C). Work quickly but gently to avoid deflating the batter.

6   Scrape the batter into the prepared tin and use the spatula to spread it evenly and smooth the top.

7   Bake the layer until it is well risen, deep golden, and firm in the centre, about 30 minutes. Immediately invert the layer to a rack, leaving the paper on the bottom; place another rack on the layer and invert the whole stack, removing the top rack, so that the layer cools right side up. Cool completely.

variations

Pistachio Sponge: Use 85g blanched unsalted pistachios in place of the almonds. To blanch the nuts, cover with water in a saucepan and bring to the boil. Drain, rub in a clean tea towel and separate the nuts from the skins. Place the nuts on a swiss roll tin and bake them at 150°C/gas mark 2 until just dry but not colouring, 7–8 minutes.

Hazelnut Sponge: Use 85g unblanched hazelnuts instead of almonds. Don't bother to remove the skins from the hazelnuts before grinding; the flecks of skin in the baked cake look appealing. Use 1 teaspoon vanilla extract instead of almond extract.

Walnut or Pecan Sponge: Use 85g lightly toasted walnut or pecan pieces. Use 1 teaspoon vanilla extract instead of the almond extract. Stir ¼ teaspoon ground cinnamon into the flour before sifting and folding it in.

A

B

C

baked meringue & nut meringue layers

Makes two or three meringue layers, depending on the size you choose to make them

4 medium egg whites, at room temperature

Pinch of salt

½ teaspoon distilled white vinegar or strained lemon juice

2 teaspoons vanilla extract

280g sugar, divided

2 baking sheets or swiss roll tins lined with baking paper or silicone pan liners and one size 5 (500mm) pastry bag fitted with a 1.25cm plain tube (Ateco size 6)

Crunchy, sweet meringue layers may be used to make a festive dessert on their own or may be coupled with sponge or butter cake layers for a truly extravagant presentation. There are three types of meringue. Making ordinary meringue, also known as French meringue, involves whisking egg whites with part of the sugar used and folding in the rest. Swiss meringue calls for combining the egg whites with all the sugar and heating the mixture over simmering water until hot, dissolving the sugar at the same time, and whisking afterwards. Italian meringue is made from whisked egg whites that have hot sugar syrup poured over them while they are whisking. The method below is a personal combination of the first two methods and results in meringue that holds its shape perfectly and bakes to a fragile texture. Meringue layers are piped out, which makes them easier to form, not more complex. If you've never tried piping before, meringue is a great place to start because unlike some other mixtures that are piped out, meringue won't flow from your pastry bag of its own accord.

1   Half fill a saucepan with water and bring it to the boil. Reduce the heat so that the water boils gently.

2   Combine the egg whites, salt, vinegar, vanilla and 140g of the sugar in the bowl of an electric mixer and whisk by hand to mix.

3   Set the bowl over the pan of simmering water and whisk constantly but slowly to keep the mixture in motion, but not to incorporate air, until the egg whites are hot, about 60°C and the sugar has dissolved, about 3 minutes.

4   Place the bowl on an electric mixer fitted with the whisk attachment and whisk on medium-high speed until cooled and increased in volume.

5   Once you can touch the bowl and feel that it has completely cooled, decrease the speed to medium and add the remaining sugar about 2 tablespoons at a time, continuing to whisk until all the sugar has been added.

6   Remove the bowl from the mixer and follow the instructions for shaping and baking below.

variation

Nut Meringue: Grind 110g almonds, hazelnuts or a combination in the food processor until medium fine; you may still have pieces of nuts as large as 3mm, but no larger or they will clog the end of the piping tube. Pour the ground nuts onto the surface of the whisked meringue and sprinkle on 1 tablespoon cornflour or potato flour. Fold the nuts and flour into the meringue (A).

A

B

C

piping meringue layers

1 Use a dark pencil to trace the shape you want, either a circle or square, onto a piece of baking paper, then invert the paper onto the prepared tin. If you're using a silicone mat, have a plate or a cardboard pattern the same size and shape you wish to make nearby to compare to the layer to gauge the correct size.

2 Fold back one third of the pastry bag and stand it in a jar or large measuring cup to fill. Spoon in one third to one half the meringue, unfold the bag and twist the top of the bag closed behind the meringue.

3 For a disc of meringue, start piping in the centre of the circle, holding the pastry bag perpendicular to the pan and about 2.5cm above it. Spiral the meringue around, moving from your waist up, and holding the bag fairly stationary while squeezing the top closed end of the bag (B and C). When you come to the end of your traced pattern, just stop squeezing and pull the tube away. You don't have to worry if the outside edge isn't perfect; it's always trimmed before use.

4 For a square or other angular-shaped layer, hold the bag at a 45 degree angle to the tin with the tube touching the surface of the paper. Start at the far side of your pattern and, while squeezing, pull the bag towards the side closer to you. Repeat, making a series of lines with the meringue that are almost touching (they'll puff a little and join while baking).

5 Squeeze out a few blobs of meringue the same height as your layers, which you'll be able to press to determine the degree of doneness later on.

baking meringue layers

1 Set racks in the upper and lower thirds of the oven and preheat to 110°C/ gas mark 1/4 for plain meringue and 150°C/ gas mark 2 for nut meringue.

2 Bake plain meringue until it is almost completely dry, which can take up to 2 hours, watching carefully that the meringue takes on no colour or as little colour as possible. After 1 1/2 hours, press one of the extra pieces of meringue; there should only be 1cm in the centre that is still soft. For nut meringue, the degree of doneness is the same, but at the higher temperature it should only take about 30 minutes. Test as above, but only continue baking another 10 minutes before testing again if it's still too soft when you press.

3 Cool the meringues on the tins on racks. Stack them on a cake board with baking paper between them and slide them into a plastic bag for storage. If the weather is very humid, they will soften. Crisp plain or nut meringues at 110°C/gas mark 1/4 for about 20 minutes, cool, and use immediately.

15
layer & moulded cakes

In this chapter we'll use the butter-based, genoise and meringue layers to create cakes both casual and elegant. Organised a little differently, the chapter starts by taking a look at the fillings and frostings most common in sandwich and layer cakes and then outlines the essential techniques for assembling layer cakes. The subsequent recipes presume that the layer is baked and ready to go, so you can follow the instructions for assembly, only having to look up the recipe for the frosting earlier in this chapter. The recipes for moulded cakes stand alone and only reference the separate cake layer. Making a slick layer cake isn't difficult, but it requires a little practise and the right tools. A sharp serrated knife for splitting layers is a requirement. A tiny and a medium palette knife make spreading fillings and frostings a breeze. And circular cake boards are essential.

perfect meringue buttercream

Real buttercream – not the kind made with vegetable fat – is light and rich at the same time and perfectly complements delicate cake layers. Meringue buttercream is on the sweet side, so it pairs well with strong flavourings such as lemon, unsweetened berries, plain chocolate and coffee. This recipe is particularly easy to prepare, but please be patient and observe all the temperature guidelines for both ingredients and mixing. I promise if you do you'll achieve a perfectly smooth and delicious buttercream.

Makes about 675g unflavoured buttercream, enough to fill and finish a 23cm 2- or 3-layer cake

4 medium egg whites

Pinch of salt

280g sugar

340g unsalted butter, very soft

Flavouring suggestions (at right)

1 Half fill a saucepan on which your mixer bowl will fit without having more than 5cm inside the pan. Bring the water to the boil over a medium heat and reduce the heat so that the water boils gently.

2 Whisk the egg whites, salt and sugar together by hand in the bowl of an electric mixer. Place over the boiling water and whisk constantly but not furiously until the egg whites are hot (about 60°C) and the sugar is dissolved, 3–4 minutes. Test a little by withdrawing the whisk and letting a little of the mixture flow onto a fingertip; it should be a smooth liquid with no sugar grit.

3 Place the bowl on the mixer fitted with the whisk attachment and whisk on medium speed until the meringue is very risen in volume and beginning to cool. The outside of the bowl should feel just slightly warm.

4 Switch to the paddle attachment and beat on the lowest speed until the meringue is completely cooled and the bowl no longer feels at all warm. This is critical; if you add the butter when the meringue is still warm it will melt and ruin the buttercream.

5 Add the butter in 6 or 8 additions immediately following each other, still mixing on the lowest speed. Scrape the bowl and beater and increase the speed to medium; beat the buttercream until it is smooth, thick and shiny, about 5 minutes. Don't be concerned if the butter-cream appears separated a little while after adding the butter; it's normal.

6 Once the buttercream is perfectly smooth, add flavourings as suggested at right. Add liquid flavourings such as lemon juice or coffee 1 tablespoon at a time, beating smooth after each addition. Thicker flavourings such as melted chocolate or reduced berry purée may be added in larger amounts, provided that they are neither chilled nor warm.

flavouring the buttercream

Lemon or Lime: Beat in 75ml freshly squeezed lemon or lime juice, strained before measuring. Add a tablespoon of kirsch or white rum if you wish.

Raspberry: Beat 110g thick, cooled raspberry purée into the buttercream. Add a tablespoon of raspberry liqueur or eau de vie if you wish. To make the raspberry purée, combine 450–560g fresh or frozen raspberries with 120ml water. Bring to the boil over a medium heat, stirring to crush the berries. Pour the crushed mixture into a bowl, rinse the pan and press the berries through a fine sieve back into the pan. Return to the simmer and cook, stirring occasionally, until thickened, 5–10 minutes. Cool completely. If you can only buy raspberries that are frozen with a small amount of sugar added, don't be concerned; it won't oversweeten the buttercream.

Coffee: Dissolve 2 tablespoons instant espresso coffee granules in 75ml warm brewed coffee. Cool completely before adding.

Chocolate: Cut 225g plain chocolate (65–70%) into 5mm pieces. Combine it with 75ml milk or water in a small saucepan and cook over a low heat, stirring constantly, until melted. Scrape into a small bowl and cool completely before adding to the buttercream. Add 1 tablespoon dark rum or 2 teaspoons vanilla extract if you wish.

Vanilla: Beat in 1½ tablespoons vanilla extract or vanilla bean paste, or 1 tablespoon vanilla extract mixed with the seeds scraped from the inside of one plump vanilla pod into the buttercream.

essential tips for meringue buttercream

- Make sure the egg whites are free of any traces of yolk or the meringue won't whisk firm.

- Cool the meringue completely. If the butter melts when it's added it might be impossible to rescue the buttercream.

- The butter has to be very soft – the consistency of mayonnaise – or it won't combine smoothly with the meringue.

- When adding a liquid, add no more than 1 tablespoon at a time. The buttercream will separate slightly, sliding away from the side of the mixer bowl. Keep beating until the liquid is absorbed and the buttercream adheres firmly to the side of the bowl again before adding more.

- If the buttercream separates after liquid has been added too quickly or too soon, try beating on medium speed for at least 5 minutes. If it remains separated, scrape the butter-cream into another bowl and beat 110g of butter in the bowl with the paddle on medium speed until it is very soft and light, about 5 minutes. Beat the separated buttercream a little at a time into the butter, beating smooth after each addition.

- For advance preparation, cover and chill unflavoured butter-cream. Let it come to room temperature before using, then beat smooth with the paddle on medium before adding flavouring.

ganache for filling & frosting

A rich filling made principally from chocolate and cream, ganache goes well with every cake layer. Dark chocolate with 50–65% cocoa solids works best for ganache, but chocolate with a higher cocoa solid content can make the ganache too bitter in contrast with a sweet cake layer. Ganache should be used as soon as it's thick enough to spread or it can be whipped to lighten it. Recipes that call for it as a filling specify which way to use it.

Makes about 675g ganache, enough to fill and finish a 23cm cake

240ml whipping cream

2 tablespoons golden syrup

400g dark (50–65%) chocolate, cut into 5mm pieces

55g unsalted butter, very soft

1 Whisk the cream and golden syrup together in a saucepan. Bring to the simmer over a low heat, about 82°C.

2 Place the chocolate in a bowl and pour the cream over. Gently shake the bowl a couple of times to submerge all the chocolate. Let melt for 2–3 minutes, then whisk smooth.

3 Cool the ganache to room temperature (about 18°C) and

essential tips for ganache

- Always use a premium brand of chocolate. Chocolate chips or baking chocolate won't make a fine-flavoured ganache.

- Only whisk enough to mix the chocolate and cream mixture. Overmixing can cause separation. In ganache for glazing, too much mixing will make a glaze riddled with air bubbles.

- Before you fill a cake with ganache, it should have the consistency of room temperature peanut butter. If it's too soft, refrigerate for a few minutes only and then stir smooth with a rubber spatula. Chilling too long can harden the ganache and it will tear through the cake layers if you try to spread it.

- If you wish to lighten the ganache more than hand whisking allows, beat it on medium-low speed with the paddle for 1 minute. Work quickly when finishing, because beating air into ganache encourages it to set quickly.

- Keep ganache overnight at a cool room temperature.

quickly whisk in the butter all at once. Use immediately or whisk by hand for 30 seconds to lighten.

variations

Ganache for Glazing: Reduce the amount of chocolate to 225g and omit the butter. Cool to about 27°C so that it's still pourable before using.

> ESSENTIAL TECHNIQUE

crème pâtissière

A starch-thickened custard cream, crème pâtissière is a versatile and delicate filling for cakes and pastries of many types. This recipe is thickened with cornflour because it allows the crème pâtissière to be whisked smooth before spreading, which might liquefy a crème pâtissière thickened with flour. Be careful to bring the crème pâtissière to the full boil when cooking it (it won't make the egg yolks scramble; the starch prevents this) or the crème pâtissière won't be thick enough to spread.

Makes about 725g, enough to
fill a 23cm cake

360ml full fat milk, divided

120ml whipping cream

70g sugar

35g cornflour

5 medium egg yolks

2 teaspoons vanilla extract

45g unsalted butter,
cut into 6 pieces

1 Set aside 120ml of the milk in a medium, heatproof bowl.

2 Combine the remaining 240ml milk with the cream and sugar in a medium non-reactive saucepan and whisk to mix. Place on a low heat and bring to the full boil.

3 Meanwhile whisk the cornflour into the reserved 120ml milk and whisk in the egg yolks.

4 Once the milk boils, whisk about one third of it into the yolk mixture. Return the remaining milk to the full boil. Beginning to whisk before pouring, pour in the yolk mixture in a quick stream, continuing to whisk constantly.

5 Cook, whisking constantly, until the crème pâtissière thickens and comes to the full boil. Cook, whisking, for 30 seconds longer.

6 Off heat, whisk in the vanilla and butter. Pour the crème pâtissière into a shallow bowl so that it cools quickly and press clingfilm directly against the surface. Refrigerate immediately. Use the crème pâtissière within 36 hours.

variations

Crème Mousseline: A cross between crème pâtissière and buttercream, crème mousseline is a delicate cake filling and unlike buttercream, it pairs well with fresh fruit. Make crème mousseline immediately before spreading it. Omit the butter from the crème pâtissière. Beat 170g soft unsalted butter with the paddle on medium speed until soft and light. Beat in the whole batch of crème pâtissière all at once and beat until well mixed, about 1 minute. Scrape the bowl and beater, increase the speed to medium high and continue beating until the cream is smooth and fluffy, about 5 minutes longer. If you wish, add a tablespoon of kirsch or light or dark rum right after scraping the bowl.

> ESSENTIAL TECHNIQUE

meringue frosting

Egg white-based frostings have always been popular for American-style layer cakes. This variation is of a classic that used to be called 'seven-minute frosting' because it was whisked with a rotary egg beater in the top of a bain marie. With the heavy-duty mixers of today, it's just a question of heating the ingredients first and then whisking them by machine.

Makes about 500g, enough to fill
and finish a 23cm cake

4 medium egg whites

Pinch of salt

295g sugar

175g golden syrup

1 Put all the ingredients in the bowl of an electric mixer and whisk by hand to mix.

2 Heat and whisk as for the Perfect Meringue Buttercream, page 156.

3 Use the frosting immediately after it's whisked up; it might still be a little warm, but that's okay.

sweetened whipped cream

Making perfect whipped cream and finishing a cake with it isn't difficult, but you have to remember a few basic rules: keep everything cold and don't over-whip. Softly whipped cream holds its shape well and doesn't disintegrate on the outside of a cake.

Makes about 800g, enough to fill and finish a 23cm cake

720ml whipping cream, ice cold

70g sugar

2 teaspoons vanilla extract

1 About 30 minutes before whipping the cream, chill the mixer bowl and whisk in the refrigerator. Take out and put the cream, sugar and vanilla in the bowl and whisk once by hand to mix. Place on the mixer fitted with the whisk attachment and whip on medium high until you see traces of the whisk holding in the cream.

2 Decrease the speed to medium and continue whipping until the cream holds a soft peak on the end of a rubber spatula.

3 Cover the bowl and chill the cream until you need it. Before using the refrigerated whipped cream, re-whip it briefly by hand to a soft peak again.

essential tips for...
...crème pâtissière

- A pointed whisk gets into the corners of the pan when cooking.
- Make sure to bring the crème pâtissière to the full boil – large bubbles that slowly burst on the surface – or it won't thicken and will have a strong starchy flavour.
- Use as soon as possible after cooking, and refrigerate any cake filled with it.

...meringue frosting

- When heating the mixture, make sure the sugar fully dissolves or the frosting will be gritty.
- Frost the outside of the cake with swirled strokes, but don't go back once you have applied; it crusts almost immediately and the surface will look rough if you go back over it.
- Adding golden syrup makes the frosting smooth and soft instead of hardening.

...whipped cream

- Remember to have everything ice cold. If it's hot in the kitchen, pour the cream into a bowl and freeze it for 15 minutes.
- Whipped cream always melts a little in the refrigerator; don't over-whip when re-whipping it.
- Keep the finished cake at a cool room temperature for only a few hours before serving. Refrigerate for longer, but no more than half a day; whipped cream rapidly acquires a stale taste. Wrap leftovers tightly in clingfilm and serve no later than the next day.

cream cheese frosting

Traditional with carrot cake or another spiced layer cake, cream cheese frosting is also perfect on cupcakes. Both the cream cheese and butter should be only slightly softened; let your mixer complete the softening while beating in some air to lighten the frosting and give it a more appealing texture.

Makes about 750g, enough to fill and cover a 2-layer 23cm cake

340g cream cheese, slightly softened

85g unsalted butter, slightly softened

340g icing sugar, sifted

2 teaspoons vanilla extract

1 Put the butter and cream cheese in the bowl of an electric mixer and beat with the paddle on medium speed until completely mixed, about 3 minutes, stopping and scraping the bowl and beater several times.

2 Decrease the speed to low and add the icing sugar one third at a time, beating until absorbed after each addition. After the last addition, the frosting might look dry.

3 Beat in the vanilla and increase the speed to low-medium until the mixture is no longer dry looking, about 2 minutes.

4 Increase the speed to medium and beat until smooth and light, 4–5 minutes. Use soon after mixing.

A

assembling layer cakes

The general directions on the right pertain no matter which of the fillings and/or frostings outlined in the previous recipes you are using.

1 To prepare a layer, turn the cake out onto the work surface and peel off any baking paper. Turn the cake right side up again.

2 With a sharp serrated knife, trim the top of the cake flat. If a dome has formed in the centre, trim it off.

3 If you need to cut one layer into more layers, hold the serrated knife perpendicular to the side of the cake about one third of the way down from the top if you are making three layers and about halfway down if you are making two layers. Use the blade of the knife to mark a shallow line all the way around the cake, turning the cake so it presses against the knife (A). Turn the cake again, cutting a little deeper this time (B). After two turns, you should have cut all the way through. If not, repeat a third time. Slide a cake board under the cut layer and remove it. Repeat if you are cutting three layers (C).

4 Invert what was the top of the cake onto a cake board. Dip a pastry brush into any syrup and sprinkle it on the layer. (Do not brush.)

5 Spread on any filling using a medium palette knife; the filling should be about 5mm thick. If you're using some jam or chocolate filling under the principal filling, use a small palette knife to spread it on before the principal filling.

6 Slide what was the middle layer of the cake to the edge of the cake board it's on so that it hangs 2.5cm over the edge. Hold that edge of the cake to the far end of the previous layer at about a 30 degree angle, pull away the cake board and let the layer fall into place. Moisten and spread with filling. Place the top layer (the former bottom of the cake) on next with its smooth side up. Moisten with syrup, if using.

7 Before frosting the outside of the cake, clean the work surface. Any crumbs lying around tend to get stuck to the outside of the cake, marring its appearance.

B   C

8 Hold the cake in your left hand (assuming you are right handed) and use a palette knife to 'mask' the side of the cake. Use about 1 tablespoon of filling at a time, and press it onto the cake, holding the palette knife at a right angle. Pat it on; do not spread smooth.

9 Place the cake on the work surface and spread the frosting over the top using the palette knife. (Reserve some frosting if you are planning to decorate the finished cake.) If any crumbs appear on the knife, wash and dry it carefully.

10 Again hold the cake in your left hand and use the palette knife to smooth the side of the cake, holding the knife steady and turning the cake.

11 Return the cake to the work surface and smooth the top, working any frosting that has accumulated on the edge of the cake in towards the centre.

12 If you are using ground nuts, hold the cake in your left hand over the work surface and use your right hand to press the nuts into the side of the cake, allowing the excess to fall away. If you are decorating with chocolate shavings, use a palette knife rather than your hand, which will melt the chocolate. Always do this before refrigerating the cake.

13 To decorate a cake, place the remaining frosting in a pastry bag and pipe a border around the perimeter.

14 To glaze the cake, refrigerate it after spreading the frosting smooth but before piping on a border or pressing anything against the side of the cake. Chill until the outside is set, then place the cake on a rack set over a tin and pour the glaze evenly and slowly over the cake in a spiral from the centre outward. Refrigerate the cake to set the glaze, then loosen the bottom edge with a small paring knife and transfer the cake to a serving plate.

essential tips for assembling & glazing

- If the outside of your cake isn't perfectly straight, apply a crumb coat to the outside to hide the imperfection. Spread a thin layer of buttercream all over the outside of the cake as thinly as you would spread butter on toast. Chill for 30 minutes before continuing, which prevents any crumbs from mixing into the buttercream as you spread them onto the outside of the cake.

- When glazing a cake with ganache, if you see any bubbles in the glaze before pouring it, put the glaze through the finest sieve you have a couple of times, which will help to eliminate the bubbles.

hazelnut meringue dacquoise

Makes one 20 or 23cm 3-layer cake, 12–16 servings

Three 20 or 23cm layers of hazelnut meringue (see page 152), baked until still moist within and cooled

1 batch coffee meringue buttercream (see page 156)

Toasted chopped hazelnuts or crumbled meringue scraps for finishing

Icing sugar for serving

Serving: A dacquoise is always a little difficult to slice and if you don't use a really sharp knife it will look as though you used a hammer to cut it. Use a long, sharp serrated knife held perpendicular to the top of the dacquoise and saw back and forth, cutting across the diameter of and through the top layer only. Wipe any buttercream off the blade (with the sharp edge held away from your hand) and repeat at a 90 degree angle to the first cut – you now have 4 wedges. Continue cutting through the top layer to make as many wedges as you need, always cutting across the entire top of the cake at the same time. After the top layer is cut, go back and follow the initial cuts in the same order, cutting through the remaining layers to the bottom and wiping the knife after each cut. A final hint: It's easier to cut the dacquoise when it's chilled, then let the slices come to room temperature before serving.

Storage: Wrap and chill leftovers and bring to room temperature before serving again.

One of the signature desserts developed by then-executive pastry chef Albert Kumin for the opening of Windows on the World in 1976, dacquoise took New York by storm and was one of the most popular desserts on restaurant menus for years afterward. James Beard, who loved the dessert and had first introduced it to the United States after he tasted it in Paris in the early 1960s, was acting as consultant to Joe Baum, the owner of the company that installed all the food service facilities in the newly opened World Trade Centre. It's my guess that this is how the confection of hazelnut meringue layers and coffee flavoured buttercream made it onto the restaurant's dessert menu, where it remained until the restaurant closed after the parking garage bombing in 1993. Dacquoise always makes me remember the early days of Windows, as we all called it, and the thrill of (over)working in the world's most talked about restaurant right at the beginning of my career.

1   Using a plate or cardboard cake board as a guide, trim the meringue layers to an even 23cm diameter. Save the one that has the best spiral pattern for the top.

2   Put a dab of the buttercream on a cake board or serving plate and place one of the layers flat (bottom) side down on it. Save the trimmed-away scraps for finishing the cake if you wish.

3   Use a medium palette knife to spread a little more than a third of the buttercream on the layer.

4   Place the second trimmed layer on top and spread on the same amount of buttercream.

5   Place the last layer on top. If you don't have a really nice spiraled layer for the top, then place it on flat side up and cover it with buttercream and meringue crumbs or chopped hazelnuts.

6   Spread the remaining buttercream to cover the side of the cake; crumble or chop the meringue scraps left from trimming the layers (use the chopped hazelnuts if you don't have enough scraps) and press them against the buttercream.

7   Lightly dust the top with icing sugar immediately before serving.

variations

Use ganache (see page 157), whipped or unwhipped, rather than coffee meringue buttercream to finish the dacquoise. Substitute chocolate shavings for the meringue crumbs or chopped hazelnuts.

Substitute plain white meringue layers and use coffee meringue buttercream or ganache to finish.

strawberry chantilly cake

Yellow cake, whipped cream and strawberries make a simple yet elegant cake that always has everyone hoping that seconds will be offered. When I was a child, retail bakeries referred to this as 'strawberry shortcake', but real shortcake is made with rich baking powder scone dough that has sugar and eggs added to it. I make this a couple of times a year and only when really sweet local berries are in season or it just doesn't have enough flavour.

Makes one 2-layer 23cm cake, about 10 servings

425g height-of-season strawberries, rinsed

Two 23cm layers yellow or golden cake (see page 124 or 125), baked and cooled

1 batch Sweetened Whipped Cream (page 159)

1 Select six of the best-looking strawberries and reserve them. Hull and slice the remaining strawberries.

2 Place one of the cake layers on a cake board or serving plate smooth side down. Spread with one quarter of the whipped cream. Arrange the sliced berries on the cream evenly.

3 Spread another quarter of cream on the berries – spread gently or all the strawberry slices will go flying.

4 Top with the other cake layer, smooth side up. Spread the outside and top of the cake with the remaining whipped cream and evenly smooth the top.

5 Slice through 5 of the reserved berries, hull and all and arrange them cut side up perpendicular to the edges of the cake and evenly spaced apart from each other. Place the last whole berry in the centre of the cake. Refrigerate until serving.

Serving: Cut wedges of the cake at the table; it needs no accompaniment.

Storage: Wrap leftovers in clingfilm and refrigerate them. Plan on serving all the leftovers within 24 hours.

variations

Substitute sweet raspberries or blackberries for the strawberries, leaving them whole.

Victoria Sandwich: Use the yellow cake on page 124, or the hot milk sponge on page 149. Stack the layers with 185g strawberry jam between them and sprinkle the top of the cake with icing sugar. You can also add a layer of whipped cream (made with 240ml cream, 2 tablespoons sugar, 1 teaspoon vanilla extract) between the cake layers and even a few sliced strawberries.

Black Forest Cake: A real Black Forest cake is made from cocoa sponge cake layers soaked with kirsch syrup and filled with whipped cream and preserved sour cherries. Bad versions turn the cherries into something that resembles tinned cherry pie filling. I like to use *amarene*, Italian sour cherries in a thick syrup that are used as a gelato topping in Italy. Failing that, sour cherry conserve is a good substitute.

Slice the cocoa genoise layer (see page 147) into 3 and place the top layer on a cake board, crust side down. Sprinkle it with one third of the rum syrup from the Russian Punch Cake (page 165), substituting 2 tablespoons kirsch for the rum. Spread with 170g sweetened whipped cream and top the cream with 185g *amarene* (if using conserve, spread on first, then top with 340g whipped cream). Spread another 170g whipped cream on the cherries. Place the middle layer on and repeat syrup, whipped cream, cherries, whipped cream. Place the last layer on, smooth side up and sprinkle with the last of the syrup. Spread the outside of the cake with the remaining whipped cream. Press milk chocolate shavings all over the cake using a palette knife. Lightly dust with icing sugar right before serving.

Some versions of the cake add a layer of chocolate whipped cream under the cherries: Melt 110g plain chocolate with 60ml whipping cream and cool to room temperature before assembling. Whisk half the chocolate mixture into the 170g whipped cream to be spread on the first layer, then repeat with the remaining chocolate mixture and another 170g whipped cream for the second layer; if you mix for both layers at the same time, it might harden before you get to the second layer.

russian punch cake

Makes one 3-layer 23cm cake, about 12 servings

RUM SYRUP

75ml water

55g sugar

60ml dark rum

One 23cm plain genoise cake (page 146)

1 batch Crème Pâtissière (page 158), chilled

VIENNESE MERINGUE FROSTING

5 medium egg whites, at room temperature

225g granulated sugar

110g icing sugar, sifted after measuring

Baking sheet or swiss roll tin

Serving: Serve wedges of this rich cake at the table; it needs no accompaniment.

Storage: Loosely wrap leftovers in clingfilm and serve within 24 hours.

This is a specialty of Demel, the great Viennese pastry shop, arguably one of the top half dozen in the world. I learned the recipe when I visited in the spring of 2008, to write an article about the shop for *Saveur* magazine, and this was one of the recipes that Dietmar Muthenthaler, the head pastry chef, had given us for the story. The elements in the cake are so simple that I was surprised at the delicate and delicious result when they were combined. The 'punch' in the name indicates the use of rum for moistening and flavouring the layers; I think calling it Russian is just a way of distinguishing it from the classic Viennese punch cake, which is filled with a mixture similar to what we would call rum balls – cake scraps, apricot jam, rum, a little chocolate – and covered with pink sugar icing.

1 For the syrup, stir the water and sugar together in a small pan over a low heat. Stir until the sugar is dissolved. Pour into a heatproof bowl and cool. Stir in the rum.

2 To assemble the cake, use a long, sharp serrated knife to split the genoise cake into 3 equal layers. Place the former top of the cake, crust side down, on a cake board. Sprinkle with a third of the rum syrup.

3 Whisk the crème pâtissière to smooth it out and use a medium palette knife to spread half on the layer.

4 Place the middle layer on the crème pâtissière and sprinkle with another third of the rum syrup; spread with the remaining crème pâtissière.

5 Place the last layer on top, smooth side up, and sprinkle with the remaining syrup. Slide the cake to a baking sheet or the back of a swiss roll tin and chill it while preparing the meringue.

6 Place the egg whites and granulated sugar in the bowl of an electric mixer and whisk by hand to mix. Place over a pan of gently boiling water (see Meringue Buttercream, page 156) and whisk gently until hot (60°C) and the sugar is dissolved, about 3 minutes. Place on the mixer with the whisk attachment and whisk on medium until increased in volume and almost cooled, 4 to 5 minutes. Decrease the speed to low and whisk in the icing sugar 2 tablespoons at a time. Increase the speed back to medium and whisk until the meringue has completely cooled.

7 Set a rack in the lower third of the oven and preheat to 200°C/gas mark 6.

8 Remove the cake from the tin it's resting on and spread a thick layer of the meringue all over the outside of the cake. Use a 1.25cm plain tube (Ateco size 6) to pipe a border of overlapping spheres at the top edge of the cake. Pipe any remaining meringue onto the side of the cake.

9 Replace the cake on the tin and bake it until the meringue is light golden, checking after about 20 seconds. If necessary, turn the cake from back to front and continue until the meringue colours sufficiently.

10 Slide the cake to a serving plate and refrigerate, uncovered, until serving time.

devil's food bombe

Makes one 20–23cm dome-shaped cake, depending on the size of the bowl used

2 layers Devil's Food Cake (page 128)

Whipped cream (page 159), made with 960ml cream and 110g sugar

60ml dark rum for sprinkling, optional

50g fresh raspberries, optional

Chocolate shavings or fine devil's food cake crumbs for finishing

One 1.5–2litre round-bottomed bowl, buttered and lined with clingfilm

This is an original and amusing presentation for plain old devil's food cake. It's sliced vertically and layered in a bowl with whipped cream. You can even sprinkle on a little dark rum and/or a handful of raspberries along the way. After spreading the outside of the unmoulded cake with whipped cream, you may press chocolate shavings against the cream or crumble any bits of leftover cake and use them instead.

1   Cut the devil's food layers into 5mm thick vertical slices.

2   Line the bowl with a single layer of the slices, patching them together if necessary. Sprinkle the slices with rum.

3   Spread a large spoonful of whipped cream on the cake slices at the bottom of the bowl.

4   Trim 2 or 3 cake slices to the diameter of the bottom of the bowl and arrange them on the cream. Sprinkle with rum and spread with more cream. If you're using raspberries, sprinkle a few on each layer.

5   Repeat, cutting enough cake slices to fit the changing diameter of the bowl as you build up higher so that they cover the previous layer of cream, until the bowl is full. Finish with a layer of cake.

6   Wrap and chill the bowl at least 4 hours or overnight. If chilling the cake overnight, only whip 720ml of the cream as in the recipe on page 159 and whip the rest for covering the cake soon before you're going to serve it.

7   Place a cake board or serving plate on the bowl and invert, then lift off the bowl. If the cake is stuck, wring out a clean tea towel in hot water and place on the bowl. This will melt the layer of butter between the bowl and the clingfilm, then you can lift off the bowl and carefully peel off the clingfilm.

8   Spread the outside of the cake with the remaining whipped cream and sprinkle with chocolate shavings or fine devil's food cake crumbs.

Serving: Since the cake is tall, it's difficult to serve even wedges. Use a sharp thin knife to cut them and use a wide cake server or other implement to transfer them to plates.

Storage: Tightly wrap leftovers with clingfilm and refrigerate and plan on serving all of it within 24 hours for best flavour.

variations

Substitute a batch of ganache (see page 157) for the cream inside the bowl. Cover the cake on the outside with Meringue Frosting (see page 158) or if you want a golden meringue, use the Viennese Meringue Frosting in the recipe for Russian Punch Cake on page 165 and bake the cake briefly as in that recipe.

chocolate pistachio orange cake

Makes one 2-layer 23cm cake, about 12 servings

ORANGE GANACHE FILLING

240ml whipping cream

2 tablespoons golden syrup

1 tablespoon grated orange zest

340g dark chocolate (50–65% cocoa solids), cut into 5mm pieces

30g unsalted butter, very soft

1 tablespoon orange liqueur, such as Triple Sec

100g candied orange peel cut into 5mm dice

ORANGE SYRUP

150ml water

70g sugar

2 tablespoons orange liqueur

2 teaspoons vanilla extract

1 batch whipped cream, made with 360ml cream, 2 tablespoons sugar, and 1 teaspoon vanilla extract

1 Pistachio Sponge cake layer (see page 150), baked and cooled (when you bake the cake layer, blanch an extra 30g of pistachios for finishing the cake)

FINISHING

Milk chocolate shavings

Candied orange peel

30g blanched pistachios, finely chopped

This is one of my favourite cakes, bar none. I first prepared it for a lunch cooked by my friend Ann Amendolara Nurse at the James Beard House in New York in the autumn of 1988. A restaurant chef had cancelled at the last minute and Ann was called in to replace him for one in a series of Italian lunches. The first thing Ann did was to phone and ask me to make a dessert and this cake was the result.

1 For the ganache, combine the cream, golden syrup and orange zest in a saucepan and bring to the boil over a low heat, whisking occasionally. Meanwhile place the chocolate in a heatproof bowl. Once the cream mixture boils, pour it through a fine mesh sieve (discard the orange zest) over the chocolate. Wait for 1 minute, then whisk smooth. Cool to room temperature and whisk in the butter, then the liqueur. About 1 hour before you intend to finish the cake, refrigerate the ganache briefly until it reaches spreading consistency.

2 Meanwhile, for the syrup, stir the water and sugar together in a small saucepan and place over a low heat. Bring to the boil, stirring occasionally. Pour the syrup into a heatproof bowl, cool to room temperature and stir in the liqueur and vanilla.

3 When you are ready to assemble the cake, whip the cream by hand or by machine with the sugar and vanilla until it holds a soft peak. Chill in the refrigerator.

4 To assemble the cake, use a sharp serrated knife to split the pistachio sponge cake layer horizontally into 2 equal layers. Invert the top of the cake to a cake board or serving plate and use a brush to moisten it with half the syrup. Whisk half the ganache by hand until lightened and spread it on the layer. Scatter the diced candied orange peel over the ganache. Remove the whipped cream from the refrigerator and re-whisk it if necessary. Spread about one third of the cream over the candied peel.

5 Invert the other layer onto the cream and peel off the paper. Moisten with the remaining syrup. Spread the top and side of the cake with the remaining whipped cream.

6 Use a palette knife to adhere the chocolate shavings to the side of the cake. Whisk up the remaining ganache and place it in a pastry bag fitted with a 1.25cm star tip (Ateco size 4). Pipe 12 rosettes around the top edge of the cake. Decorate each rosette with a small disc or shred of candied orange peel. Scatter the chopped pistachios all over the top of the cake.

Serving: Serve thin wedges of this rich cake.

Storage: If you are serving the cake within a few hours, keep it at a cool room temperature. Or cover loosely with clingfilm and refrigerate. Bring to room temperature for a couple of hours so that the ganache inside the cake isn't hard when it's served.

mocha
walnut
cake

Makes one 23cm 3-layer cake,
about 12 servings

COFFEE SYRUP

3 tablespoons sugar

120ml hot brewed coffee (don't heat cold
coffee; it will turn bitter)

2 teaspoons vanilla extract

One 23cm Walnut Sponge cake layer
(page 150), baked and cooled

1 batch Perfect Meringue Buttercream
(page 156), coffee flavoured

140g walnut pieces, lightly toasted, cooled
and finely chopped, but not ground

Coffee and walnuts make an excellent combination of flavours and I like to intensify it by using a vanilla and coffee syrup on the walnut cake layers. See the variations at the end of the recipe for adding a note of chocolate to this cake.

1   For the syrup, stir the sugar into the coffee until it dissolves, let cool and stir in the vanilla.

2   Use a sharp serrated knife to cut the cake layer into 3 thin layers. Place the top layer of the cake crust side down on a cake board and sprinkle it with one third of the syrup. Use a medium palette knife to spread about one quarter of the buttercream on top.

3   Place the middle layer on top and repeat with another third of the syrup and another quarter of the buttercream.

4   Place the last layer on the cake, smooth side up and sprinkle with the remaining syrup.

5   Spread the outside of the cake with the remaining buttercream. Press the chopped walnuts all over the side of the cake, then sprinkle the remaining walnuts on top. Use a medium palette knife to sweep across the top of the cake to even it off, letting the excess walnuts fall onto the work surface.

Serving: Cut the cake into wedges. This rich cake needs no accompaniment.

Storage: Keep the cake at a cool room temperature until serving. If it's cool indoors, you can keep leftovers under a cake dome or loosely wrapped in clingfilm. Or wrap and refrigerate the cake and bring it to room temperature before serving again.

variations

Chocolate Mocha Walnut Cake: Prepare $1^1/_2$ times the recipe for ganache glaze on page 157. Refrigerate one third of the glaze until it's thick enough to spread, 10–20 minutes. Spread half the chilled ganache on the bottom layer after the syrup, then spread with the buttercream. Repeat with the middle layer. Top with the last layer and sprinkle with syrup. Spread the outside of the cake with the buttercream, reserving about 8 tablespoons for decorating the cake, then chill it for an hour. If necessary, gently reheat the glaze until it is pourable, but not above 32°C or it will melt the buttercream. Place the chilled cake on a rack over a clean tin and pour the glaze over it in a spiral, starting at the centre of the cake and ending at the top edge (A and B). Quickly sweep across the top of the cake using a medium palette knife to remove excess glaze (C); quickly check to see that the sides are evenly covered. If not, use some of the glaze that has dripped into the tin to patch. Let the glaze set, then pipe the reserved buttercream into a dozen or so rosettes with a 1.25cm star tip (Ateco size 4) at the top edge of the cake. Dust 12 walnut halves with icing sugar and arrange them on the rosettes and tilted toward the centre of the cake.

If you wish, use a plain or cocoa genoise (see page 146) for the cake in either variation above and omit the walnuts. If using a cocoa genoise and not glazing the cake, press chocolate shavings against the side of the cake.

A

B

C

A   B

raspberry meringue wedge

Makes one 23 x 23 x 33cm triangular cake, about 16–20 servings

Two 23cm square meringue layers, plus the rest of the meringue piped into a rectangle on another tin (page 152), baked and cooled

1 batch raspberry meringue buttercream (page 156)

Multicoloured curling ribbon, optional

In the autumn of 1986 I was teaching my first career-training intensive baking course at Peter Kump's New York Cooking School when I learned that Peter's birthday was a few days away. I asked Gaynor Grant, our registrar, what kind of cake I should make for Peter and she told me that he absolutely adored the raspberry meringue cake from Maurice Bonté's patisserie, then the best pastry shop in Manhattan. So I took a walk over after class and with the pretext of buying some cake yeast, which they were always happy to sell to us. I asked Mme. Bonté about the unusual triangular cake covered with chunks of broken meringue with a bright pink buttercream showing through beneath and two narrow corners festooned with thin multicoloured curling ribbons. Yes, it was all meringue layers, and yes, it was raspberry buttercream, were her answers. I returned to the school to start preparations, happy that the recipe had cost me so little. I was very flattered when Peter refused to believe we hadn't bought the cake from Bonté.

C

D

1 Trim each of the meringue layers to an even 23cm square, then carefully cut through each diagonally with a sawing motion to make 4 triangles; only 3 will be used to assemble the cake (A).

2 Use a chef's knife to chop the least even of the triangles and the extra rectangle into 5mm–1cm pieces.

3 Cut a cake board that will fit under one of the layers and use a dab of the buttercream to secure a layer in place, flat (bottom) side down. Spread the layer with one third of the buttercream.

4 Place the second triangle on top, flat side down and spread with another third of the buttercream (B).

5 Place the last layer on top, again flat side down and gently press into place (C). Spread the entire outside of the triangle with the remaining buttercream.

6 Press the broken meringue chunks against the buttercream all over the top and sides of the triangle (D).

7 If you want to decorate the triangle with ribbon, cut about twelve 40cm lengths and bunch six together. Tie them around one of the narrow corners of the triangle, then scrape a table knife or a single blade of a pair of scissors against them to curl. Repeat with the remaining ribbon on the opposite narrow angle. Chill the cake to set the buttercream.

Serving: Snip the ribbons away and cut slices from either narrow end of the cake inward. Once the slices are very long, cut the remaining cake in half lengthways to make more manageable slices.

Storage: Keep the cake refrigerated, but bring it to room temperature for 1–2 hours before serving. Wrap and refrigerate leftovers and bring to room temperature again before serving.

variations

This will work well with any flavor of buttercream as well as with ganache. For a triangle filled with ganache, dust the meringue shards on the outside of the cake with a very light coating of cocoa powder.

assembling moulded cakes

Some of the moulded cakes in this chapter have a cake layer as a base underneath the fillings, as in the case of this cheesecake.

1 To prepare the layer, turn it out onto a clean work surface and peel away any baking paper. With a sharp serrated knife, trim the crust and any domed portions from the cake so that it is flat.

2 To cut one layer into two or three, see page 160.

3 The tin used for moulding the cake should be 2.5cm wider in diameter than the cake layer so that when the filling is added it automatically finishes the side of the cake.

4 Place a trimmed layer in the bottom of the tin to be used as a mould. Dab on about half the syrup, if using, with a pastry brush.

5 Pour on about half of the filling and smooth it with a small palette knife, making sure that some of it fills in the gap between the side of the tin and the side of the cake layer.

6 If there is a second layer, place it on top of the first. Again, moisten it by dabbing with syrup. (If the cake just has one layer, skip to the last sentence of the next step.)

7 Scrape the rest of the filling onto the top layer and use the same palette knife to spread it over the top, again making sure that it fills in the gap between the side of the tin and the side of the layer. To finish off the top of the cake, use a palette knife or the back of a knife whose blade is longer than the diameter of the mould to scrape across the top of the mold and make the filling perfectly even.

8 Refrigerate the cake, uncovered, until the filling starts to set on the outside, about a couple of hours. After that, loosely cover the mould with clingfilm and keep the cake refrigerated until it's completely set, at least 4 hours (overnight works best).

9 To unmould a cake, warm the side of the tin/mould with a cloth dipped in hot water and wrung out. Run the tip of a sharp, thin knife between the side of the cake and the tin, pushing against the tin. Then unbuckle the outside of the springform and carefully lift it away without touching the cake. Leave the cake on the base of the springform tin, but transfer to a serving plate to serve.

10 If you like, you can finish the sides of the cake, once unmoulded, with nuts or chocolate shavings. You can also decorate the top with slices of fruit, meringue or piped whipped cream.

no-bake cheesecake

The only baking involved in this cheesecake recipe is for the cake base. You can shave a thin layer from a genoise you're using for a layer cake or from almost any other plain cake layer you wish. If you make one of the other moulded cakes in this chapter, you'll automatically have a single thin genoise layer left over; just wrap and freeze it until you want to make this. The filling here is a cream cheese mousse, but its flavour and texture are that of an incredibly light and delicate cheesecake.

Makes one 23 or 25cm cheesecake, about 16 servings

One 5mm thick 23cm layer of plain genoise (see page 146), or any other firm cake layer in Chapter 11

CHEESECAKE

675g cream cheese, very soft

225g soured cream or natural low fat yogurt

1 tablespoon lemon juice, strained

2 teaspoons vanilla extract

75ml water

4 teaspoons unflavoured powdered gelatine

4 medium egg whites

Pinch of salt

170g sugar

One 23 or 25cm springform tin, 6.25–7.5cm deep

1 Arrange the cake layer in the bottom of the tin and set aside.

2 Beat the cream cheese in the bowl of an electric mixer fitted with the paddle attachment on medium speed until smooth, about 1 minute. Scrape the bowl and beater and beat again, then scrape again.

3 Beat in the soured cream, lemon juice and vanilla until smooth. Stop, scrape, and beat again until lightened, about 2 minutes. Scrape the cream cheese mixture into a large bowl and wash the mixer bowl in hot soapy water, then rinse and dry it.

4 Pour the water into a small shallow bowl and use a fork to stir in the gelatine, making sure that all the granules are moistened. Set aside so that the gelatine evenly absorbs all the water.

5 Half fill a small saucepan on which your mixer bowl will fir without having more than 5cm inside the pan, and bring the water to the boil. Reduce the heat so that the water boils gently.

6 By hand, whisk the egg whites, salt and sugar together in the mixer bowl. Set the bowl on the pan of boiling water and whisk gently until the egg whites are hot (60°C) and the sugar is dissolved, about 2 minutes. Scrape the gelatine into the egg whites and whisk it in. Continue to heat for 30 seconds longer to melt the gelatine.

7 Place the meringue on the mixer with the whisk attachment and whisk on medium-high speed until white and fluffy but not completely cooled, 4–5 minutes.

8 Vigorously whisk one third of the meringue into the cream cheese mixture, then whisk the cream cheese mixture, more gently this time, back into the remaining meringue in the mixer bowl.

9 Pour the cheese mixture into the prepared tin and refrigerate immediately.

10 After the mixture has set in the tin, 2–3 hours, loosely wrap the tin in clingfilm and chill until you wish to unmould the cake, up to 2 days.

11 To unmould the cake, insert a thin paring knife between the side of the cake and the side of the tin and, pressing it against the tin, loosen the cake. Unbuckle the side of the tin and lift it off. Use a wide palette knife to slide the cake from the springform base to a serving plate. Keep the cake chilled until serving.

Serving: Cut the cake into wedges at the table, wiping the knife after each cut. Serve with some crushed sweetened strawberries or mixed berries.

Storage: Keep the cheesecake refrigerated, loosely covered with clingfilm.

variations:

Chocolate Cheesecake: Omit the lemon juice. Add 225g dark chocolate, melted with 75ml water or milk and cooled, to the cream cheese mixture, whisking it in by hand, then pick up the recipe above at step 4.

Devil's Food Cheesecake: Cut one layer devil's food cake, page 128, horizontally into two layers. Put one in the springform tin and make sure it's tight. Omit the lemon juice and divide the cream cheese mixture into two bowls, one with slightly more. Melt 110g dark chocolate with 3 tablespoons water and cool; whisk into the bowl with slightly less cream cheese. Prepare the gelatine and meringue as above, then whisk half into each of the mixtures. Pour the chocolate mixture into the prepared pan and set the other cake layer on it. Pour the plain mixture over and chill and unmould.

apple & calvados bavarian cake

Makes one 25cm cake, about 16 servings

APPLE PURÉE

1.1kg Golden Delicious apples, pared, cored, and diced

120ml water

225g sugar

CALVADOS SYRUP

75ml water

55g sugar

60ml Calvados

1 teaspoon vanilla extract

POACHED APPLE WEDGES

480ml dry white wine or cider

110g sugar

2 7.5cm pieces lemon zest

4 large (about 900g) Golden Delicious apples

One 23cm plain genoise cake layer (page 146), baked and cooled

APPLE BAVARIAN CREAM

560g apple purée, above

60ml Calvados

60ml poaching liquid from the apple wedges

4½ teaspoons unflavoured powdered gelatine

600ml whipping cream, whipped to a soft peak and refrigerated

APRICOT GLAZE

225g apricot jam

2 tablespoons water

FINISHING

120ml whipping cream, whipped to a soft peak

2 tablespoons toasted flaked almonds

One 25cm springform tin and one 30cm pastry bag fitted with a 1.25cm star tip (Ateco size 4)

Calvados, or aged French apple brandy, is produced in Normandy, one of the world's great centres of apple cultivation. Sweet, tart and bitter apples are first pressed and fermented into cider, then the cider is distilled into Calvados that's aged in oak barrels for a minimum of two years, often much longer for premium brands. Two-year-old Calvados is fine for making desserts, as is American applejack, which is made in a similar manner. This cake is for a special autumn or winter occasion; it's not only delicious, but beautiful as well. Crowned with a ring of apple wedges poached in white wine and glazed with apricot jam, it's so impressive that everyone will ask you for the recipe.

Plan ahead: This dessert has a lot of elements, all of which can be prepared in advance. Bake the cake layer and refrigerate it for up to five days. Make the syrup and refrigerate it in a covered jar and prepare the apple purée several days in advance. Cook the apple wedges the day before and leave them in their syrup, covered, in the refrigerator. You can even assemble the cake in its mould beforehand, but only unmould and decorate it the day you intend to serve it.

1   For the apple purée, combine the apples, water and sugar in a large saucepan or enameled iron casserole with a tight-fitting lid. Place on a medium heat and bring to the boil. Reduce the heat, cover the pan and let the apples cook, uncovering and stirring occasionally, until they have completely disintegrated. Cool the apples and purée them in a food processor or blender. Pack the apple purée into a plastic container, cover and refrigerate. Remember to remove the apple purée from the refrigerator 1–2 hours before preparing the filling.

2   For the syrup, bring the water and sugar to the boil in a small saucepan, stirring occasionally to dissolve the sugar. Pour into a small bowl, cool and stir in the Calvados and vanilla. Cover and refrigerate if not using on the same day.

3   For the poached apple wedges, combine the wine, sugar and lemon zest in a wide, shallow sauté pan. Bring to the simmer and remove from the heat. Pare, halve, and core the apples and cut each half into 6 wedges, adding them to the syrup as soon as they are cut. When all the apple wedges are in the pan, jostle them around so that they are in a single layer and add water to cover. Cut a piece of baking paper the same diameter as the inside of the pan and cut a hole in the centre. Press the paper into the liquid so that it is completely submerged and will in turn keep the apple wedges submerged. Bring the liquid to the simmer and cook until the apple wedges are tender when pierced with a fork. Use a slotted spoon to remove them from the hot liquid and cool them on a plate. Refrigerate the leftover liquid in a shallow bowl to cool quickly, then store the apple wedges covered in the cold liquid until you need them. Drain thoroughly on a tin covered with kitchen paper before finishing the cake.

4   To assemble, cut the genoise layer into 3 layers. Wrap and freeze one of the layers for another use, such as a base for the No-Bake Cheesecake on page 175. Place one of the layers in the bottom of a springform tin and use a brush to sprinkle it with less than half of the Calvados syrup.

5   For the apple Bavarian cream, put the apple purée into a large mixing bowl. Put the Calvados and poaching liquid into a small heatproof bowl and use a fork to stir in the gelatin. Half fill a small saucepan or sauté pan with water and place over a low heat. Once the gelatine has absorbed all the liquid and is wet looking, place the bowl in the water and let the gelatine melt. Once the gelatin has melted, remove the bowl from the hot water. Quickly re-whip the cream. Whisk 1 cup of the apple purée into the dissolved gelatin to cool it and whisk the gelatin mixture into the bowl of apple purée. Quickly use a large rubber spatula to fold in the whipped cream.

6   Pour half the Bavarian cream over the cake layer in the springform tin, spreading it with a medium palette knife and making sure it also covers the side of the layer Quickly place the second layer on top and sprinkle on the remaining syrup. Pour the remaining Bavarian cream over the layer and spread smooth. Cover with clingfilm and refrigerate until set, preferably overnight.

7   To finish the cake, insert a thin paring knife between the side of the cake and the side of the tin and, pressing against the tin, loosen the cake. Unbuckle the side of the tin and lift it off. Use a wide palette knife to slide the cake from the springform base to a platter. >

8 For the glaze, stir the jam and water together in a small pan and bring to the simmer over a low heat. Strain into a bowl, rinse out the pan and return the glaze in the pan to a low heat to reduce slightly, about 5 minutes.

9 Arrange the drained apple wedges around the top edge of the cake and brush them with the apricot glaze. Re-whip the decorating cream and use the pastry bag to pipe a series of stars into the centre area of the cake top not covered by the apples. Sprinkle with a few pieces of sliced almonds. Refrigerate until ready to serve.

Serving: Use a sharp knife to cut the cake into wedges. Serve a sparkling cider or slightly fizzy Moscato d'Asti with the cake.

Storage: Wrap and refrigerate leftovers.

variations:

Apricot Bavarian Cake: Really sweet, perfect apricots would make a perfect substitute for the apples. For the top of the cake, poach unskinned apricot halves and cool them. If the skin slips off easily, remove it; if not, don't be concerned. You'll need about 900g apricots rinsed and stoned for the purée and a dozen medium apricots to ring the border of the cake. Substitute white rum for the Calvados.

Raspberry or Strawberry Bavarian Cake: Use 675g fresh or frozen raspberries or 840g strawberries for the purée (rinse and hull strawberries). Use sweetened raspberry liqueur in place of the Calvados for raspberries and 2 tablespoons kirsch for strawberries. For both, use water in place of the poaching liquid. Decorate the top of the cake with perfect berries, uncooked, of course; they don't need to be glazed.

suggestions for pairing cake layers, fillings, and frostings

- Though butter- and oil-based cake layers are richer in general than sponge and meringue layers, they may still pair successfully with rich fillings such as buttercream or ganache, as long as the filling is used with restraint. This is why in the past these types of cake layers were almost always finished with meringue frosting.

- When using a neutral-flavoured cake layer such as a plain genoise or a white or yellow cake, choose a filling and frosting that will impart both colour and flavour to the finished cake. Vanilla buttercream and plain whipped cream are both excellent fillings, but using them to finish a yellow cake doesn't bring out the best qualities of either.

- The addition of fruit can make a simple presentation more colourful and appealing. Remember that fresh fruit pairs best with crème pâtissière and whipped cream, both of which have a texture that better serves as a backdrop than the richness of buttercream or ganache.

- There's nothing wrong with choosing a filling that's different from the frosting. Just remember when preparing the filling and frosting that you'll need only half of the quantities stated in the recipes.

- Liqueurs and brandies make excellent flavourings or adjuncts to flavourings in fillings, frostings, and syrups used for moistening sponge layers. It's better not to mix and match here, and if you're using a particular liqueur or alcohol in one element of the cake, use the same one throughout. No matter which element of the cake it appears in, liqueur should be used with restraint and should have a subtle flavour and you should never be able to detect the bitterness of alcohol as a result.

- Spreading the outside of a cake smoothly takes a little practise to master. Covering the outside of a cake by adhering toasted sliced almonds, chocolate shavings, or even flaked coconut camouflages little imperfections in the frosting beneath. Just make sure that whatever you choose to press against the outside of the cake harmonises with what's inside.

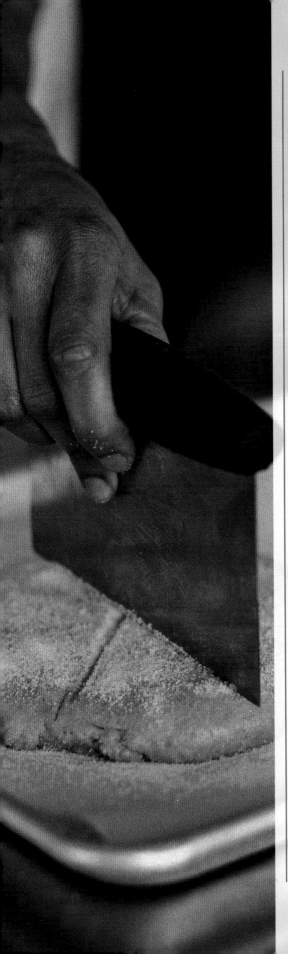

16

scones

'Quick breads' became popular during the 19th century due to the invention of baking powder. Primitive baking powders caused aeration in doughs by combining an acid, usually cream of tartar, with bicarbonate of soda, a strong alkali. Acids and alkalis throw off carbon dioxide gas in the presence of water, thus causing a leavening somewhat similar to what takes place in a yeast-risen dough. Baking powder biscuits originated in the American South, while scones have a British origin. Each region of the United Kingdom has its own particular version of scones. The scones in this chapter are made in a manner very similar to a pastry dough and are easy to prepare in the food processor or by hand.

A B C

American 'biscuits'

Biscuits and scones are prepared in a similar manner, though contemporary versions of the latter are quite a bit sweeter. They both require careful handling, but as long as it's cool in the kitchen and you don't over-knead the dough, it's easy to turn out excellent versions of both.

Makes about 12 biscuits, depending on the size of the cutter used

390g plain flour

2 tablespoons baking powder

1 teaspoon salt

200g unsalted butter, cold and cut into 12 pieces

300ml full fat milk

2 baking sheets or swiss roll tins lined with baking paper or foil

Serving: Serve the biscuits in a napkin-lined basket with butter, honey and your favourite jam or marmalade.

Storage: Biscuits are a little like a soufflé – they have to be served immediately and are less delicate once they've cooled. Leftover biscuits become a little hard, but you can split and lightly toast them instead of throwing them away. Since the biscuits made from this recipe contain a large amount of butter, they reheat more successfully than biscuits normally do. I reheat them in a toaster oven for a couple of minutes on the lowest toaster setting.

1 Set a rack in the centre of the oven and preheat to 220°C/gas mark 7.

2 Combine the flour, baking powder and salt in the bowl of a food processor fitted with the metal blade and pulse several times to mix.

3 Add the butter and pulse again repeatedly until no visible pieces of butter remain and the mixture is still cool and powdery, but not pasty.

4 Invert to a mixing bowl and carefully remove the blade. Add the milk and use a rubber spatula to scrape upward from the bottom of the bowl and moisten the dough as evenly as possible.

5 Turn the contents of the bowl out onto a floured work surface (A). Press the dough into a 15–18cm square (B), then fold it in three: Fold the bottom third of the dough closest to you up over the middle third (C), then fold the top third down over that. Press it out again a little longer in the length and repeat the folding into thirds, this time from the short ends (D through F). Press the dough back out into a 15–18cm square (G).

6 Use a 5–6.25cm plain round cutter, flouring it before each cut, to stamp out the biscuits (H). Cut straight down and don't twist the cutter or the biscuits won't bake straight-sided. Cut them close together to avoid generating too many scraps.

7 Press the scraps together into a rectangle only as wide as your cutter and three times as long. Cut out three more biscuits and discard the remaining scraps.

8 Arrange the biscuits about 2.5cm apart on the prepared tins. For advance preparation, cover the tins with clingfilm and chill the biscuits for up to 2 hours before baking, then bake them straight from the refrigerator, without returning them to room temperature. If you intend to prepare the biscuits in advance, preheat the oven only about 20 minutes before baking.

9 Bake the biscuits until they are deep golden and well risen, 15–20 minutes. Let the baked biscuits cool for a couple of minutes on the tin before serving.

variations

Buttermilk Biscuits: Substitute buttermilk for the milk, adding 1/2 teaspoon bicarbonate of soda to the dry ingredients.

Drop Biscuits: Increase the milk to 420ml. Use a 5cm diameter ice cream scoop or a large soup spoon to drop mounds of the dough on the prepared tin and bake immediately as for the biscuits above. Some Southern cooks like to bake these in a

D E F

G H

round cake tin, positioning them close together, so they have soft sides when pulled apart after baking. This amount of dough will fill two 20–23cm round tins. You can accomplish the same soft sides by arranging the mounds of dough close together on a baking sheet and that way you can make some soft and some crusty biscuits too.

Old-Fashioned Southern Biscuits: Substitute good-quality lard for the butter in the recipe. Don't even think of using vegetable fat.

Potato or Sweet Potato Biscuits: Bake a large (225–340g) baking potato or sweet potato at 200°C/gas mark 6 until it is tender, about 1 hour. (To minimise last-minute fuss, it's better to do this the day before.) Cool, peel, and coarsely mash the potato. Weigh 170g mashed potato for this recipe. Start by puréeing the potato in a food processor fitted with the metal blade, scraping and pulsing several times. Mix the flour with the baking powder and salt in a bowl and add the dry ingredients and butter to the food processor bowl at the same time. Resume the recipe at step 3.

Cheese Biscuits: Before adding the butter, add 70g coarsely grated mature cheddar, aged Gouda or Gruyère cheese to the work bowl. Pulse until finely mixed into the dry ingredients before adding the butter. Cheese biscuits are great split and filled with some thick-sliced baked ham.

essential tips for scones

- Biscuit and scone doughs need to be made slightly smoother and a little elastic before being cut, but don't overdo the folding too much or they'll be tough and chewy after baking.

- Biscuit and scone doughs respond well to a gentle patting out to the right thickness. Only use a rolling pin to smooth out the top of the dough if necessary.

- As with all doughs, use pinches of flour on the work surface and on the dough. You can add as many pinches as you need without adding too much flour to the dough. Flouring with handfuls, rather than pinches, will make the dough absorb so much flour it will increase the proportion of flour in the dough and make the results dry after baking.

- Biscuits are best hot from the oven, but the recipes here can stand to be cooled and filled, or even reheated, without becoming dry.

- Don't twist: Dip your cutter into a small bowl of flour before each cut, then cut straight down without twisting the cutter for attractive straight-sided biscuits that rise well in the oven.

- All the scone recipes included here may be served after cooling; they're the cakey variety and don't need to be served immediately after baking.

cream cheese scones

Cream cheese adds a note of richness and some flakiness to these simple scones.

Makes sixteen 6.25–7.5cm triangular scones

390g plain flour

55g sugar

1 tablespoon baking powder

¾ teaspoon salt

110g cream cheese, cold and cut into 20 pieces

85g unsalted butter, cold and cut into 12 pieces

2 medium eggs, cold

75ml full fat milk, cold

Baking sheet or swiss roll tin lined with baking paper or foil

1 Set a rack in the centre of the oven and preheat to 220°C/gas mark 7.

2 In a bowl, mix the flour, sugar, baking powder and salt and set aside.

3 Place the cream cheese, butter and eggs in the bowl of a food processor fitted with the metal blade and pulse 6–8 times to combine; the mixture will look a little curdled.

4 Use a thin palette knife to scrape down the bowl. Add the dry ingredients and milk. Pulse 3 times and scrape again.

5 Pulse 3 more times and turn the dough out onto a floured work surface. Carefully remove the blade. Fold the dough over on itself several times to make it smoother.

6 Divide the dough into 2 equal pieces and press each into a 15cm disc. Arrange them on the prepared tin about 7.5cm apart.

7 Use a dough scraper or a large knife to mark each square of dough into 8 triangles, cutting about halfway through .

8 Bake the scones until they are well risen and deep golden, about 15 minutes.

9 Cool the baked scones on the tin for a few minutes, then use a knife to separate them at the marked divisions.

Serving: Serve immediately with jam or marmalade; these don't need any cream or butter.

Storage: These keep better than biscuits because of the tenderness imparted by the sugar and the higher fat content. Wrap and freeze for up to 1 month. Defrost and reheat for 7–8 minutes at 190°C/gas mark 5 and serve immediately.

milk chocolate scones

Reducing the milk and dark chocolates to a powder before adding the remaining dry ingredients eliminates the need to melt the chocolate separately. Orange marmalade, raspberry jam or sour cherry conserve are great when paired with a chocolate scone like this one.

Makes sixteen 6.25–7.5cm triangular scones

390g plain flour

1 tablespoon baking powder

½ teaspoon salt

¼ teaspoon ground cinnamon

110g milk chocolate, cut into 5mm pieces and chilled for 20 minutes

110g dark (65–70% cocoa solids) chocolate, cut into 5mm pieces and chilled for 20 minutes

55g flaked almonds

55g unsalted butter, cold and cut into 12 pieces

1 medium egg, cold

240ml full fat milk, cold

Baking sheet or swiss roll tin lined with baking paper or foil

1 Set a rack in the centre of the oven and preheat to 220°C/gas mark 7.

2 In a bowl, mix the flour, baking powder, salt and cinnamon and set aside.

3 Place the chocolate and almonds in the bowl of a food processor fitted with the metal blade and pulse to grind fine. Stop if you see any signs of the chocolate melting.

4 Add the dry ingredients to the work bowl and pulse again to combine. Add the butter and pulse to mix in fine.

5 Quickly whisk the egg and milk together and add to the food processor bowl.

6 Pulse 3 times and then turn the contents of the bowl out onto a floured work surface. Carefully remove the blade. Press the dough together and fold it over on itself several times to make it smoother.

7 Divide the dough into 2 equal pieces and press each into a 15cm disc. Arrange them on the prepared tin about 7.5cm apart. **>**

8 Use a dough scraper or a large knife to mark each square of dough into 8 triangles, cutting about halfway through the dough.

9 Bake the scones until they are well risen, firm, and dull rather than shiny, about 15 minutes.

10 Cool the baked scones on the tin for a few minutes, then use a knife to separate them at the marked divisions. Cool them completely on a rack.

Serving: Serve the scones in a napkin-lined basket; they need no accompaniment.

Storage: Use immediately or wrap and freeze for up to 1 month. Defrost and reheat for 7–8 minutes at 190°C/gas mark 5 and serve immediately.

variation

If you'd like to add some chocolate chips, invert the contents of the work bowl to a mixing bowl at the end of step 4, add the chips, use a rubber spatula to quickly mix them through the dry ingredients and then use the same spatula to mix in the egg and milk mixture by hand.

orange & almond scones

Almond paste adds richness and an elusive flavour to these sweet scones. If you only have marzipan, which has about a third more sugar in it than almond paste, decrease the sugar in the recipe by 2 tablespoons.

Makes sixteen 6.25–7.5cm triangular scones

390g plain flour

55g sugar

1 tablespoon baking powder

½ teaspoon salt

110g almond paste (or marzipan), cut into 1cm cubes

85g unsalted butter, cold and cut into 12 pieces

1 medium egg

150ml full fat milk

1 tablespoon finely grated orange zest

Egg wash: 1 egg well beaten with a pinch of salt

½ cup whole unblanched almonds, coarsely chopped

Baking sheet or swiss roll tin lined with baking paper or foil

1 Set a rack in the centre of the oven and preheat to 220°C/gas mark 7.

2 Place the flour, sugar, baking powder and salt in the bowl of a food processor fitted with the metal blade and pulse to mix. Add the almond paste and pulse again until the mixture is powdery looking.

3 Add the butter and pulse again until finely mixed in.

4 In a small bowl, whisk the egg with the milk and orange zest and add to the food processor bowl. Pulse 3 times and turn the contents of the bowl out onto a floured work surface. Carefully remove the blade. Press the dough together and fold it over on itself several times to make it smoother.

5 Divide the dough into 2 equal pieces and press each into a 15cm disc. Arrange them on the prepared tin about 7.5cm apart.

6 Use a dough scraper or a large knife to mark each square of dough into 8 triangles, cutting about halfway through the dough. Brush the tops with the egg wash and sprinkle with the chopped almonds, then gently press in the almonds.

7 Bake the scones until they are well risen, firm, and deep golden, about 15 minutes.

8 Cool the baked scones on the tin for a few minutes, then use a knife to separate them at the marked divisions. Cool them completely on a rack.

Serving: Serve the scones in a napkin-lined basket; they need no accompaniment.

Storage: Use immediately or wrap and freeze for up to 1 month. Defrost and reheat for 7–8 minutes at 190°C/gas mark 5 and serve immediately.

17

tea breads
& muffins

Tea breads, minimally sweet loaves leavened with baking powder, deserve to be more popular again. A mainstay of home baking of the last century, they're now neglected in favour of richer, sweeter cakes. Perfect with a thin spread of cream cheese or butter, tea breads can pass from the 'I feel like baking something' stage to the table in a little more than an hour. And nothing is better than a homemade muffin. As a veteran of more airport breakfasts than I care to remember, I can attest to the fact that commercially and industrially made muffins often taste as though they've been made with recycled frying oil. Muffins mix up quickly and are ready for the table before you know it. They also freeze beautifully, so you can get them ready in advance for a breakfast or brunch when you might need to be concentrating on cooking or baking other things.

old-fashioned cornbread

Makes one 23cm round cornbread, about 8 servings

130g plain flour

130g stone-ground white or yellow polenta

3 tablespoons sugar

1 tablespoon baking powder

1 teaspoon salt

2 medium eggs

180ml full fat milk

110g unsalted butter, melted

One 23 x 5cm round tin, buttered and the base lined with a disc of baking paper

essential tips for quick breads & muffins

- Easy does it. Overmixing the batter could make the results tough and chewy after baking.

- Check for doneness at the three-quarter point in the baking time; a lean batter doesn't tolerate any overbaking without becoming much too dry.

- For best results, use standard size (120ml capacity) muffin tins – not the aluminium foil reinforced papers, which may flatten out.

- Brush the top of the muffin tin with some butter or grease with vegetable cooking spray. That way, even if the muffins rise above the top of the hole, they won't stick to the top of the tin.

The only thing to use for cornbread is stone-ground polenta. Industrially milled polenta that you find in the supermarket has been degerminated. The small sprouting end of the corn kernel has been removed because it contains some fat and there's a remote possibility that it could make the polenta turn rancid. Unfortunately, a lot of flavour is in the corn germ and it's lost after removal. Use either yellow or white polenta; they taste exactly the same, but some American Southern and New England cooks prefer the white variety.

1 Set a rack in the centre of the oven and preheat to 200°C/gas mark 6.

2 Stir the flour, polenta, sugar, baking powder and salt together in a large bowl.

3 In another bowl, smoothly whisk together the eggs, milk and melted butter.

4 Add the liquid to the bowl of dry ingredients and use a large rubber spatula to quickly fold everything together. Scrape the batter into the prepared tin and smooth the top.

5 Bake the cornbread until it is well risen and light golden on top, feels firm in the centre, and the point of a paring knife inserted in the centre emerges clean, about 25 minutes.

6 Cool in the tin on a rack for 5 minutes, then loosen the cornbread from the side of the tin with a small paring knife if necessary and invert it to another rack. Peel off the paper and replace it with a serving plate. Invert the whole stack, lift off the rack and serve immediately.

Serving: Serve warm with butter and honey for breakfast, brunch or tea.

Storage: Best as soon as it comes out of the oven, leftover cornbread may be reheated or toasted.

variations

Corn Muffins: Bake the batter in a standard muffin tin, lining the holes with paper cases. Divide the batter evenly among the 12 holes in the tin and bake as above for about 20 minutes. These are best immediately after they're baked.

Buttermilk Cornbread: Omit 1 egg and substitute 240ml buttermilk for the milk. Add 1/4 teaspoon bicarbonate of soda to the dry ingredients.

Savoury Cornbread: To serve the cornbread with a meal of American-style food (like barbecued ribs or fried chicken), reduce the sugar to 1 tablespoon or omit it entirely. If you're making cornbread for a crowd, double the recipe and bake the cornbread in a 23 x 33 x 5cm tin – the baking time is approximately the same. Cut the cornbread into 5 or 7.5cm squares in the tin and use a wide palette knife to lift them out.

Cornbread for Turkey Stuffing: When I cook Thanksgiving dinner, I always bake a cornbread stuffing alongside the bird. To make the cornbread for that, use the Savoury Cornbread variation and add 1 tablespoon each of rubbed sage and poultry seasoning directly to the dry ingredients. Visit my website for the stuffing recipe.

perfect banana walnut bread

Makes one 23 x 13 x 7cm loaf, about
16 slices

300g plain flour

170g sugar

2½ teaspoons baking powder

½ teaspoon salt

2 medium eggs

450g bananas, peeled and mashed (use a
potato masher or a fork), about 3 medium

110g unsalted butter, melted

2 teaspoons vanilla extract

110g walnut pieces, coarsely chopped and
tossed with 1 tablespoon flour

One 23 x 13 x 7cm loaf tin, buttered and
the base lined with baking paper

There are only two secrets to making perfect banana bread: Use very ripe bananas with spotted or darkened skin and measure the quantity of mashed banana. All too often, home bakers mash a couple of bananas and just throw the resulting quantity into a batter – and usually it's either too much or too little. I like to add some chopped walnuts for texture; you could add raisins, dried currants, or even flaked sweetened coconut.

1 Set a rack in the centre of the oven and preheat to 180°C/gas mark 4.

2 In a large mixing bowl, stir together the flour, sugar, baking powder and salt.

3 In another bowl whisk the eggs to break them up, then whisk in the bananas, butter and vanilla one at a time, whisking smooth between additions.

4 Pour the liquids into the bowl of dry ingredients and use a large rubber spatula to fold them in. Fold in the floured walnuts.

5 Scrape the batter into the prepared tin and smooth the top.

6 Bake the bread until it is well risen and golden in colour and the point of a paring knife inserted in the centre emerges clean, 55–60 minutes.

7 Cool in the tin on a rack for 10 minutes, then unmould, remove the paper, and cool the loaf right side up.

Serving: Serve the bread plain with tea or coffee, or add a little butter or cream cheese.

Storage: Wrap the loaf in clingfilm after it has cooled completely and store it that way. For advance preparation, double wrap and freeze, then unwrap and bring to room temperature before serving.

lemon coconut tea bread

Makes one 23 x 13 x 7cm loaf, about
16 slices

260g flour

140g sugar

2½ teaspoons baking powder

½ teaspoon salt

45g unsweetened desiccated coconut

2 medium eggs

120ml full fat milk

85g unsalted butter, melted

2 tablespoons lemon juice, strained
before measuring

1 tablespoon finely grated lemon zest

One 23 x 13 x 7cm loaf tin, buttered and
the base lined with baking paper

Unsweetened desiccated coconut imparts both sweetness and richness to this easy tea bread. If you can only find sweetened coconut, reduce the sugar in the recipe by 2 tablespoons and pulse the coconut in the food processor to make it finer.

1 Set a rack in the centre of the oven and preheat to 180°C/gas mark 4.

2 In a large bowl, stir together the flour, sugar, baking powder, salt and coconut.

3 In another bowl, whisk the eggs to break them up, then whisk in the milk, butter, lemon juice and zest one at a time, whisking to combine between additions.

4 Pour the liquids into the bowl of dry ingredients and use a large rubber spatula to fold them in.

5 Scrape the batter into the prepared tin and smooth the top.

6 Bake the bread until it is well risen and golden in colour and the point of a paring knife inserted in the centre emerges clean, 55–60 minutes.

7 Cool in the tin on a rack for 10 minutes, then unmould, remove the paper, and cool the loaf right side up.

Storage: Wrap the loaf in clingfilm after it has cooled completely and store it that way. For advance preparation, double wrap and freeze, then unwrap and bring to room temperature before serving.

treacle gingerbread

Makes one 23cm round gingerbread, about 8 servings

260g plain flour

2 teaspoons ground ginger

½ teaspoon ground cinnamon

¼ teaspoon ground cloves

110g unsalted butter, cut into 8 pieces

140g dark brown sugar

4 tablespoons treacle

240ml water

1 teaspoon bicarbonate of soda

One 23 x 5cm round tin, buttered and the base lined with a disc of baking paper

Gingerbread's long history pretty much concludes in the British Isles, where it is a standard. This is an adaptation of a 1940s British recipe. As soon as spices became commonly available in Europe in the late Middle Ages, all sorts of spiced honey cakes, the most common example of which is probably the *Lebkuchen* of German-speaking countries, began to appear. Gingerbread is both a descendant and a variation of those kinds of cakes, most of which are more biscuit-like. This type of gingerbread is about 3.75cm thick after baking, and it certainly qualifies a little bit more as a cake than a bread due to its sweetness. You can masquerade it as a dessert by serving some whipped cream with it or you can serve it with butter for breakfast or brunch.

1   Set a rack in the centre of the oven and preheat to 180°C/gas mark 4.

2   Stir the flour and spices together in a large bowl.

3   Melt the butter in a medium saucepan over a low heat, then (still on low heat) stir in the brown sugar, treacle and most of the water, leaving a couple of tablespoons in the measuring cup. Stir together to combine and increase the heat to medium. Bring to the simmer, stirring occasionally.

4   Stir the bicarbonate of soda into the remaining water. Remove the butter mixture from the heat and pour the bicarbonate of soda mixture into it.

5   Add the liquids to the bowl of dry ingredients and use a large rubber spatula to quickly fold everything together.

6   Scrape the batter into the prepared tin and smooth the top.

7   Bake the gingerbread until it is well risen and feels firm in the centre and the point of a paring knife inserted in the centre emerges clean, 25–30 minutes.

8   Cool in the pan on a rack for 5 minutes, then loosen the gingerbread from the side of the tin with a small paring knife if necessary, and invert it to another rack. Peel off the paper and replace it with a rack, then invert the stack and remove the top rack. Cool completely before serving.

Serving: Serve gingerbread for breakfast, brunch or tea.

Storage: This is a good keeper well wrapped at room temperature.

all-purpose muffins

I love a recipe like this one, that can be varied in infinite ways. Here the basic muffin batter can be altered to make a dozen different types of easy-to-prepare muffins. Thanks to my dear friend Cara Tannenbaum for sharing her recipe. The recipe that follows is the basis for making muffins with the flavourings and other enhancements listed in the variations below it; this recipe is not meant to be made as is.

Makes 12 standard-size muffins

260g plain flour

110g sugar

1 tablespoon baking powder

1/4 teaspoon salt

110g unsalted butter, melted and slightly cooled

1 medium egg

240ml full fat milk

Other ingredients as per the variations below

One 12-hole standard-size muffin tin with paper liners

1 Set a rack in the centre of the oven and preheat to 190°C/gas mark 5.

2 In a medium bowl, mix the flour, sugar, baking powder and salt and set aside.

3 Pour the butter into a mixing bowl (scrape out the butter pan with a rubber spatula) and thoroughly whisk in the egg; whisk in the milk.

4 Whisk about one third of the flour mixture into the liquid until the liquid is absorbed. Whisk in another third, again until the liquid is absorbed. Use a rubber spatula to fold in the last of the flour mixture.

5 Gently fold in any solid enhancements to the batter and distribute the batter into the muffin pan.

6 Bake the muffins until they are well risen and golden and the point of a paring knife inserted in the centre of one muffin emerges dry, about 20 minutes.

7 Cool the muffins in the tin on a rack and lift them out only after they have cooled completely.

Serving: This style of sweet, cake-like muffin needs no accompaniments.

Storage: Wrap the muffins individually in clingfilm and freeze after the day they're baked. Defrost and bring to room temperature before serving.

variations

Blueberry Muffins: Add 1 teaspoon grated lemon zest to the liquids. After mixing the batter, fold in 200g rinsed, dried, and picked-over blueberries. Sprinkle the tops of the muffins with 2 tablespoons sugar mixed with 1/4 teaspoon ground cinnamon right before baking.

Lemon Poppy Seed Muffins: Add 2 tablespoons poppy seeds to the flour mixture, and add 1 tablespoon of finely grated lemon zest to the liquids.

Apple Raisin Muffins: Pare 225g Golden Delicious apples and grate them on the largest holes of a box grater. Turn the shreds into a sieve and place the sieve over a bowl to drain. Press clingfilm against the surface of the apple so that it doesn't darken too much. Add 1/2 teaspoon ground cinnamon to the dry ingredients. After mixing the batter, fold in the grated apple along with 120g raisins. Sprinkle the tops of the muffins before baking with cinnamon sugar as in Blueberry Muffins, above.

Chocolate Chip Muffins: Add 2 teaspoons vanilla extract to the liquids. After mixing the batter, fold in one 170g milk or dark chocolate chips. Sprinkle the tops of the muffins before baking with 2 tablespoons unflavoured sugar.

Old-Fashioned Jam Muffins: Add 2 teaspoons vanilla extract and 2 teaspoons finely grated lemon zest to the liquids. Half fill the holes in the muffin tins and drop 1 teaspoon of your favourite jam in the centre of the batter. Add the rest of the batter, being careful to cover the jam completely.

18
biscuit bars & brownies

If you ever have to make a lot of biscuits in a hurry, turn to biscuit bars, a slab of baked biscuit dough, often with a topping or filling, that's easy to cut into squares – and even very small squares if you really need to stretch the quantity. Biscuit bars are great for rounding out the festive biscuit assortment, too: You can wrap and freeze the whole slab and then cut them after they're defrosted. Brownies are the quintessential biscuit bar – a square of moist, fudgy indulgence that has you wondering by the time you're halfway through one whether you're eating a biscuit bar or a chocolate bar. Some people like cakey brownies: I consider them totally inedible; a brownie is all about chocolate and richness, and that's good enough for me.

A   B   C   D   E

golden almond bars

I know I say it about far too many recipes, but these are a real favourite. In fact, I seldom bake them much in advance of serving them because I can't be trusted around them – they are that addictively good. This is loosely based on a recipe shared by my old friend Jayne Sutton, who's been attending my classes for over thirty years. Light toasting brings out the flavour in almonds. Just be careful to toast them very lightly; they'll be in the oven again and will continue to toast then.

Makes 24 square biscuits

1 batch Sweet Pastry Dough (page 14), chilled

ALMOND TOPPING

140g unsalted butter

70g granulated sugar

70g light brown sugar

3 tablespoons golden syrup

⅛ teaspoon salt

60ml whipping cream

390g slivered almonds, lightly toasted

One 23 x 33 x 5cm tin lined with buttered baking paper

variations

Pecan pieces, crushed skinned hazelnuts or coarsely chopped honey-roasted peanuts are all wonderful in place of the almonds. I once made a batch of these bars with odds and ends of nuts I had in the freezer and they were delicious. Whatever type of nut or combination you choose, just make sure they are in 5mm–1cm pieces or they won't cover the dough evenly enough.

1   Place the dough on a floured surface and gently knead it until it is pliable and slightly softened. Form the dough into a rectangle and flour the work surface and the dough again. Roll the dough, occasionally adding pinches of flour under and on it, to a 30 x 40cm rectangle. Gently fold the dough into quarters and line up the folded corner with the centre of the tin. Unfold the dough into the tin and gently ease it down into the tin. Use your fingertips to make sure that the dough moulds to the angle between the base and side of the tin and into the corners. Trim away all but about 3.75cm of dough on the sides of the tin. Chill.

2   For the topping, melt the butter in a large saucepan over a medium heat. Stir in the sugar, brown sugar and golden syrup one at a time, stirring to combine between additions. Add the salt and bring the mixture to the full boil, stirring occasionally. At the boil, add the cream a little at a time (the mixture will bubble up). Continue cooking for 1 minute, stirring frequently. Most of the water in the cream should evaporate. Stir in the almonds and scrape the mixture into a buttered bowl to cool slightly.

3   Set a rack in the lower third of the oven; preheat to 180°C/gas mark 4.

4   Use a large kitchen spoon to deposit mounds of the topping all over the chilled crust. Then use the point of a spoon to join the mounds and make a fairly even layer of topping. Concentrate on distributing the almonds evenly; the syrupy part of the topping will come to a boil while the bars are baking and even itself out.

5   Bake until the dough is baked through and the topping is gently bubbling, 25–35 minutes.

6   Cool on a rack for at least 1 hour.

7   To unmould and cut the bars, cover the tin with another rack and invert (A). Lift off the tin and peel away the paper (B). Place a chopping board on the back of the bars and invert the whole stack (C). Lift off the top rack. Neatly trim away the sides of the bars (D) and use a ruler to mark (E), then cut into 5cm squares.

essential tips for biscuit bars & brownies

Pastry-Based Bars

- I like to use a 23 x 33 x 5cm tin for biscuit bars. If you want to double any of the recipes in this chapter you can use a 28 x 43 x 2.5cm tin, or a standard commercial 30 x 40 x 2.5cm half-sheet tin.

- Here's a quick way to line a deep tin with aluminium foil that I learned from Maida Heatter: Tear off a sheet of foil that's equal to the base of the tin plus the sides and mould it over the back of the tin. Invert the tin. The foil, which now has sharp corners, will press into place.

- Always line part of the tin's side to keep toppings from sticking to it or running under the crust.

- Chill bars with a topping before cutting to minimise breakage.

- Always use a really sharp knife and a ruler for cutting; nothing looks worse than a plate of biscuit bars that are different sizes.

Brownies and Cakey Bars

- These are best left uncut until shortly before serving because the exposed sides dry out easily. For advance preparation, cut the whole baked slab in half, wrap in clingfilm and freeze until needed (the stacked halves take up less room and are less likely to break). Defrost and cut while still cold.

- Dust unglazed bars and brownies with a little icing sugar before serving.

lemon crumb bars

This is possibly the most popular non-brownie biscuit bar ever. I wanted to experiment with adding a crumb topping to the tart lemon filling and I love the result, but it does add some extra work. Feel free to omit the crumbs if you're pressed for time.

Makes 24 squares

1 batch Sweet Pastry Dough (page 14), chilled

CRUMB TOPPING

165g plain flour

110g sugar

1 teaspoon baking powder

Pinch of salt

110g unsalted butter, melted

LEMON TOPPING

3 medium eggs

1 tablespoon finely grated lemon zest

60ml fresh lemon juice, strained before measuring

280g sugar

One 23 x 33 x 5cm tin lined with buttered foil for the bars and one swiss roll tin lined with baking paper or foil for baking the crumb topping

1   Set racks in the upper and lower thirds of the oven and preheat to 180°C/gas mark 4.

2   Line the tin with the dough as in the recipe for Golden Almond Bars on page 194. Trim away all but 1cm of the dough on the sides of the tin. Chill the crust while preparing the crumb topping.

3   For the topping, in a medium mixing bowl stir together the flour, sugar, baking powder and salt. Use a rubber spatula to stir in the butter. Let the mixture stand for a few minutes, then use your fingertips to break the mixture into 5mm–1cm crumbs. Scatter the crumbs on the prepared tin.

4   Press a rectangular sheet of baking paper into the crust and weigh down with dried beans. (See page 29 for more on blind baking a crust.)

5   Bake the crust in the lower third of the oven and the crumb topping in the upper third. After 10 minutes, remove the paper and beans from the crust and place it on the upper rack and the crumbs on the lower one.

6   Continue baking the crust until it is dry and light golden, about another 5 minutes. Bake the crumb topping until it is deep golden and firm, 10–15 minutes more.

7   Cool the crust and the topping on racks. If the crumbs have grown together during baking, let them cool completely and then use a dough scraper or table knife to coarsely chop them.

8   Reset the rack to the centre of the oven.

9   For the lemon topping, whisk the eggs and lemon zest in a mixing bowl. In a small bowl stir the lemon juice and sugar together to dissolve the sugar as much as possible. Add the juice mixture to the egg mixture and use a rubber spatula to gently stir them together.

10 Pour the lemon topping into the crust and bake until the topping is set, 15–20 minutes.

11 Remove the tin from the oven and scatter over the crumb topping. Bake for another 5 minutes.

12 Cool the bars on a rack in the tin for 15 minutes. If you have someone to help you do this, each lift 2 corners of the foil on the wide ends of the tin and quickly transfer the bars to a chopping board; let them cool completely. Then use a ruler to mark and cut the bars into 5cm squares. If you're on your own, let the bars cool completely in the tin and mark and cut them there, then lift them out with a wide palette knife.

Serving: Arrange the bars on a serving plate to serve; these aren't good to stack up because of the soft lemon filling.

Storage: Store in a tin or plastic container with a tight-fitting lid. They don't need to be refrigerated because the acidity of the lemon juice prevents the eggs from spoiling.

lemon ginger bars

Makes 24 bars—see page 198 for photo

GINGER BARS

325g plain flour

170g sugar

2 tablespoons ground ginger

2 teaspoons baking powder

225g unsalted butter

1 medium egg, lightly beaten

4 tablespoons finely chopped crystallised ginger

2 tablespoons honey

2 teaspoons finely grated lemon zest

LEMON GLAZE

225g icing sugar, sifted after measuring

3 tablespoons lemon juice, strained before measuring

One 23 x 33 x 5cm tin lined with buttered foil

These are about as gingery as you can get, so consider yourself forewarned if you're not a ginger lover. Actually these bar cookies make a lot of converts to the pleasures of ginger, because they have a strong ginger flavour but since they're made with ground ginger and crystallised ginger, they have little of the burning spiciness that fresh ginger can impart. Lemon zest in the bars and lemon juice in the glaze add a note of contrast.

1 Set a rack in the centre of the oven and preheat to 190°C/gas mark 5.

2 Mix the flour, sugar, ground ginger and baking powder in a medium bowl.

3 Melt the butter over a medium heat and immediately add to the dry ingredients; use a large rubber spatula to stir to a smooth, shiny dough. Add the egg, crystallised ginger, honey and lemon zest and beat vigorously to make a smooth dough.

4 Scrape the dough into the prepared tin and use the palm of your hand to press it evenly over the bottom of the tin. Don't be concerned if the dough looks greasy, as though some of the butter has separated out.

5 Bake the bars until well risen, firm and lightly golden, 20–25 minutes.

6 While the bars are baking, use a small rubber spatula to beat the icing sugar and lemon juice together. If it's too thick to spread, thin by adding 1/2 teaspoon water at a time until it's right.

7 As soon as the bars are baked, place a chopping board on the tin and use oven mitts to invert the hot bars to the board. Remove the tin and foil. Immediately use a small palette knife to spread the lemon glaze on the bars so that it sets as the bars cool.

8 Use a ruler to mark, then cut into 5mm squares.

Serving: Arrange the bars on a serving plate; the icing is dry, so they can be stacked.

Storage: Keep the bars in a tin or plastic container with a tight-fitting lid between sheets of baking paper.

florida brownies

This is my take on a famous Maida Heatter recipe called Palm Beach Brownies. Once when we taught a class together Maida added a layer of miniature chocolate mint patties between two halves of this batter. I cringed when I saw her do it, but I have to admit they were delicious.

Makes 24 square brownies

225g unsalted butter

225g premium unsweetened chocolate, cut into 5mm pieces

5 medium eggs, at room temperature

1 tablespoon vanilla extract

¼ teaspoon salt

850g sugar

215g plain flour

One 23 x 33 x 5cm tin lined with buttered foil

1 Set a rack in the centre of the oven and preheat to 190°C/gas mark 5.

2 Melt the butter in a medium saucepan over a medium heat. Let the butter get hot and start to sizzle after it's melted. Remove the pan from the heat and add the chocolate all at once. Gently shake the pan to submerge all the chocolate in the butter. Set aside.

3 Combine the eggs, vanilla and salt in the bowl of an electric mixer fitted with the whisk attachment. First whisk by hand to mix. Whisk in the sugar by hand.

4 Whisk on medium-high speed for 10 minutes, until very light.

5 Whisk the butter and chocolate smooth and scrape into the mixer bowl. Whisk on lowest speed just until smooth, then stop the mixer.

6 Sift the flour onto a piece of paper, bend the paper, and slide the flour into the bowl. Mix again on lowest speed until the flour is absorbed – no longer.

7 Remove the bowl from the mixer and use a large rubber spatula to give a final mixing to the batter.

8 Scrape the batter into the prepared tin and smooth the top.

9 Bake the brownies until they are firm but not dry and the point of a paring knife inserted in the centre of the tin emerges with moist crumbs clinging to it, about 35 minutes.

10 Cool in the tin on a rack. Unmould the brownies to a chopping board and remove the tin and paper. Cover with another board and invert the whole stack. Remove the top board and wrap the brownies on their board in a double thickness of clingfilm. Keep the brownies at a cool room temperature or in the refrigerator overnight before cutting. Use a ruler to mark, then cut the brownies into 5cm squares.

Serving: Pile the brownies on a serving plate to serve.

Storage: If you don't intend to serve all the brownies at once, only cut what you need; the whole slab will keep better wrapped in the refrigerator. Individual brownies tend to dry out quickly if they're not wrapped in clingfilm.

truffle brownies

These are so named because they're almost as rich as chocolate truffles. They are best cut the day after being baked so they have time to firm up.

Makes 24 square brownies—see photo opposite

225g unsalted butter

280g dark chocolate (65–70% cocoa solids), cut into 5mm pieces

450g light brown sugar

130g plain flour

¼ teaspoon salt

4 medium eggs

2 teaspoons vanilla extract

One 23 x 33 x 5cm tin lined with buttered baking paper or foil

1 Set a rack in the centre of the oven; preheat to 180°C/gas mark 4.

2 Melt the butter in a medium saucepan over a medium heat. Let the butter get hot and start to sizzle after it's melted. Add the chocolate all at once and gently shake the pan to submerge all the chocolate in the butter. Set aside.

3 Combine the brown sugar, flour and salt in the bowl of an electric mixer fitted with the paddle. Beat with the paddle on lowest speed until evenly mixed together.

4 Add 2 eggs to the mixer and continue to beat just until they are absorbed. Stop and scrape the bowl and beater. Repeat with the remaining 2 eggs.

5 Remove the bowl from the mixer and stir in the vanilla.

6 Whisk the butter and chocolate smooth and scrape it into the bowl. Use a large rubber spatula to mix it in thoroughly.

7 Scrape the batter into the prepared tin and smooth the top.

8 Bake the brownies until they are firm, but not dry and the point of a paring knife inserted in the centre of the tin emerges with moist crumbs clinging to it, about 30 minutes.

9 Cool in the tin on a rack. Invert the brownies to a chopping board and remove the tin and paper. Cover with another board and invert the whole stack. Remove the top board and wrap the brownies on their board in a double thickness of clingfilm. Keep the brownies at a cool room temperature or in the refrigerator overnight before cutting.

10 Use a ruler to mark, then cut the brownies into 5cm squares.

variations

Walnut Crunch Brownies: Place 140g coarsely chopped walnut pieces in a bowl. Whisk an egg white until it's just beginning to foam and add 2 teaspoons to the bowl. Rub the walnuts between the palms of your hands to coat them all over with the egg white. Use a large rubber spatula to toss the moistened walnuts with 70g sugar. Scatter the walnut crunch on top of the brownie batter before baking. Gently press the walnuts in with the palm of your hand. Bake, cool and cut.

Walnut or Pecan Brownies: Fold 225g coarsely chopped walnut or pecan pieces into the batter right before scraping it into the tin.

piped & drop biscuits

Drop biscuits are among the simplest to prepare. As their name implies, you just drop the dough from a spoon onto a tin and you're finished shaping. Piped biscuits take the method a small step further and drop the dough onto the tin through a plain or decorative tip fitted in a pastry bag. Piping biscuits isn't difficult, but like any new technique, it takes a bit of practise to master. Besides the information and photos here, we have a video about piping on my website, www.nickmalgieri.com, so you can easily see the steps and motions involved.

butter rosettes

Makes about 30–40 biscuits, depending on the size you pipe them

225g unsalted butter, very soft

70g sugar

2 teaspoons vanilla extract

1 medium egg

295g plain flour

2 baking sheets or swiss roll tins lined with baking paper or foil

These are fragile and buttery and easy to pipe because the dough is rather firm. The dough is also fine for putting through a biscuit press if you have one. These biscuits don't need to be finished off with anything before or after baking, but there are a few suggestions after the recipe if you're so inclined.

1　Set racks in the upper and lower thirds of the oven and preheat to 180°C/gas mark 4.

2　Combine the butter, sugar and vanilla extract in the bowl of an electric mixer fitted with the paddle attachment. Beat on medium speed until just combined.

3　Stop the mixer, add the egg and scrape down the bowl and beater. Beat again on medium speed until smooth.

4　Stop and scrape again, then beat in the flour on the lowest speed. Remove the bowl from the mixer and use a large rubber spatula to give a final mixing to the dough.

5　Pipe the dough (full instructions at right) onto the prepared tins using a 1.25cm star tip (Ateco size 4), leaving about 2.5cm between the biscuits in all directions.

6　Bake the biscuits until they are light golden, 10–12 minutes. The best test for doneness is to turn one of the biscuits upside down: If it's light golden on the bottom too, they're ready. Since the baking time is so short, it's not necessary to change racks midway through baking, but stack 2 tins together for the bottom rack if you know your oven gives strong bottom heat to prevent the biscuits from burning.

Storage: Keep the biscuits between sheets of baking paper in a tin or plastic container with a tight-fitting lid. These last well for a week or so, after which the buttery flavour starts to go stale. Freeze for longer storage.

variations

Very lightly dust the outside of the biscuits with cocoa powder before baking.

Sprinkle the tops of the biscuits with some crushed sliced almonds or plain or multicoloured chocolate sprinkles (hundreds and thousands).

Place a chocolate chip flat side up or a quarter of a glacé cherry in the centre of each.

Use a floured fingertip to make a small indentation in the centre of each biscuit, bake and cool. Carefully spoon in some strained reduced raspberry or apricot conserve (see page 118) after the biscuits have cooled.

piping biscuits

1   Piped biscuits are formed using a pastry bag with a metal tip. Fold back the cuff of the bag and spoon a third of the dough into the bag (A). It can be useful to place the bag in a jar or glass to hold it steady. Twist the bag above the dough to force the dough down toward the tip. You want the dough to be a single smooth mass so that it will pipe neatly.

2   Hold the bag directly behind the dough with the hand you use to write. Press your other index finger against the side of the bag to steady and guide it. Use your writing hand to squeeze the bag and force the dough through the tip.

3   For most shapes, you will be holding the tip perpendicular to the surface and about 2.5cm above it. To pipe a rosette, start with the tube only about 5mm above the tin and at a 60 degree angle. Begin squeezing, and when the dough touches the tin, keep the pressure steady and curl around to the left as if writing a cursive letter C (B). Once you've completed the movement, stop squeezing and pull away parallel to the tin instead of lifting the bag straight up, which would leave a point.

4   If using a nylon or cloth bag, wash it immediately in hot soapy water when you are finished. Pastry bags can also be cleaned in the top rack of a dishwasher or in a washing machine with other kitchen laundry.

A

B

chocolate meringue 's' biscuits

Makes about 40–50 biscuits, depending on the size you pipe them

4 medium egg whites

Pinch of salt

280g sugar

140g dark chocolate (70–75% cocoa solids), melted and slightly cooled

2 baking sheets or swiss roll tins lined with baking paper

Storage: Keep the biscuits between sheets of baking paper in a tin or plastic container with a tight-fitting lid. They last indefinitely, but will only be moist inside on the day they're baked.

These are a mainstay of almost every pastry shop in Switzerland. They are a sweet biscuit, as anything meringue-based tends to be. In the past I always used unsweetened chocolate to make them, but I once accidentally substituted some premium dark chocolate and the biscuits were already in the oven before I realized my mistake. Though still sweet (the sugar in the chocolate didn't really make them appreciably sweeter), they had a much more complex flavour because of the superior quality of the chocolate. An 'S' shape is traditional for these, but of course you may pipe them in any shape you wish.

1 Half-fill a saucepan on which your mixer bowl will fit without having more than 5cm inside the pan, with water. Bring the water to the boil over a low heat.

2 Place the egg whites in the bowl of an electric mixer and whisk by hand to break them up. Whisk in the salt and sugar.

3 Set the bowl over the pan of water so only a small part of the base is submerged and whisk gently to keep the mixture moving so that it doesn't set on the bottom; whisking too vigorously can tighten the mixture and prevent the sugar from melting. Continue whisking until the egg whites are hot (54°C) and the sugar has dissolved. Lift the whisk and let a little of the mixture run over a fingertip to test the temperature and smoothness. While heating the mixture, occasionally scrape the side of the bowl with a rubber spatula to keep sugar from accumulating there.

4 Place the bowl on the mixer and whisk with the whisk attachment on medium-high speed until the meringue is very increased in volume and looks like marshmallow, about 3 minutes. Stop whisking when the side of the bowl feels just slightly warm.

5 Use a large rubber spatula to fold the chocolate into the meringue. Be careful not to fold so much that the meringue liquefies from contact with the fat in the chocolate. If there are a few streaks of white remaining, ignore them.

6 Half-fill a pastry bag fitted with a 1.25cm star tip (Ateco size 4) and pipe the meringue onto the tins in 'S' shapes: hold the bag almost perpendicular to the tin and inclined slightly towards you with the end of the tube close to the tin. Start to squeeze out an 'S' shape; when you come to the end, pull away parallel to the tin, not straight upward, to avoid leaving a point.

7 After piping the biscuits, let them dry at room temperature for a couple of hours so they retain their shape better and they form the characteristic 'foot' at the bottom (see the photograph on page 205).

8 About 20 minutes before you're ready to bake the biscuits, set racks in the upper and lower thirds of the oven and preheat to 180°C/gas mark 4.

9 Bake the biscuits until they are matt looking but still a little moist within (press one with a fingertip), 8–10 minutes. Cool on the tins on racks.

french lemon discs

Makes about 35–40 biscuits

BISCUIT BATTER

110g unsalted butter, softened

110g sugar

2 teaspoons finely grated lemon zest

1 teaspoon vanilla extract or ¼ teaspoon seeds scraped from a split vanilla pod

2 medium eggs, at room temperature

130g plain flour

1 batch Lemon Glaze (page 197)

2 baking sheets or swiss roll tins lined with baking paper or foil

The French name for these biscuits, *palets des dames*, is one I've always translated as 'ladies' discs', not really knowing what the name referred to. After close to forty years of making these biscuits, I decided to look up *palet* in a dictionary; I found that it refers to a discus, the flat round object thrown by an athlete. Does the French name mean that ladies throw biscuits as a competitive sport? In any case, these are much better when inserted into the mouth than when thrown at a target. Dried currants are often added to the batter (they distort the shape of the baked biscuits) or three are arranged in a little triangle atop each biscuit. If you want to add currants in or on, go ahead; you'll need about 100g for the batch below. If the currants are in the dough, you'll have to spoon it onto the tin neatly rather than pipe it because the currants will clog the tip.

1. Set racks in the upper and lower thirds of the oven and preheat to 180°C/gas mark 4.

2. Combine the butter, sugar, lemon zest and vanilla in the bowl of an electric mixer fitted with the paddle attachment. Beat on medium speed until lightened, 3–4 minutes.

3. Add the eggs, one at a time, beating smooth between additions.

4. Scrape down the bowl and beater and beat for a further 30 seconds. Scrape again and add the flour.

5. Restart the mixer on the lowest speed and mix only until the flour is absorbed.

6. Use a large rubber spatula to give a final mixing to the batter. (Add the currants, if using.)

7. Use a pastry bag fitted with a 1.25cm plain tip (Ateco size 6) to pipe the batter in 2cm mounds, keeping them about 5cm apart all around to allow for spreading.

8. Bake the biscuits until they have spread and are golden and firm, about 12 minutes. If your oven gives strong bottom heat, bake the biscuits on the lower rack stacked on a second tin for insulation.

9. While the biscuits are baking, make the glaze if you haven't already.

10. Immediately after taking the biscuits out of the oven, set the tins on racks and brush the glaze over the hot biscuits so that it sets as they cool. Let the biscuits cool completely.

Serving: These are very good with tea or with a custard dessert.

Storage: Keep the cooled biscuits between sheets of baking paper in a tin or plastic container with a tight-fitting lid.

the original chocolate chip cookie

Makes about 40 cookies

295g plain flour

1 teaspoon bicarbonate of soda

1 teaspoon salt

225g unsalted butter, slightly softened (see Note)

170g granulated sugar

170g light brown sugar

1 teaspoon vanilla extract

2 medium eggs, at room temperature

225g coarsely chopped walnut pieces

340g dark chocolate chips

3 baking sheets or swiss roll tins lined with baking paper or foil

Note: If the butter is too soft, the cookies will spread too flat.

Chocolate chip cookies were first made by a New England dietitian, Ruth Wakefield, some time in the late 1920s. Wakefield and her husband were the proprietors of an inn that had originally been a way station between Boston and New Bedford, and that's how both the inn and the cookies came to bear the Toll House name. The story goes that Wakefield added cut-up chunks of chocolate to a brown sugar-based cookie dough, expecting the chocolate to melt into the dough resulting in a chocolate cookie. The rest is history. This is the recipe from Ruth Wakefield's book with two differences: The bicarbonate of soda is added to the flour and not dissolved in water (as it makes absolutely no difference), and chips are now ready-made, so you don't have to cut up bars of chocolate unless you want to. Chocolate chip cookies are like fried eggs: everyone has a preferred version. Ruth Wakefield's cookies are fairly thin and crisp; if you like them chewy, bake a couple first as a test. Take them out when they're still soft and slide the paper off the tin to cool them. If they're as chewy as you like, bake the rest for the same amount of time. Chilling the dough first will also help. If you want thicker cookies, add another 45g flour. Increase the chips, leave out the walnuts, add raisins, or do anything you like as it won't affect the texture. Finally, don't overmix. Beating air into this cookie will make it rise to great heights, then fall into a wrinkled wafer, not unlike a gingersnap.

1 Set racks in the upper and lower thirds of the oven and preheat to 190°C/gas mark 5.

2 Stir the flour together with the bicarbonate of soda and salt; set aside.

3 Combine the butter, granulated sugar, brown sugar and vanilla in the bowl of an electric mixer fitted with the paddle attachment. Beat on medium speed until just combined. Add the eggs, one at a time, beating smooth between additions.

4 Stop and scrape the bowl and beater and start the mixer again on the lowest speed. Beat in the flour mixture. Once absorbed, beat in the walnuts and chocolate chips.

5 Use a large rubber spatula to give a final mixing to the batter and drop it by tablespoons onto the prepared tins, keeping the mounds of dough about 7.5cm apart in all directions.

6 Bake the cookies until they are deep golden all over, 12–14 minutes. Cool the cookies on the tins on racks.

Storage: Keep the cooled cookies between sheets of baking paper in a tin or a plastic container with a tight-fitting lid.

A   B

almond lace biscuits

Makes about 30 biscuits

55g unsalted butter, very soft

110g sugar

1 teaspoon vanilla extract

⅛ teaspoon salt

1 medium egg

3 tablespoons plain flour

45g ground blanched almonds

3 baking sheets or swiss roll tins, buttered with soft butter

Fragile and delicate in the extreme, these biscuits are a labour of love to make because you need to bake them one tin at a time on the centre rack of the oven. If you have a double oven, start to bake another tin a couple of minutes before the first tin is ready to come out. These spread best on a bare buttered tin; brush the tins with very soft but not melted butter. If you don't mind biscuits that are a little thicker, you may use silicone mats to bake them.

1 Set a rack in the centre of the oven and preheat to 180°C.

2 In a small mixing bowl use a medium rubber spatula to stir together the butter, sugar, vanilla and salt. Add the egg and beat until smooth.

3 Add the flour and almonds and stir smooth.

4 To save time, deposit all the batter on the tins straight away. Drop level measuring teaspoons of the batter onto the tins at least 7.5cm apart in all directions (A). Put 10–12 mounds of batter on each tin.

5 Bake one tin of biscuits until they have spread, come to a simmer on the tin and are deep golden in colour, 5–7 minutes.

6 Remove the tin from the oven and immediately place another tin in to bake.

7 Let the biscuits cool for about 20 seconds, then slide a wide thin-bladed palette knife under the edge of the biscuit closest to you and gently work the knife back and forth to pry the biscuit off the tin and move it to a parchment covered tin or wire rack to cool (B). Repeat with remaining biscuits. Don't get nervous, but you have to do this quickly while the biscuits are still warm or they'll shatter when you try to lift them from the tin.

Serving: Plan on serving the biscuits the day you bake them; they are too fragile to try to store. These are perfect to accompany any elegant mousse or custard dessert, or serve them with after-dinner coffee.

peanut drops

Makes about 40 biscuits

130g plain flour

1 teaspoon baking powder

¼ teaspoon salt

140g unsalted butter, softened

70g granulated sugar

70g light brown sugar

1 teaspoon vanilla extract

1 medium egg, at room temperature

110g honey-roasted peanuts, coarsely chopped, plus more for sprinkling

2 baking sheets or swiss roll tins lined with baking paper or foil

Honey-roasted peanuts are the secret to the intense flavour of this biscuit. Ordinary peanuts just don't do the trick. These are addictively good, though sometimes I'm not sure whether they're really a confection or a biscuit. It's always best to purchase a fresh supply of peanuts if you want to prepare these. Unless you store your honey-roasted peanuts in the freezer, they become stale-tasting pretty quickly and would ruin the delicate sweetness of these biscuits.

1   Set racks in the upper and lower thirds of the oven and preheat to 190°/gas mark 5.

2   Mix the flour with the baking powder and salt and set aside.

3   Combine the butter, sugars and vanilla in the bowl of an electric mixer fitted with the paddle attachment. Beat on medium speed until soft and light, 3–4 minutes.

4   Beat in the egg and continue beating until smooth.

5   Stop the mixer and scrape down the bowl and beater. Beat on the lowest speed and add the flour about one third at a time, beating to incorporate between additions, followed by the chopped peanuts.

6   Use a large rubber spatula to give a final mixing to the batter. Set a small bowl of water near your work surface.

7   Drop the batter by heaping teaspoons onto the prepared tins, keeping them 5–7.5cm apart in all directions. After all the batter is on the tins, moisten your fingertips and flatten the biscuits slightly. Sprinkle the tops with more chopped peanuts.

8   Bake the biscuits until they have spread and are deep golden, 12–15 minutes. Slide the biscuits on the papers from the tins to racks to cool the biscuits.

Storage: Keep the biscuits between sheets of baking paper in a tin or plastic container with a tight-fitting lid.

variation

Melt 110g milk chocolate, let it cool, and then sandwich the biscuits bottom to bottom with it.

20
rolled &
sandwich
biscuits

Nothing can make you look more like an accomplished baker than a beautiful – and symmetrical – assortment of rolled biscuits. The little cutter does all the work and we get to take all the credit. Rolling is even easy, once you know the essential secret of rolling out soft doughs: rolling small pieces of dough at a time so it never gets a chance to soften too much before you've got those perfectly shaped biscuits safely on your baking tin. Sandwich biscuits are the biscuit lover's dream – the politest way to eat two biscuits at the same time without appearing greedy (well, not too greedy).

A

B

C

crisp brown sugar wafers

All good biscuits are addictive, but these are particularly dangerous. As if their shatteringly crisp texture weren't enough, their buttery flavour is accentuated and deepened by brown sugar. Unlike most cut out biscuits, these spread quite a bit while they're baking.

Makes about 40 biscuits

295g plain flour

½ teaspoon bicarbonate of soda

¼ teaspoon salt

170g unsalted butter, softened

340g light brown sugar

2 teaspoons vanilla extract

1 medium egg

1 medum egg yolk

2–3 baking sheets or swiss roll tins lined with baking paper or foil

1   Stir the flour, bicarbonate of soda and salt together and set aside.

2   Beat the butter, brown sugar and vanilla with the paddle attachment of an electric mixer on medium speed until well mixed, about 1 minute. Beat in the egg and yolk one at a time, beating smooth between additions. Scrape the bowl and beater and beat again for 30 seconds.

3   Stop the mixer, add the flour mixture and beat on the lowest speed to incorporate. Remove the bowl and use a large rubber spatula to give a final mixing to the dough.

4   Scrape the dough onto a large piece of clingfilm, fold the clingfilm over it and press the dough to about 1cm thick. Refrigerate until ready for baking, up to 2 days.

5   When you are ready to bake the biscuits, set racks in the upper and lower thirds of the oven and preheat to 180°C.

6   Remove the dough from the refrigerator and cut it into quarters. Return three of the pieces to the refrigerator. Place the single piece of dough on a floured work surface and use a rolling pin to press the dough firmly in close parallel strokes (A) until it is slightly softened and pliable.

7   Flour the dough again and gently roll it out to 5mm thick (B). Use a 5–6.25cm round cutter to cut biscuits, placing them on one of the prepared tins about 7.5cm apart in all directions to allow for spreading (C).

8   Repeat with the next piece of dough, incorporating the scraps from the previous piece as you knead it. Continue cutting out biscuits and repeat adding the scraps with the remaining pieces of dough. When you have nothing but scraps left to roll, form the dough into a sausage shape and roll it to a rectangle as wide as the cutter you are using. Cut out more biscuits and discard the last few scraps.

9   Bake the biscuits until they are firm and dry looking, 12–15 minutes. If your oven gives strong bottom heat, bake the tin of biscuits on the lower rack stacked on another tin for insulation.

10 Slide the biscuits on the papers from the tins to racks to cool.

Storage: Keep the biscuits between sheets of parchment paper in a tin or plastic container with a tight-fitting lid.

Variations: Add 85g blanched almonds, pecans, or honey-roasted peanuts, chopped into 5mm pieces to the dough along with the flour.

essential tips for rolled & sandwich biscuits

Rolled Biscuits

- Always chill the dough until it's firm. Flattening it to a thin sheet on a piece of clingfilm before refrigerating it will make it chill more quickly.

- Roll about a third or a quarter of the dough at a time and leave the rest refrigerated; if the dough softens back to its original consistency you won't be able to roll or cut it.

- Before rolling the dough, squeeze and knead it a few times until it has a clay-like consistency but is still cool. If you try to roll the chilled dough directly from the refrigerator it will just break apart.

- Flour under and on the dough with pinches of flour, not handfuls. You can add as many pinches of flour as you like without toughening the dough.

- Roll with gentle pressure; even the chilled dough is relatively soft and it lacks the elasticity of a flaky or puff pastry dough.

- Flour the cutter between cuts and always cut straight down without twisting the cutter.

- Use a wide spatula like a pancake turner to lift the biscuits off the work surface and transfer them to the tin.

Sandwich Biscuits

- Look over the baked biscuits and choose the best-looking ones to be the upper biscuit of the sandwiches.

- Invert the others so that the smooth bottom of the biscuit is upward and apply the glaze or filling to them.

- If you want to use jam for filling biscuits, bring it to the boil and let it reduce to evaporate excess moisture for a couple of minutes or it will soften the biscuits.

- Don't overdo the filling or the biscuits will turn into a mess. For most biscuits, 1/2 teaspoon of filling is the perfect amount.

- When putting the top biscuit in place, press gently to make the filling spread to the edge of the bottom biscuit.

A

B

C

swiss
bull's eyes

The Swiss name for these biscuits is *Ochsenaeugli*, or 'oxen's eyes'. This dough has no eggs in it – it's just a flour-sugar-butter dough that's very fragile after baking. The traditional filling is apricot jam, but use any flavor you like, or even some apricot or prune Danish filling (see page 119). Thanks to my friend Thea Cvijanovich from Berne for this typically Swiss recipe.

Makes about 24 sandwich biscuits

BISCUIT DOUGH

225g unsalted butter, softened

110g icing sugar, sifted after measuring

Large pinch of salt

2 teaspoons vanilla extract

350g plain flour

FINISHING

365g apricot jam

Icing sugar for sprinkling

2 baking sheets or swiss roll tins lined with baking paper or foil

1 Beat the butter, icing sugar, salt and vanilla with the paddle attachment of an electric mixer on medium speed until well mixed, about 1 minute. Stop the mixer, add the flour, and beat on the lowest speed. Remove the bowl and use a large rubber spatula to give a final mixing to the dough.

2 Scrape the dough onto a large piece of clingfilm, fold the clingfilm over it and press the dough to about 1cm thick. Refrigerate for up to 2 days.

3 When you are ready to bake the biscuits, set racks in the upper and lower thirds of the oven and preheat to 180°C/gas mark 4. Remove the dough from the refrigerator and cut it into thirds. Return two of the pieces to the refrigerator. Place the single piece of dough on a floured surface and gently knead it until it is slightly softened and pliable.

4 Flour the dough again and gently roll it out to just under 5mm thick. Use a 5–6.25cm plain cutter to cut biscuits, placing them on one of the prepared tins about 7.5cm apart in all directions to allow for spreading.

5 Repeat with the next piece of dough, incorporating the scraps from the previous piece. Continue cutting out biscuits and adding the scraps. When you have nothing but scraps left to roll, form the dough into a sausage shape and roll it to a rectangle as wide as the cutter. Cut out more biscuits and discard the last few scraps.

6 Use a small cutter to make a 1–2cm hole in the centre of half of the biscuits. Lift out the cutout pieces of dough and bake them with the biscuits if you wish.

7 Bake the biscuits until they are firm, dry and very light golden, 12–15 minutes. If your oven gives strong bottom heat, bake the tin of biscuits on the lower rack stacked on another tin for insulation.

8 Slide the biscuits on the papers from the tins to racks to cool.

9 Bring the jam to the boil in a small saucepan over a low heat. Strain into a bowl, rinse the pan, and return the jam to the pan. Return to the boil over a low heat and cook until thickened, 2–3 minutes.

10 Shake a light coat of icing sugar over the biscuits with holes in the centres (A). Turn the biscuits without holes upside down and spread about ½ teaspoon of the jam on each, immediately covering the jam with one of the biscuits with a hole in the centre (B and C). After you have sandwiched all the bases, use a ½-teaspoon measure to add more jam to the opening in each biscuit.

Storage: These have to be kept in a single layer to avoid marring the icing sugar on them. If you don't serve all the biscuits straight away, finish off what you need and store the baked bases.

lemon vanilla pod shortbread

Makes about 24 biscuits, depending on the size of the cutter you use

225g unsalted butter, softened

110g sugar

¼ teaspoon salt

2 teaspoons finely grated lemon zest

1 Madagascar Bourbon vanilla pod

325g plain flour

2–3 baking sheets or swiss roll tins lined with baking paper or foil

A classic Scottish biscuit, shortbread is all about butter. A little bit of lemon zest and the seeds scraped out from the inside of a vanilla pod serve to accentuate the already buttery flavour of these biscuits. For a classic shortbread, omit the lemon and vanilla. In both the lemon-vanilla and plain varieties, the delicate caramelised flavour of sugar and butter baked together is predominant and is what makes these simple biscuits so good. For best results, do not use any kind of extra high-fat butter to make these or they will be overly fatty, will spread while baking and will have an unappetisingly greasy texture.

1 Set racks in the upper and lower thirds of the oven and preheat to 160°C/gas mark 3.

2 Combine the butter, sugar, salt and lemon zest in the bowl of an electric mixer fitted with the paddle attachment.

3 Split the vanilla pod lengthways and scrape out the seeds with the point of a paring knife. Add them to the bowl. Wrap and reserve the remainder of the vanilla pod for another use. (If the vanilla pod is too hard, pulverise a quarter of it with the sugar in a blender, or grate it into the sugar with the tiniest holes of a box grater.)

4 Beat on medium speed until soft and light, about 5 minutes.

5 Remove the bowl from the mixer and use a large rubber spatula to stir in the flour by hand.

6 Scrape the dough to a floured surface and press it into a rough rectangle.

7 Cut off one quarter of the dough, place it on the work surface and flour on and under it. Gently roll to 5mm thick. Use a plain round cutter 6.25–7.5cm in diameter to cut out biscuits, placing them on one of the prepared tins about 2.5cm apart all around.

8 Incorporate the scraps from the first piece of dough into the next piece before rolling it. Repeat until all the dough and the final scraps have been used.

9 Bake the biscuits until they are very pale golden, 20–25 minutes. If your oven gives strong bottom heat, bake the tin of biscuits on the lower rack stacked on another tin for insulation.

10 Slide the biscuits on the papers from the tins to racks to cool.

Storage: Keep the biscuits between sheets of baking paper in a tin or plastic container with a tight-fitting lid. Don't try to store them for more than a few days or the freshness of the butter flavour will be lost.

chocolate raspberry sandwiches

Makes about 24 sandwich biscuits, depending on the size of the cutter used

COCOA BISCUIT DOUGH

260g plain flour

25g alkalized (Dutch process) cocoa powder, sifted through a fine-mesh sieve after measuring

225g unsalted butter, very soft

110g sugar

¼ teaspoon salt

2 teaspoons vanilla extract

RASPBERRY FILLING

225g seedless raspberry jam

2 tablespoons sugar

2 baking sheets or swiss roll tins lined with baking paper or foil

Be sure to use the best cocoa powder you can find for these biscuits. Thanks for this recipe to my old friend Tim Brennan, who makes them at Cravings, his bakery-café in St. Louis.

1 For the dough, stir the flour and cocoa powder together and set aside.

2 Combine the butter, sugar, salt and vanilla in the bowl of an electric mixer. Beat with the paddle on medium speed until lightened, about 5 minutes.

3 Scrape the bowl and beater and restart the mixer on the lowest speed. Add the flour mixture in thirds, mixing smooth after each addition.

4 Scrape the dough to a floured surface and squeeze it together into a fat cylinder, then divide it into 4 equal pieces. This dough doesn't need to be chilled before rolling.

5 Set racks in the upper and lower thirds of the oven and preheat to 180°C/gas mark 4.

6 Flour one quarter of the dough and gently roll it out to 5mm thick. Use a 5–6.25cm plain cutter to cut biscuits, placing them on one of the prepared tins about 7.5cm apart in all directions to allow for spreading.

7 Repeat with the next piece of dough, incorporating the scraps from the previous piece as you knead it. Continue cutting out biscuits and repeat adding the scraps with the remaining pieces of dough. When you have nothing but scraps left to roll, form the dough into a sausage shape and roll it to a rectangle as wide as the cutter you are using. Cut out more biscuits and discard the last few scraps.

8 Bake the biscuits until they are firm and dry looking, 12–15 minutes. If your oven gives strong bottom heat, bake the tin of biscuits on the lower rack stacked on another tin for insulation.

9 Slide the biscuits on the papers from the tins to racks to cool.

10 After the biscuits have cooled, make the filling by stirring the jam and sugar together in a small saucepan. Bring to the boil over a low heat and reduce, stirring occasionally, for 2 minutes.

11 Invert half the biscuits so that the flat bottom sides are upward. Top one with a generous ½ teaspoon of the filling and place another biscuit on it, flat-side down. Repeat with the remaining biscuits.

Storage: Keep the biscuits between sheets of baking paper in a tin or plastic container with a tight-fitting lid.

ginger lemon sandwich biscuits

Makes about 30 sandwich biscuits

GINGERSNAP BASES

195g plain flour

1½ teaspoons bicarbonate of soda

¼ teaspoon salt

2 teaspoons ground ginger (see Note)

1 teaspoon ground cinnamon

140g unsalted butter, softened

170g sugar

1 medium egg, at room temperature

85g treacle

LEMON BUTTER FILLING

85g unsalted butter, softened

225g icing sugar, sifted after measuring

2 tablespoons lemon juice, strained
before measuring

3 baking sheets or swiss roll tins
lined with baking paper or foil

Note: The amount of ginger in the recipe
can vary. If your ground ginger is from
a freshly opened jar, 2 teaspoons will be
enough. If you opened the jar more than
a few weeks before baking the biscuits,
use 3 teaspoons.

This variation on a traditional gingersnap is good on its own or sandwiched with a lemony butter filling as it is here. To add a note of lemon to the biscuit bases themselves, grate the zest from a lemon before you squeeze the juice for the filling and add it to the biscuit dough. The baking process for gingersnaps is rather odd. The biscuit dough spreads and then rises quite a bit, only to fall eventually and become the crisp biscuit we recognise as a gingersnap. Sometimes I hasten the process along by opening the oven at the point where the biscuits are very risen and lifting the closest side of the tin a few centimetres off the oven rack and then letting it drop back down to encourage the biscuits to fall and become crisp.

1   Set racks in the upper and lower thirds of the oven and preheat to 180°C/gas mark 4.

2   Mix the flour with the baking soda, salt and spices; set aside.

3   Combine the butter and sugar in the bowl of an electric mixer fitted with the paddle attachment. Beat on medium speed for 2 minutes, then add the egg. Continue beating until the egg is well absorbed. Use a large rubber spatula to scrape the bowl and beater.

4   On the lowest speed, beat in half the flour mixture until it is absorbed. Beat in the treacle and the remaining flour mixture, continuing to beat just until the dough is smooth. Remove the bowl from the mixer and use a large rubber spatula to give a final mixing to the dough.

5   Use a rounded (not heaped) measuring teaspoon to drop small balls of the dough on the prepared tins about 7.5cm apart in all directions to allow for spreading.

6   Bake the biscuit bases until they have spread and darkened and their surfaces are crackled, 12–15 minutes. Halfway through baking, switch the tins from the top rack to the lower one and vice versa, turning the tins back to front at the same time. If your oven gives strong bottom heat, bake the biscuits on the lower rack on two tins stacked together.

7   Cool the biscuits on the tins on racks; they become crisp as they cool.

8   While the biscuits are cooling, prepare the filling. Combine the butter and icing sugar in the bowl of an electric mixer fitted with the paddle attachment. Beat on low speed until smooth, then increase the speed to medium and beat until the filling is fluffy, 3 to 4 minutes more. Beat in the lemon juice a little at a time, continuing to beat until the filling is soft and smooth.

9   To fill the biscuits, flip over half the cooled biscuits and spread with 2 teaspoons of the filling. After spreading all the bottoms with the filling, top with another biscuit, flat side down, gently pressing them together to adhere.

Storage: Store the biscuits between sheets of baking paper in a tin or plastic container with a tight-fitting lid.

afterword

Much of what we think of as skill in baking depends on accurately executing techniques. In fact, the 'essentials' that follow most of the recipes in this book often give the reasons why you're mixing, rolling or cutting in a specific way that's essential to success. Yet baking is undoubtedly a creative pursuit. If it weren't, we wouldn't be able to enjoy the millions of variations – just think of how many different cheesecakes or brownies exist. The truth is that creativity in baking carries some responsibility with it. You can infinitely vary the flavour of buttercream or the type of fruit you use in a tart, but you really can't do much to alter the way you keep track of the temperatures in your buttercream or how thin you roll your dough. With this in mind, I've added variations where appropriate, though you needn't stop with my suggestions. Take off on your own and remember that creativity in baking, as in all the arts, is governed by experience and a certain degree of restraint. And above all, enjoy the process.

index

acknowledgements

What a pleasure it has been, every step of the way, to work on this, my first effort for Kyle Cathie. Kyle welcomed me on board with warmth and grace and all the hours spent planning and working with my publisher and editor Anja Schmidt have been as enjoyable an experience as I can remember. Of course nothing here would exist without three other important people, my agent, Phyllis Wender, my own freelance editor, Natalie Danford, and Rose Kaplan, who helped test all the recipes. A big thank you to all for your support, kindness and generosity.

On the production side, thanks are due to designer Dirk Kaufman, photographer Quentin Bacon and his assistant Lauren, prop stylist Roy Finamore, food stylist Liz Duffy and copy editor Janet McDonald.

At the Institute of Culinary Education in New York, my thanks to owner and president Rick Smilow; career baking program director Andrea Tutunjian; director of purchasing Josh Pappas and all his crew, especially Jaime Olenick; schedule and operations manager Mary Bartolini; and the dozens of other faculty and staff who make it such a pleasure to be there. Thanks also to students Samantha Neal and Ana Borrero who volunteered to help with food preparation for photography, and to the students pictured in the photographs: Joan Ferng, Samantha Neal, Bianca Bianco, Kyle Warendorf and Justin Wender.

Thanks to friends and colleagues who contributed or inspired recipes: Michael Ayoub, Tim Brennan, Leah Chase, Thea Cvijanovich, Kyra Effren, Maida Heatter, Albert Kumin, Dietmar Muthenthaler, Ann Nurse, Roberto Santibañez, Amy Scherber, Jayne Sutton, Cara Tannenbaum and Carole Walter. Special thanks to my dear friend Kyra Effren for help with recipe testing and to Ciril Hitz, of Johnson & Wales University, for answering my countless questions about bread baking.

And a final thank you to Ron Longe and to all my cooking school friends all over North America for helping to promote the book.